Raising Capital or Improving Risk Management and Efficiency?

Fabiano Colombini
Editor

Raising Capital or Improving Risk Management and Efficiency?

Key Issues in the Evolution of Regulation and Supervision in European Banks

palgrave
macmillan

Editor
Fabiano Colombini
Department of Economics and Management
University of Pisa
Pisa, Italy

ISBN 978-3-030-10104-6 ISBN 978-3-319-71749-4 (eBook)
https://doi.org/10.1007/978-3-319-71749-4

Softcover re-print of the Hardcover 1st edition 2018

Cover illustration: Steve Cavalier / Alamy Stock Photo

Printed on acid-free paper

This Palgrave Macmillan imprint is published by the registered company Springer International Publishing AG part of Springer Nature
The registered company address is: Gewerbestrasse 11, 6330 Cham, Switzerland

To Lorenzo, Chiara, and Edoardo

Contents

List of Contributors

Fabiano Colombini Department of Economics and Management, University of Pisa, Pisa, Italy

Antonella Cappiello Department of Economics and Management, University of Pisa, Pisa, Italy

Paola Ferretti Department of Economics and Management, University of Pisa, Pisa, Italy

List of Figures

List of Tables

CHAPTER 1

Introduction

Fabiano Colombini

This book aims to analyse the potential choice between the raising of capital and the improving of risk management and efficiency in commercial banks in Europe. Given that capital requirement is becoming more and more important for regulatory authorities as a prudential tool and, at the same time, for supervisory authorities as a discretional tool, it is relevant to raise the question of the viability for individual banks and the banking system.

From the theoretical point of view, there is a discrepancy between the prudential view included in the regulatory measures based on Basel agreements and the discretional view included in the supervisory measures based on decisions taken by the supervisory authorities. It is by no means easy to obtain a clear understanding of this twofold approach, which reveals different and dialectically opposing views.

The regulatory and supervisory measures represent a heavy burden for commercial banks in Europe, and the discrepancy has repercussions on choices of individual banks. Is this authoritarian framework justified in the attempt to ensure sound bank management? Finding a reply is not easy. It is worth to point out that application of Basel agreements leads to a rise in costs which needs to be matched by additional revenue in order to maintain the previous economic situation at an individual bank level. At the same time,

F. Colombini (✉)
Department of Economics and Management, University of Pisa, Pisa, Italy

F. Colombini (ed.), *Raising Capital or Improving Risk Management and Efficiency?*, https://doi.org/10.1007/978-3-319-71749-4_1

supervision requires system costs arising from the presence of supervisory authorities.

Considering the importance, the spreading effects and the time length of financial crises of recent periods, crisis resolutions involve additional costs for taxpayers in different countries. This is the case both in a bail-in and in a bail-out, as depositors are called upon to contribute in accordance with their deposits and tax position. Will banks survive as fears of systemic risk spreading throughout the system become more pressing? Who correctly estimates the level of systemic risk?

One point is very clear by comparing European banks to American banks: public tools have been called upon to deal with financial and economic crises that have been more serious and more protracted in Europe, whereas considerably shorter periods were involved in the USA. Furthermore, there have been different repercussions on financial and economic systems: American economy did recover in a few years and did continue to grow from solid foundations; European economy did spend a long time before recovering and going through a growing path. It is worth to point out the positive transmission effect from the economy in good shape to the banking system.

In this context, help for recovery from shifts and shocks has been the primary task attributed to public authorities and especially to monetary authorities in order to overcome the critical points in the economic set-up and the bank situation. Establishing strategies for instruments and business areas is of paramount importance on account of the link to cost and revenue and therefore to profit.

Identification, measurement and management of risks associated with financial instruments and business areas constitute the premises for a sound management. This is the strategic issue for banks and financial intermediaries and is the key to positive results and therefore profits or—in contrast—leads to negative results and therefore losses.

This is straightforward for achievement of efficiency in cost, revenue and profit and in scale and scope: it is a complex process which increases the soundness of individual banks by building up a solid system.

Financial crises, which have been particularly severe in Europe over a prolonged period of time starting from 2007, together with related economic crises, have given rise to non-performing loans spreading throughout European banks. This book underlines the need to address and solve the problem in question, which continues to have negative repercussions on the economic growth of the European Union, above all because it has meant lower loans to the economy and especially to small- and medium-sized enterprises.

In this context, particular attention is devoted to the introduction and spread of the so-called bad bank, which takes the bad assets and, at the same time, leaves the good assets in the previous bank in a sort of "cleaning up" of the asset side of the banks' balance sheets. The cleaning up and the full return to good banks represent the steps towards better conditions for the financing of the economy and economic growth. The greater the rates of return on investments for the good banks in the European Union, the better will be the premises for lending.

Regulation and supervision are typical aspects of the complexity and distinctive features of banks. It is worth pointing out the over implementation of rule constraints on the banking business and especially on capital levels, which are important from the point of view of covering losses but not from the point of view of a rational and sound management of banking risks and business areas. This is the critical point, especially with reference to improving risk management and efficiency. These two aspects are crucial in the development of individual banks and banking systems in different countries in Europe.

In this context, the Single Supervisory Mechanism and the Single Resolution Mechanism, which brought into operation the so-called bail-in from the beginning of 2016, are examined by focusing on weaknesses and critical aspects that involve the evolution of commercial banks and by singling out confidence risks and instability risks. Financial crises have been the cause of many critical points and instability factors as well as the application of the "bail-in" can recreate financial instability. In the past years, states spent a large amount of money for rescue purposes, which has now led to an incorrect use of state aid according to the interpretation given by the European Commission, which considers many cases as state aid when they are not, in fact, genuine state aid. This is misleading as it tends to increase the financial instability risks arising from the application of the bail-in.

This book examines risk management issues in the context of the bank and evolution of the banking business. Attention focuses on non-performing loans and on bad bank as well as the selling of loans to remove obstacles to economic growth on a European scale; at the same time, attention is also paid to rules and single supervision for the removal of excessive restrictions and their inner irrationality on a European scale: thus critical points and weaknesses are identified.

Such circumstances are of considerable importance where bank reinforcement is concerned, as well as banks' capacity to lend credit to the economy. Lending represents the point of return to satisfactory rates of economic growth in the European countries, particularly the weaker ones.

Therefore, this book aims to analyse relationships between risk management, credit risk, banking efficiency, regulatory and supervisory capital constraints, bank regulation and supervision in Europe, monetary policy, supervisory policy and economic growth in Europe, capital raising and bank performance, regulation and supervision in the USA, raising capital or improving risk management and efficiency. The contents focus on a wide range of topics and provide suggestions for the evolution of the European banking system.

This book is subdivided into 11 chapters. Chapter 1, "Introduction", considers a range of topics included in the different chapters and provides a guideline for the topics included.

Chapter 2, "Risk Management and Banking Business in Europe", examines risk management issues in the context of banks and evolution of the banking business, by focusing on identification, measurement and management of all the risks linked with financial instruments and business areas in order to achieve sound management. This is a key issue in devising strategies for banks and financial intermediaries: it can lead to positive results and therefore profits or negative results and therefore losses; in the latter case, the outcome allows identification of critical points and weaknesses.

Chapter 3, "Credit Risk Management and Banking Business in Europe", examines credit risk and credit risk management issues in the context of banks and evolution of the banking business, focusing on non-performing loans. Such topics are of considerable importance where bank reinforcement is concerned and also influences the capacity of banks to lend credit to the economy and especially to small- and medium-sized enterprises. The latter aspect represents the point of return to satisfactory rates of economic growth in the European countries, particularly the weaker ones.

Financial crises, which have been particularly severe in Europe over a prolonged period of time starting in 2007, together with related economic crises, have given rise to non-performing loans that have spread throughout European banks. This chapter underlines the need to deal with and solve the problem in question, which still has negative repercussions on the economic growth of the European Union, above all because it has meant fewer loans to the economy and especially to small- and medium-sized enterprises.

In Chapter 4, "Banking Efficiency in Europe", the efficiency of banks is examined in the framework of production evolution, banking business and business areas, taking into account inputs and outputs and the impact on costs, revenue and profits. Improving banking efficiency constitutes a structural reinforcement in the economic conditions and therefore in the economic account, creating the best premises for bank survival.

Evolving production and business areas and competition between small- and medium-sized banks and great banks, as well as the shocks and shifts induced by financial crises of recent years, tend to improve the strength and solidity of best banks.

Chapter 5, which focuses on "Capital Constraints by Regulation in Europe", considers the evolution of bank capital rules. Capital constraints are important from the point of view of covering losses but not from the point of view of a rational and sound management of banking risks and business areas.

The chapter aims to describe the evolution of the capital adequacy framework for banks, with reference to the international scale: from Basel I to Basel III and the forthcoming Basel IV. As is known, the main reasons for the introduction of Basel III link back to financial crises, overcoming the inability of banks to deal adequately with the consequences. This difficulty was mainly due to operational distortions that have characterised the banking business in the last decades. In particular, in the years preceding the financial crises, banks of many countries had built up excessive on- and off-balance sheet leverage; this was accompanied by a gradual erosion of the level and quality of the capital base. At the same time, many institutions were holding insufficient liquidity buffers. The banking system was therefore unable to absorb trading and credit losses. Financial crises were further amplified by a procyclical deleveraging process and by the interconnection of systemic institutions through an array of complex transactions.

In order to respond to financial crises, the current framework focuses on provision of higher quantity and better quality own funds, introduction of countercyclical buffers, the discipline of rules for managing liquidity risk and containment of leverage. However, Basel III provisions have aroused considerable debate. In particular, with regard to capital requirements, questions have been raised as to their real effectiveness in ensuring the soundness of banks. Hence it is important to ascertain the extent to which the increase in capital levels genuinely ensures bank solvency. Such considerations are useful for a critical assessment of Basel III provisions, especially as far as the latest proposals on the capital adequacy framework are concerned. Accordingly, since the finalisation of Basel III, the Basel Committee has continued to work on various aspects of the detailed capital requirements. These changes (the so-called Basel IV framework in progress) will have a substantial effect on the size of the risk-weighted assets against which capital has to be held and, therefore, the total *quantum* of bank capital. It is worth to point out that capital constraints are imposed following a line of prudential regulation.

Chapter 6, "Capital Constraints by Supervision in Europe", turns to an examination of capital requirements designated by supervisory authorities for individual banks. This chapter aims at providing an overview of additional capital requirements demanded by the Supervision Unit of the European Central Bank in accordance with the appraisal or asset quality review of the economic situation of individual banks. Additional capital requirements can be imposed by an asset quality review or by a stress test indicating bank situations in a crisis or near crisis. This additional constraint considers a number of situations in which the supervisory authorities establish the need for additional capital. It should be underlined that extreme discretion is exercised in relation to decisions concerning additional capital by supervision, which may be required in addition to capital by regulation that is calculated in accordance with Basel III and the forthcoming Basel IV. However, this points to an issue of overlapping rules and uncertainties in the regulatory and supervisory criteria used for calculating and creating the required level of capital for individual banks.

Pursuing additional capital can distract from the real objective, which is the stability of banks throughout Europe: raising capital needs time, and resolution delays underline the worsening of asset and liability values and economic conditions. This in turn leads to increasing levels of capital required in order to restore a bank's situation and enable it to remain on the market.

In Chapter 7, "Banking Regulation and Supervision in Europe", the main focus of attention concerns the evolution of rules applied to European banks as a means of reducing financial instability. Regulation and supervision are typical aspects of the complexity and distinctive features of banks.

Financial crises have been the cause of a considerable number of critical points and financial instability. In the past years, states spent a large amount of money for rescue purposes. Now, according to the European Commission's interpretation, the current situation displays an incorrect use of state aid. However, the Commission's interpretation considers many cases as state aid when they do not genuinely fall into this category. Thus the Commission's approach is misleading as it tends to increase financial instability.

In contrast, this chapter outlines the best result of a process of restructuring banks in the evolution of production and business areas, taking into account the relevant competition between small- and medium-sized banks and great banks and all adjustments induced by financial crises of recent years.

The Single Supervisory Mechanism, introduced on the basis of the lessons learnt from financial crises, entered into operation in November 2014. Although its statement did not explicitly refer to the banking union or to any other "pillars" of the latter, there was an implicit reference to the fact that supervision was a precondition for bringing other elements of the banking framework up to the European level, notably in the area of crisis resolution.

This chapter underlines that although the framework is comprehensive and well advanced, it remains incomplete, and several challenges still need to be addressed. First, it should be noted that while a single resolution authority, established in 2015, assumed full responsibilities in 2016, a single deposit insurance, despite having been recognised as an integral part of the construction in question, does not exist yet, nor there is an agreed time frame for its implementation. Yet this further step is necessary to complete and harmonise the Single Resolution Mechanism in the euro area.

Furthermore, some issues pertaining to regulatory changes still remain to be addressed by banks and supervisors. The legislative framework, which underpins banking supervision, allows several elements of flexibility, available to supervisors or member states. Moreover, the need of transposition into national legislation opens the door to legislative differences between countries and prevents a truly level playing field within the European banking union.

Finally, this chapter examines critically the relationship between capital rules and other supervisory measures, within a risk-based regulatory framework aiming to ensure the safety and soundness of banks.

In Chapter 8, "Monetary Policy, Banking Supervisory Policy, and Economic Growth in Europe", a description of the definition and trend of monetary policy is given, with a focus on critical issues related to the interaction between monetary and supervisory policy in the euro area in recent years.

Currently, in a context of uncertainty, the monetary policy easing of the ECB may be considered adequate, though opinions differ as to its genuine effectiveness in helping to achieve growth and inflation goals. In the perspective of economic growth, the crucially important point is that the financial system must be able to relay monetary policy impulses efficiently to the economy. In the euro area, the transmission mechanism has been impeded repeatedly in the past, initially by rising risk premia due to doubts concerning the survival of the euro area, and later by widespread bank deleveraging. In this respect it is necessary to discuss and evaluate the consequences of restrictive banking regulation and the supervisory policy with regard to the capital adequacy framework. A supervisory policy should go well beyond the new capital and liquidity regulatory framework, supporting rather than delaying the effectiveness of monetary policy measures.

Chapter 9, "Capital Raising in European Banks", examines the recapitalisation process of the European banking system. Particularly, this chapter seeks to give an overview of recapitalisation operations for a sample of European banks during the years 2012 to 2016. The analysis is designed to assess whether the capital increase genuinely contributed to the soundness of banks or whether a more balanced solution would be to focus jointly on different drivers to achieve this goal, *in primis* the improvement of risk management and efficiency policies.

Chapter 10, "Banking Regulation and Supervision in the USA", considers features of regulation and supervision in the USA. This chapter gives an overview of the financial regulation and supervision applied by US authorities, by pointing out the key features as well the main tools used for examining the safety of banks. In particular, the focus is on CAMELS ratings; the acronym refers to the six components of a bank's condition that are assessed: capital adequacy, asset quality, management, earnings, liquidity and sensitivity to market risk. These supervisory ratings are commonly viewed as summary measures of the private supervisory information gathered by examiners regarding banks' overall financial conditions, although they also reflect available public information.

In the light of banking crises in recent years worldwide, CAMELS can be considered as a useful tool to examine the soundness of banks and help mitigate the potential risks which may lead to bank failures.

Chapter 11, "Raising Capital or Improving Risk Management and Efficiency", takes into consideration the raising of capital from time to time or the improving of risk management and efficiency from one period to another in the context of banks.

The raising of capital is the main tool used by regulation on a prudential application and by supervision on a discretional application in order to maintain the viability of the banking system. Capital requirements are calculated through Basel III and the forthcoming Basel IV; they are also imposed as an additional tool through discretional decisions by supervisory authorities. This can be viewed as a form of "recurrent stressing" to be imposed on banks as a means of pursuing the stability objective. It is important to point out that capital raising is useful only in order to hedge the solvency risk at the specific date examined and only if the solvency risk is correctly estimated at that time.

Looking at only the capital level at a given point of time can be misleading as it cannot create the premises for a sound and stable bank at some future point of time. Improving risk management through the identification, measurement and management of all risks linked to bank instruments and bank business areas is the best strategy in order to achieve structural reinforcement and therefore to assure the soundness of individual banks and the banking system both in the medium and the long term.

This strategy can be carried out by improving efficiency in a wide range of areas, with particular emphasis on the aspects of cost, revenue and profit, in parallel with the structural premises for sound and viable conditions. Taken together, these improvements will lead to better frameworks for the economic account of banks in Europe and in the world from one period of time to another.

CHAPTER 2

Risk Management and Banking Business in Europe

Fabiano Colombini

2.1 Introduction

In an increasingly global competitive context characterised by a number of changes and financial innovations, banks are experimenting with risk management.

Net interest income reductions force bank intermediaries to reinforce non-interest income through a range of products which is wider and has a higher added value. This results in a broadening of instruments and business areas, with the consequent increase in risks and mutual interrelations.

It is therefore indispensable to set in place an adequate risk management function which can manage complex factors through processes able to transform risks into profit opportunities. There are, however, two unavoidable elements that must be taken into account in order to achieve this target: competence and tools.

On closer inspection, these are two sides of the same coin as each propels the other. Mathematical and statistical knowledge is the *conditio sine qua non* for accomplishing the tasks attributed to risk managers, but at the

F. Colombini (✉)
Department of Economics and Management, University of Pisa, Pisa, Italy

F. Colombini (ed.), *Raising Capital or Improving Risk Management and Efficiency?*, https://doi.org/10.1007/978-3-319-71749-4_2

same time it must be supported by adequate human resources. Competence and tools must perfectly align in order to maximise the benefits achievable from their synergies.

Financial engineering has achieved remarkable progress, originating tools for a real quality leap in the results obtainable through risk management strategies. Among these, the main strategy is represented by derivatives which, despite their origins that date a number of years, still find wide use in the banking world of today. Their diffusion has been, to say the least, very impressive, as attested by the growth of the markets of reference.

As well as being used for a range of purposes, the aforementioned financial instruments play a key role in covering risks, there being several hedging techniques in use. In a bank context in which risk management represents the heart of all existing business areas, derivatives find an almost natural collocation, to the point that their use has become an almost everyday procedure. Thus banks adopt risk management policies which allow them to carry on their risk-taking function over financial markets and, at the same time, to use these financial instruments to reduce their risk exposure.

Hence the need for adequate management skills to prevent negative outcomes related to experimentation with derivatives, because the ratio of assets to capital as is generally the case in the financial sector, will be very high. This implies measurement of the leverage, including fears of excess hedging, which may in the end result in pursuing objectives that do not genuinely constitute hedging but are better described as speculation, thereby increasing rather than reducing the range of risks.

2.2 Risk and Bank

Risk identification, measurement and management represent the heart of bank enterprises, and the ability to control these aspects in a situation of asymmetric information is a fundamental bank function for the attainment of management results (Colombini, 2008; Colombini & Calabrò, 2011). In-depth analysis of what is meant by risk is not strictly necessary, but it is translated into a determining element to trace precisely the frame of reference for the bank.

In economic theory, risk tends to identify the variability of results around an expected value, and its existence is correlated with the presence of uncertainty. The latter constitutes a push towards progress, although progress through change generates uncertainty in return. Despite there being a close relation between the concepts of risk and uncertainty, it is necessary not to confuse them. This labelling issue has been discussed in economic theory since the beginning of the twentieth century, but only around the 1920s was it given an exhaustive explanation by identifying two different types of uncertainty, characterised by their being measurable (measurable uncertainty) or unmeasurable (unmeasurable uncertainty) (Knight, 1921).

The onset of a phenomenon and the period of its manifestation are not known beforehand according to clear results, but it may involve several different values depending on a determined probability distribution. The calculation of probability must lead to a result other than 0 as the latter would represent a cost and not a risk, and at the same time different from 1 as this would mean a certain event.

If it is possible to estimate and identify the possible factual event and its deviation from the expected value, one can talk about risk, otherwise about uncertainty. Along the same lines are the remarks of other economists who believe similarly that risk is the only element that can constitute a focus of investigation within the economic discipline, because risk is quantifiable, unlike uncertainty (Arrow, 1951; Lucas, 1981). These assumptions can be seen as part of the neoclassical financial theory, which, since the 1970s, has been built on the supposition of the absolute rationality of economic agents: the latter are held to be limited only by lack of knowledge about the possible risk manifestations, due to the randomness of events. The spread of studies on the theory of information re-assesses uncertainty, seeking to take into account the effects of limited human rationality within a system where the role of information and of its acquisition becomes pre-eminent.

Hence it follows that risk or stochastic variability pertains to the randomness inherent in events, whereas uncertainty concerns lack of knowledge or information. The distinction between risk and uncertainty may appear to be lacking practical outlines, but not if one takes into account an interesting consideration which holds that choices presuppose distribution of probability depending, at least partially, on subjective elements. Thus even in the presence of one and the same event, decisions taken may differ on the basis of the operator (Arrow, 1951). This is due not only to the different attitude to risk characterising each individual, but also to the different professional skills in identifying, measuring and managing a specific risk. In contrast, by virtue of their resources and their skills, bank intermediaries are better able than others to adequately manage risk-related issues.

The twofold expression ***risk-cum-bank*** is an inseparable concept, which can lead to a variety of results depending on the rate of accuracy of the risk assessment process by the risk management function. Despite the association of the common concept of risk solely with the negative side of event distribution—that is, concerning unfavourable situations—in actual fact the risk factor of a certain scenario can represent an opportunity for revenue compared to merely financial, rather than pure, risks.

In this context, the importance of risk managers becomes even clearer, as not only can they prevent the destruction of value through correct risk management, but they may also create it, to the point that risk management becomes the real "profit engine" of the banking business (Masera & Mazzoni, 2007).

2.3 Risk Management: Function and Processes

Considering the major world banks, the true discriminating factor in identifying successful banks lies in their capacity to deal correctly with the evolution of risky phenomena.

In the financial literature, two different approaches to this theme can be found. One refers to the organisational description of the risk management function, while the other is related to the processes which the latter sets in motion (Schroek, 2002). In actual fact, however, organisation and processes are two sides of the same coin, as it is only through their correct co-penetration that the best results can be achieved.

Risk management by a bank intermediary implies the function of risk management. Located in the organisation chart as an autonomous unit, the risk management function is transversely related to the whole organisational structure, acquiring strategic information from the top management and gathering information from each single business unit in order to identify risk exposure, propose suitable levels of capital to allocate and gather information concerning any critical issue relating to any of the above items. In the first instance we could define the processes involved as "top down", given that they are indeed traced by the board of directors. Though not completely mistaken, this consideration needs to be reformulated, because the definition of certain strategies implies a close-meshed relation between the board of directors and risk management.

Strategies cannot avoid considering the risk management capacity with regard to specific financial instruments and business areas, in order to avert the possibility of starting a given operation in the wake of a great commercial idea without then being able to manage the related critical issues. It has been pointed out that such a *modus operandi* does not give sufficient value to the theme of risk, even though for years this has represented the way many banks work. In contrast, the current context does not allow the top management to begin any strategic operation without considering risk management peculiarities, given the exponential increase in the range of risks and also the acquired awareness of correct risk management in the production of value.

The role attributed to the latter can be seen as that of a crossroads. It represents the main barycentre of the whole complex structure of the banking organisation chart (Bessis, 2015).

The autonomy of the risk management function means that it needs not be linked to a specific business. This makes it possible to approach risk management from an integrated perspective. Setting a determined area to control each risk factor is not genuinely farsighted, because the task of dealing with the possible correlations among the different factors would cause additional expense and would also lose its evaluative effectiveness.

In risk management, and in all related capital allocation issues, it is necessary to take into account the processes linked to the management of risk:

- identification;
- measurement;
- monitoring and reporting;
- management.

Clearly, the execution of strategies implies preventive risk identification for its measurement and management (Mikes, 2009). This consideration might seem banal, but very often in operational practice it is from this first step that difficulties arise. Frequently, the multifaceted nature of banking activity means that an individual operation can be subject to several risks, which can be confusing. The correct match between risks and business lines represents a key element to risk management success.

Each identified risk has to be classified according to event frequency and potential impact, as this is an important reference parameter for the final step: management itself. During identification and classification, all data are gathered and organised into informative databases. This sets the stage for the actual risk measurement, the heart of the whole process quantifying the risk exposure of the business units and of the bank as a whole. Usually the trend is for risk managers to be assigned tasks that consistently follow a particular logic, in order to ensure that risk analyses carried out during the life of a bank will be homogenous and comparable. This is done with the introduction of the *ex ante* screening and *ex post* monitoring.

Risk exposure monitoring ensures that management will never lose track of the risk exposure of individual business units, constantly allocating the correct amount of capital and identifying for each the most appropriate risk-return profile according to the targets fixed by top management. Attention should also be paid to the reporting phase, which provides useful information to risk managers, with results coming from the measurement system adopted. This allows accurate assessment of the whole process and the correction of any gaps.

As clearly emerges from the above picture, risk management is a dynamic activity that needs to take shape in accordance with market scenarios and related risk events and is carried out with close and constant scrutiny of the bank business in its entirety (Crouhy, Galai, & Mark, 2014).

2.4 Risk Management: Objectives

Risk management plays a role of primary importance in the creation of value in bank intermediaries. As can be imagined, the focal issue in the understanding of the importance of such a complex—and thus proportionally so expensive—structure is to identify the benefits.

In order to understand the logic connecting the production of value to risk management, it is necessary to consider the reason that prompts a bank intermediary to deal with risk management and acquire profound insight with regard to the targets pursued. The latter are contained in the following categories:

- adoption of the most appropriate strategy for risk management;
- reduction of the variability of economic outcomes;
- capacity for a suitable response to stakeholders' expectations.

The most appropriate strategy for risk management implies the link between risk management and the production of value. In short, this implies the need to determine whether or not to hold a certain risk in the balance sheet. On this matter, with special regard to the capital level for supervisory purposes, the need to assess whether or not it is advantageous to hold a specific risk prompts the bank to adopt diametrically opposed management strategies. The moment a specific critical issue is analysed, it becomes fundamental to understand its cost in terms of capital and—above all—the possible benefits.

This phase, despite being inserted in the risk identification, measurement and management process, involves elements of monitoring and reporting. It should be noted that a good deal of the costs to be borne with the acquisition of a certain risky position is related to its control *ex post*. This further expense needs to be added therefore to the initial evaluation and parameterised to the possible scenarios capable of influencing the position in question.

With regard to the supply of management skills, the overall cost of a risk-taking strategy needs to be estimated, and the more skills the bank proves to have with regard to that specific business risk, the lower the cost will be. However, there are risks for which a risk-taking strategy will turn out to be more expensive than a covering derivative strategy. In such contexts it is necessary to have recourse to the practice of hedging. Basically, the dynamic modelling between risk taking and risk covering allows the activation of a flexible and dynamic managing policy, which can optimise capital and producing value (Culp, 2011).

Thus, risk identification and management, transfer and removal of choices are related to the bank management's strategic competence with regard to the financial instruments, business areas and operations that are to be considered central for the bank intermediary's mission. The final decision will tend to incorporate both business strategy and risk strategy, which need to operate together in order to achieve the solution that best suits the bank in question.

Risk management activity, as empirical evidence makes clear, has a profound impact on the reduction in volatility of cash flow and profit. When the aim is to avert serious financial shocks arising from financial markets, the strategies introduced will seek to ease the potential losses which, as well as eroding profit margins, cause instability in the worst-case scenarios, with heavy repercussions on investment strategies (Gatzert, Schmeiser, & Schuckmann, 2008).

Reduced availability of resources for lending credit means that the main bank activity is penalised, with all the effects that may result. As in a vicious circle, such a circumstance has repercussions on the profits and on the level of the bank's competitiveness. Not only does the bank experience a rise in the cost of fund raising due to deterioration of the market's confidence, but—in the search for a higher net interest income—there may be a tendency to increase the bank's lending interest rates, with the effect of—once again—losing existing customers and failure to acquire potential new customers. The overall conclusion is that the bank's level of competitiveness tends to decrease, and with it the production of value.

Therefore the effects of a mismanaged risk trigger mechanisms and impacts which are not limited to the current procedure, but basically produce effects—and this is the worst aspect—also in the medium and long term.

In the absence of an adequate risk management system, not only are cash flows and profits eroded due to the losses attributed to an underestimated risk, but it also becomes necessary to undertake a revision of the business strategies projected to intervals of a much larger scale. The reduction of cash flow and profit variability is a primary target which can be achieved only with a sound risk management.

There are a number of categories of stakeholders for whom risk managers need to find answers. Considering that the bank institution's target is value maximisation, the shareholders are the first to feel the effects of risk reductions. To confirm this, one need only consider that in rating each individual bank's performance, risk-adjusted performance measurement (RAPM) indicators are used more and more often, which identify risk adjustment as the discriminating element in a comparison among different banks.

It would be pointless to consider on equal terms two banks which imply completely different risks, because in this case we would not grasp the logic that underlies different investing strategies played out by operators with different risk profiles. Yet even in this case an adequate risk management system becomes the determining factor to align shareholders' performance expectations to the results actually achieved.

As indicated, reduction of profit volatility is a primary target for a bank that aims to be competitive on the financial markets, so much so that many operators seek to achieve this reduction in order to achieve value maximisation (Crouhy, Galai, & Mark, 2014). However, this aspect may not be equally important for all types of shareholders. For instance, especially for the so-called scalpers, higher exposure to bank risks would increase the risk-return profile and would better fit an investment logic of a purely speculative nature and oriented to the short term. On the other hand, a small portion of shareholders believe that risk reduction and profit stabilisation are key elements for a correct response to the majority of shareholders' expectations.

Maintenance of a certain risk profile permits the achievement of a financial reputation that is of benefit to all stakeholders—a critical factor for success in banking. This result arises from the idea of trust, whereas the lack of trust, caused by an increase in default probabilities, can lead to a downturn in the standard business areas.

Consider, for instance, the case of a depositor who feels there is a problem affecting the financial solidity of his own bank, and even before ascertaining the possible seriousness of the situation, he hurries to the cashier's desk to withdraw what he has previously deposited. In contrast, a correct and sound risk management represents the founding element of a bank that wants to enjoy a healthy relationship with all its stakeholders.

2.5 Enterprise Risk Management

Models which can be framed in the context of enterprise risk management (ERM) lead to an integrated risk approach, more effectively pursuing the following targets (Bessis, 2015; Fraser & Simkins, 2010; Nocco & Stulz, 2006):

- more efficient capital allocation to individual business units;
- identification of the relations between the range of risks and the performance achieved by the different areas of banking business;
- better planning and control of banking and financial products which include many and complex risks, thus focusing attention on active monitoring of the interrelations.

Integrated risk management allows a relation between the concept of value and the concept of regulatory capital. Basel III application maintains a risk-based approach between allocation of capital and risk. This risk-based logic brings with it a rethink of the whole organisational and management structure, which needs to be moulded in order to perform more manageable and flexible risk management actions. The close link between the function in question and the internal audit needs to achieve its maximum expression in the ERM.

Risk becomes, as it was, the key variable retracing the whole organisational and management structure of the control procedures. Risk management and internal audit are two sides of the same coin, to which management and control give continuous feedback concerning the interaction between the cost of resources and means-related expenses and their effectiveness. Such a relationship becomes the crucial element on which bank strategies and management policies are based. This is particularly important in order to remould controls that proved to be inadequate and/or to reinforce them if they already successfully support the evolution of the intermediary's operative capacity. The truly crucial element to achieve these aims goes beyond the risk management function and processes. Namely, it involves the development of a "risk culture" such that its management is not just a problem for risk managers.

Accordingly, starting from the board of directors, every single area of the bank management must follow risk-based logic, regardless of whether a specific function is set for this target. It is possible to produce data and information by giving risk managers an exhaustive picture of the risk exposure of the intermediary in question. In this regard, to ensure the success of the risk management process it becomes essential to build up an integrated information system and to have operators capable of adjusting the system in response to changes in demand arising from the evolution of different economic and operational contexts.

A continuous flow of information moving like a circulatory system delivers to the heart of the structure—the risk management function—all the necessary elements to put into effect an adequate risk management policy. Without information it is impossible to plan, let alone to engage in quantitative studies as a means of monitoring and controlling uncertainty, as the neoclassicists intended, to an *epsilon* percentage of the entire own exposure to stochastic variability. It is thus necessary to produce as much significant data as possible.

Hence the fundamental role played by human resources, whereby each person's skills, from the board of directors to the front office, can become critical factors for success of the risk identification process and for risk measurement and management. The professional capacity to set in place small precautions in order to eliminate further risk sources is crucial.

Identification, measurement and management of the risks which burden financial instruments and business areas of each bank are of crucial importance in a context of medium- and long-term profit achievement strategies, regardless of the regulatory measures that need to be complied with.

2.6 Bank Business: Evolution and Shifts

Banks pursue the objective of expansion of on- and off-balance sheet instruments and volumes over time in order to create the premises for profits and positive performance. Banking balance sheets have grown rapidly in a low interest rate environment and in the presence of a surge in innovative instruments (Richardson, Smith, & Walter, 2010).

Traditionally, banks take deposits and make loans to individuals and firms (commercial banking). Some banks engage in underwriting, dealing, market making of securities and derivatives, management of personal and real estate property, consultancy, mergers and acquisitions, financial planning, custody and administration of securities, intermediation and selling of securities, derivatives, investment trusts and real estate investment trusts, pension funds and insurance policies (investment banking).

The growth of the banking business has underlined the shift from commercial banking to investment banking, and therefore an increase in the range of risks and in total risk. The process of identification, measurement and management of risks is of crucial importance in creating and maintaining conditions for profit and solvency. The above-mentioned shift is evident when looking at the asset side, the liability side and income sources as the share of net interest income falls and non-interest income rises (Liikanen, 2012).

The universal model in the banking sector combines commercial banking with investment banking and can be regarded as a critical issue for managing risks at a sustainable level for the individual institution and for the whole financial system.

Large banks tend to apply the universal banking model in the European Union (EU) for production diversification and also for risk diversification, adopting jointly the instruments of commercial banking and investment banking. Moreover, the expansion of business areas leads to a corresponding increase in the range of risks, with the result that risk management assumes a progressively more significant role. As a consequence of the links among different business areas, a bank may encounter difficulty in estimating its total risk exposure; accordingly, many banks engage in risk transfer as a practice for management of asset classes that involve a higher credit risk.

The systematic use of this practice has negative repercussions on the two classical banking activities: screening and monitoring. Screening and monitoring reduce or—in a very optimistic assumption—completely eliminate the problems, respectively, of information asymmetry *ex ante* and, therefore, of adverse selection and the problem of information asymmetry *ex post* and, therefore, of moral hazard.

Screening and monitoring activities, together with the information content of bank loans, the uncertainty of return and of the value of their assets and the "certainty" of remuneration and of the value of their liabilities, as well as the specific nature and depth of financial transformation, underline the importance of banks and, at the same time, highlight their differences in comparison with other financial intermediaries (Colombini, 2008).

A considerable number of banks have undertaken the development of business areas which are parallel to the classical areas of raising and lending funds. Many of these developments frequently involve high leverage areas, as in the case of derivatives (Colombini, 1999, 2004; Colombini & Calabrò, 2011). Restoring rational choices in the context of commercial banks constitutes a requirement for medium and long period financial stability, with less importance awarded to growth of their capital.

Over time, the dealing and market making of securities and derivatives and proprietary trading have become increasingly important. There has also been a remarkable growth in derivatives, especially in the over-the-counter (OTC) market (Colombini & Calabrò, 2011; King, 2016; Oldani, 2008; Savona, 2010). Since the beginning of the third millennium, securitisation markets have grown rapidly and created the phenomenon of the shadow banking system, built up essentially by special purpose vehicles (SPVs) and structured investment vehicles (SIVs).

Extensive recourse to leverage and, at the same time, the development of the shadow banking system (Claessens, Pozsar, Ratnovsky, & Singh, 2012; Gorton & Metrick, 2010; Lemma, 2016; Stein, 2010) imply avoidance of capital requirements in a banking context, through the constitution of off-balance sheet vehicles. The latter, in particular, run up debts on the market of commercial papers such as short-term securities and use the resources thereby achieved to purchase long-term securities, such as asset-backed securities (ABS). The difference between return on purchased securities and the cost of financing through commercial papers makes it possible to obtain profits by means of special purpose vehicles.

Changes and innovations in rules should be accompanied by adequate levels of controls on bank practices of regulatory avoidance through off-balance sheet items (OBSIs). For banks, the shadow banking system represents one of the main ways in which a vast quantity of risk that is generated and transferred is rendered opaque (Pozsar, Adrian, Ashcraft, & Boesky, 2012). It is important to bring greater transparency into financial intermediaries' balance sheets, above all as regards OBSIs, which, in the light of financial crises on a global scale, highlight irrationalities in the management of banks.

In this framework, the subprime mortgage financial crisis causes negative repercussions, because the liquidity crisis affecting banks does not allow special purpose vehicles to satisfy their continuous demand for refinancing through commercial papers.

It is worth pointing out that the paralysis of asset-backed securities markets, due to the collapse of the real estate market and of the underlying assets characterising these securities, does not allow special purpose vehicles to raise funds to cope with their short-term commitments.

In their desire to reassure the markets of the commercial papers, banks are forced to re-enter the special purpose vehicle assets and the enormous losses recorded in the balance sheet perimeter. The repercussions are devastating and banks experience heavy write-downs both on the lending portfolio and the financial instruments portfolio, recording losses and bank failures.

National responses to financial and economic crises, together with years of waste in public resource management, cause a rise in public expenditure and imbalance in the major Western countries' public accounts, leading the way to a sovereign debt crisis. Essentially this means a credit risk for the country due to the non-payment of its debt maturity (debt default), or the intervention of an international financial authority, such as International Monetary Fund (IMF), to adjust deadlines and amounts of those payments as defined in the debt contract (debt restructuring).

2.7 Bank Business: Range of Risks

Considerable diversity in business areas, financial instruments and the associated range of risks can be observed among banking intermediaries. Typical financial risks include liquidity, solvency, credit, the interest rate and exchange rate. A typical pure risk consists of operational risk. Such risks affect banks and are similar to those that affect other financial intermediaries. However, they do not exhaust the range of bank risks, as it is necessary to analyse and make comparisons among different instruments and the respective business areas, in order to assess the complete range of risks affecting the various areas. Additionally, this circumstance presupposes appropriate management capacity in the process of risk identification.

2.7.1 Liquidity Risk

Liquidity consists in the capacity to repay debts at maturity. This, in turn, presupposes the availability of sufficient monetary resources for current business. Availability is measured by the ratio between liquid assets and total deposits or total assets. Such a concept implies that monetary outflows will occur at various dates when payments fall due. Therefore, this involves the need to identify and maintain proportions among liquid asset aggregates and total liabilities or assets (Revell, 1975).

The liquidity risk refers to the capacity of a bank to settle its debts at the various expiry dates. There would be no liquidity risk under the hypothesis that the bank could achieve a perfectly symmetrical composition of its assets and liabilities with respect to the values and maturities involving the classes of instruments that appear in its balance sheet. However, such a hypothesis is rather remote; in addition, it would disregard capital or the eventuality of missed interest payments or missed loan reimbursements. Naturally, the pursuit of liquidity by synchronising deadlines concerning assets and liabilities would presuppose the ability of a given bank to reconstruct and obtain knowledge of loan and debt maturities (Revell, 1973; Ricci, 1988).

Let us suppose that a given bank has exact knowledge of its maturities t_i with $i = 0, 1, \ldots, n$; let us also assume that it is capable of replicating and matching values and maturities of assets and liabilities, reducing values as maturities increase with $a_{t_i} = l_{t_i}$ and $\sum_{i=0}^{n} a_{t_i} = \sum_{i=0}^{n} l_{t_i}$. This would achieve a perfectly balanced situation.

Apart from the almost insuperable obstacles in this regard, if many banks and, even more strikingly, almost the total number of banks present within the banking industry of a given country were to achieve perfect symmetry in maturities and in the values of the respective financial instruments, this would end up by eliminating the financial transformation that is typical of financial intermediaries and, above all, of banks themselves. In such a manner, the supply of liquidity to the economic system would be reduced or annulled (Diamond & Dybvig, 1986; Freixas & Rochet, 1997; Wallace, 1996).

Cases where loan utilisation and conversion of deposits into money involve amounts and times that are not easily foreseeable affect above all the liquidity risk, causing pressures involving monetary outlays.

Since banks make use of the fractional reserve system, there exists no perfect equivalence between volume of sight deposits and volume of liquid reserves. Such a situation leads to problems arising from unexpected, rapid and massive demands for conversion of deposits into money or from unexpected large increases in loan utilisations.

A decline in the general public's trust tends to increase the liquidity risk, which can turn into an insolvency risk.

In order to estimate the demand for liquidity, it is necessary to forecast monetary receipts and outflows for given intervals of time, so as to quantify excess outflows as compared to monetary receipts. This allows identification of the appropriate monetary resources to cover imbalances. The estimate in question requires reconstruction of the monetary flows associated with the various asset, liability and off-balance sheet items.

In the evolution of the banking business, matching and management of maturities involving instruments dealing with assets, liabilities and off-balance sheet items cannot be separated from liquidity management.

In particular, interest rate movements influence the conditions negotiated for the raising or use of additional liquidity over time. Even the very presence of an interest rate risk that can be associated essentially with the different maturities and the difference in repositioning of the rates on asset and liability instruments should be considered by means of appropriate variations in the types of instruments available to the banks and also in the interest rates.

It can thus easily be seen that there exists a close link between liquidity problems and solvency problems, even if different time periods are taken into consideration.

2.7.2 Solvency Risk

Solvency concerns the ability to honour one's debts at any cost. This, in turn, presupposes the availability of monetary resources during crisis periods. Solvency is measured by the ratio between capital and total deposits or total assets or assets exposed to risk (Revell, 1975). The latter basically replicates that of capital adequacy.

However, leverage ratios measured as capital over total assets (unweighted) were better in predicting bank failures during financial crises than the more sophisticated risk-weighted measures of capital (King, 2016).

The solvency risk concerns the differentiated ability of banks to settle their debts at any cost. Solvency is thus achieved by means of systematically higher asset values as compared to liabilities, thereby indicating positive levels of the bank's capital. This highlights the problem of growth of profit and of banks' recourse to market instruments in order to develop its capital.

On closer inspection, insolvency arises from an excessive risk level, which brings about reductions in value of financial assets (Johnson, 1993; Kohn, 2004; Saunders & Cornett, 2008). This testifies to a problem of appropriate choices for risk identification, measurement and control, as well as the need to minimise the impact on a bank's capital and to ensure its survival on the market.

Maintenance of solvency presupposes management choices based on appropriate principles of rigour and, above all, on accuracy in credit risk assessment. It is also necessary to ensure creation of a loan portfolio which, over time, will prove capable of restoring and renewing cash flow, together with the ordinary cash flow arising from interest collection.

Solvency has close links to liquidity because the sources of liquidity arise from asset, liability and off-balance sheet items (OBSIs) and from the costs and revenue trend, because the sources of solvency are directly affected by asset and liability values and by achievement of profit.

Solvency is also linked to management of the other risks, as their impact influences the economic outcome and the fluctuations in the value of assets and liabilities.

2.7.3 Credit Risk

The credit risk concerns failure to pay interest and/or capital associated with a bond or a bank loan.

Bonds issued by states within industrialised economies are widely present, with a low risk. However, the credit risk can be restricted by investment in high-rated bonds. The credit risk can be further reduced by granting loans to high-quality customers. On closer inspection, it's the rating level which can be attributed to bond issuers or loan customers to define the risk level involved in related financial instruments and total portfolio.

In this framework, credit risk is examined essentially with reference to bank loans' portfolio. As far as loans to clients are concerned, loans to excellent or low-quality enterprises are equally present, with lowering or raising of the credit risk. A rigorous analysis should be carried out prior to the financing of investment projects, in order to ascertain the extent to which the project has the capacity to produce income. Basically, this is equivalent to an assessment of the credit capacity (Bianchi, 1992; Caprara, 1954; Dell'Amore, 1965; Dematté, 1974; Forestieri, 1991). This type of assessment is always regarded as necessary. The temporal horizon and the methodologies used are different in the hypothesis of short-term as compared to medium-term or long-term credit.

Application of the most modern risk analysis techniques is necessary in order to rationalise choices concerning the granting of credit to clients and, at the same time, to avert problems of adverse selection and moral hazard (Colombini, 2001; Hubbard, 2008; van Damme, 1994).

Such problems can be reduced or eliminated by production of information before and after the granting of financing. The content of the information produces uncertainty regarding the value of the loans and the value of assets; this, in turn, causes fluctuations in the capital and economic values.

Adverse selection arises when monetary resources are destined to risky investment projects that were not fully evaluated, leading to difficulties in the loan repayment. Moral hazard, on the other hand, arises from a different use of monetary resources as compared to that which was originally planned: this likewise creates difficulties for the loan repayment.

Modern screening and monitoring activities play a fundamental role in containing or eliminating the problems associated with adverse selection and moral hazard, which inevitably pose a risk for the granting of credit. Consequently, these aspects also affect management of loan portfolios and can lead to reduction in value and lower return on assets, more contained interest on assets and also credit losses in the income statement. Naturally, such phenomena result in lower or even null profit. The credit risk can however be lessened by means of investment in high-rated loans.

2.7.4 Interest Rate Risk

Asset and liability management (ALM) presupposes simultaneous management of balance sheet assets and liabilities and includes problems of matching assets and liabilities, matching and mismatching of maturities, costs and revenue, as well as interest rate structure. Possible scenarios and the ensuing reflexes on income statement and on capital are examined. ALM aims to pursue objectives of risk control and management, with particular reference to the interest rate risk (Bergendahl, 1996).

In this context, the interest rate risk has an effect on costs and revenue and on assets and liabilities that are linked to changes in the market rates. The impact on the profit and loss account and on the asset and liability statement can likewise become positive by increasing profits and capital or negative by reducing profits and capital.

A closer examination reveals that the financial transformation and the consequent mismatching that is an intrinsic aspect of the different maturities, interest rates, flow periodicity and index-linking parameters exert an influence on the rise and evolution of the interest rate risk (Bessis, 2015; Colombini, 1994; Cucinotta & Moretti, 1988; Gardner & Mills, 1994; Kidwell, Peterson, & Blackwell, 1997; Saunders & Cornett, 2008).

The risk examined here is linked essentially to differences in maturities (for fixed rates) and in the dates of revision of the rate (for variable rates), due to the different reflexes of repricing. Such differences lead to fluctuations in costs and revenue, assets and liabilities, thereby also affecting profit and capital on account of unexpected variations in the market rates.

Similarly, imperfect correlation in adjustment of asset rates and liability rates in reference to different instruments but with similar price revisions likewise leads to changes in the yield differentials.

Furthermore, asymmetries in financial instruments that have an option right also create management problems and constitute an additional risk with regard to the interest rate (Wright & Houpt, 1996).

Assets and liabilities that are sensitive or insensitive to interest rate variations can easily be distinguished. The former involve fixed rate expiry positions and variable interest rate, while the latter include only fixed rate positions.

Changes in external market rates are not transmitted to an identical extent onto sensitive assets and liabilities, due to the non-parallel displacements in the yield curve, the set of internal rates involved and the contractual position of the individual banks on the given markets. This leads to upward or downward movements of the interest income and/or of capital.

2.7.4.1 *Measurement: Gap Management Models and Duration Model*

Measurement of the interest rate risk can be carried out basically by two different approaches: current earnings and the economic value of capital. These methods are applied, respectively, in the gap management models and the duration model (Colombini, 1994; Drago, 1998; Rose, 1989; Sinkey, 1992).

The current earnings approach considers the impact of variations in the market rates on the interest income and, therefore, on the profit and loss account (Flannery, 1981). In particular, in the context of remunerative assets and onerous liabilities, the interest rate risk derives from the gap between sensitive assets and liabilities, which consist of expiring fixed rate positions or variable rate positions. This approach gives an indication of the impact of market rate movements on short-term income.

In contrast, the economic value approach takes into consideration the impact of interest rate movements on the market value of assets and liabilities and, therefore, on capital. This approach awards importance to capital sensitivity concerning future modifications in market rates, with reference to the entire time period of repricing. In this regard, the balance sheet items are calculated at current value for determination of the economic value of capital. Interest rate variations affect the value of capital as a result of the different level both of interest flows and the discount rate.

Considering the potential impact of interest rate variations on the current value of all future financial flows, the economic value approach offers a broader view of the potential medium- and long-term effects on the bank's overall situation.

2.7.4.2 Measurement: Simulation Model

In order to set up a simulation model, hypothetical economic and financial scenarios are devised, and the resulting reactions affecting the balance sheet values are examined. The various hypotheses concern the economic, financial and asset and liability statement of the bank, with attention focusing on the extent to which the results are affected by changes in the environmental variables and the management policies. While the resulting scenarios suggest approaches and solutions concerning the problem of exposure to the interest rate risk, they presuppose reliable data, correct hypotheses, as well as a valid internal organisational structure. The latter is in any case necessary for the functioning of an ALM system and for management of the interest rate risk (Toevs & Haney, 1986).

The construction of a simulation model implies that several phases must be set up, such as definition of the problems that constitute the object of the simulation, formulation of the required hypotheses, definition of the logical-mathematical relations, data collection, estimation of the model and, finally, acceptance or rejection of the model that has been set up.

Acceptance of the model leads to definition of various different sets of hypotheses concerning the future trend of the variables under consideration and, accordingly, of the reference scenarios that produce divergent results. Construction of the simulation model provides a range of answers concerning interest rate trends, market conditions and bank management policies.

This model allows measurement and management of the interest rate risk by formulating a number of distinct hypotheses on the trend and structure of the interest rates and on modifications in the volume and composition of assets and liabilities. It follows that despite the complexity of the procedure adopted for setting up and using a simulation model, such a model proves to be a suitable tool for control of the interest rate risk in its divergent manifestations and, above all, in its dynamic aspects.

Naturally, simulation models are quite complex both as regards their construction and their use. However, they can suggest a range of solutions for management problems and for the interest rate risk. The validity of such models is linked above all to the reliability of their input data and of the hypotheses underlying the associated mathematical equations.

Two fundamental aspects play an important role: the interest rate risk must be set in the context of a logical-formal representation of banking and financial activity and, at the same time, estimates must be performed using a correct forecast of market rate trends.

2.7.4.3 Derivatives and Securitisation

Derivatives, such as swaps, options and futures, have created the conditions allowing an expansion of capital market activity as well as changes both in balance sheet and off-balance sheet items, in line with control of the interest rate risk. These instruments can be used to cover price and coupon fluctuations within specific asset classes. Therefore they effectively contribute to reduction of the interest rate risk. This implies that the swap can be negotiated for changes from a fixed rate to a variable rate, or vice versa. In this manner, a positive influence on relations between rate sensitive assets (RSAs) and rate sensitive liabilities (RSLs) is achieved. Options and, likewise, futures can be negotiated in order to block the future price of securities, thereby exerting a positive influence on potential interest rate changes.

Furthermore, securitisation applied to asset classes can be used for reduction of the interest rate risk, by disinvestment of fixed rate and longer maturity positions.

Choices and use of derivatives and securitisation are tested in the context of gap management, duration or simulation models. Such models provide indications concerning the interest rate risk exposure and, consequently, on suitable approaches to risk reduction. It is worth noting that derivatives and securitisation can be used in order to reduce and transfer a portfolio's credit risk by a credit derivative or by creating asset-backed securities (ABS) and loan classes. The latter solution also leads to a reduction in the loan portfolio and to a rise in liquidity.

2.7.5 Foreign Exchange Risk

The exchange risk originates from assets and liabilities and from revenue and costs expressed in different currencies, which at times have a marked effect on levels of profit and capital.

The exchange risk can be measured by net exposure in exchanges. In this regard, net foreign exchange exposure (*NFXE*) for each currency *i* is obtained by summing the difference between assets and liabilities in currency *i* together with the difference between purchases and sales of currency *i*. This can be indicated by the following expression:

$$NFXE_i = \left(FX\,\text{assets}_i - FX\,\text{liabilities}_i\right) + \left(FX\,\text{bought}_i - FX\,\text{sold}_i\right)$$

In any case, overall exchange risk exposure does not correspond to the sum of net positions in the different currencies, because of the compensation effect in currency movements. The exchange risk can be reduced by utilisation of covariance among different currency positions (Campbell & Kracaw, 1993; Santomero & Babbel, 1997; Saunders & Cornett, 2008).

Furthermore, the exchange rate risk can be cancelled by expressing assets and liabilities as well as revenue and costs in the same currency. The exchange risk can be lowered or eliminated by means of appropriate derivative instruments which result in partial or total transfer to other parties.

2.7.6 Operational Risk

Operational risk arises from inadequacies or deficiencies in internal processes, human behaviour, technological systems and external events. Such situations lead to cost increases and/or lower revenue and therefore a decrease in profit. Operational risk can be addressed by considering a series of internal and external factors for risk identification, measurement and management. This definition includes the legal risk, but excludes strategic and reputational risk.

Operational risk involves the problem of loss and, at the same time, the problem of steps to be taken for correction of internal and external procedures and for reduction or minimisation of negative effects.

2.8 Bank and Financial Crises

Financial crises can be examined in the framework of crises involving financial markets, crises affecting financial intermediaries, sovereign debt crises and currency crises. Careful examination of the issues involved shows that financial crises are the result of interrelations among a number of circumstances: adverse trends on the financial markets, adverse situations affecting financial intermediaries, tensions focusing on the public debt and turmoil in the exchange markets.

Financial crises have effects that ripple through financial markets, financial intermediaries, financial instruments, states and central banks, thus highlighting correlations and interdependencies as well as financial instability (Colombini & Calabrò, 2011). In short, financial crises have repercussions of marked intensity that are projected in the short, medium and long term over financial systems and, at the same time, over economic systems. For example, the subprime mortgage financial crisis calls for state aid measures in support of crisis-ridden financial intermediaries; the sovereign debt crisis implies the need for action to restore balance in the public finances; the economic crisis necessitates economic stimulus initiatives which diverge from the measures suggested in the previous two cases and may indeed be in conflict with them.

One aspect that clearly emerges is the importance of a scale of priorities concerning the volume of public resources required. Decisions on priorities must take into account the margins for public expenditure without causing excessive imbalance in the public budgets.

It likewise becomes clear that the irrational strategies based on innovative finance must be downsized or abandoned, in favour of restoring the concept of cultural and regulatory financial responsibility. Profits should be achieved by rational risk management, rather than arising from practices inspired by a separation between risk and return which ends up offloading the negative impact of risk onto the state budgets, while the positive impact of returns is inserted into the balance sheets of individual banks.

These improper practices tend to exacerbate the risks weighing on the entire financial system, thereby undermining savers' confidence in financial intermediaries. The latter thus tend to be regarded as incapable of reducing the information asymmetries present on the financial markets. The move towards excessive risk taking has been allowed to creep in partly on account of failure by the supervisory authorities to exert proper control over the individual financial intermediaries and over the placement of financial market instruments; however, it is partly also ascribable to systematic attribution of decidedly positive ratings that are totally mistaken in their quantification.

The subprime mortgage financial crisis can be identified as originating above all from the practice of selecting and transferring the credit risk associated with poor-quality mortgage loans, thereby intensifying and transferring the overall credit risk. The collapse of the real estate market has led to markedly negative and widespread repercussions on the assets of banks and financial intermediaries that are characterised by significant levels of very bad mortgage loans and which, additionally, have made use of financial instruments of equally poor quality.

The sudden drop in house prices has induced adverse effects on the economy, triggering a recessive process of notable extension. A very worrying aspect is the situation of many families who are facing rising levels of unemployment and thus experience difficulty in meeting their mortgage instalment payments.

Thus on the one hand, the subprime mortgage financial crisis has made it necessary for governments to intervene in support of financial systems threatened by an unprecedented crisis, while on the other it has focused attention on the fragility of public budgets. Admittedly, massive resources have been made available to crisis-ridden banks in the different countries, but it is equally true that the shaky conditions of the public finances cannot exclusively be attributed to the subprime mortgage financial crisis.

Bailout plans to address the subprime mortgage financial crisis and expansionary policies designed to tackle the economic crisis have led to a marked deterioration in the public finances. However, the dramatic condition of the public finances should be ascribed not merely to the above described exceptional measures but also to unbridled public expenditure that has risen to unsustainable levels. The most critical elements affecting the public finances involve the following aspects: rising pension and healthcare expenditure due to an ageing population; fairly high expenditure on the national, regional and local level in matters pertaining to political affairs; intensity of tax evasion; amount of the public debt and its composition in terms of maturities and apportionment between residents and non-residents; private debt levels and degree of solidity of the banking systems.

The elevated levels of public indebtedness create the premises for the sovereign debt crisis, leading to an increase in the returns that the markets demand on bonds issued by states perceived as being at risk and thereby bringing about an increase in spreads between the bonds of an individual state and those of the German state. This, in turn, exacerbates the fragility of the budgets of crisis-ridden states and makes it difficult, if not impossible, to intervene with measures aimed at economic recovery (Acharya, Philippon, Richardson, & Roubini, 2009; Adrian & Shin, 2010; Allen & Carletti, 2010; Bernanke, 2015; Blanchard, Dell'Ariccia, & Mauro, 2010; Boccuzzi, 2011; Bolton & Jeanne, 2011; Calabria, 2009; Capriglione & Semeraro, 2012; Cassidy, 2009; Claessens, Dell'Ariccia, Igan, & Laeven, 2010; Colombini, 2011; Colombini & Calabrò, 2011; Crescenzi, 2010; Davies, 2010; Dowd & Hutchinson, 2010; Duffie, 2010; Eichengreen, 2008; Estrella & Schich, 2011; FCIC, 2011; Franke & Krahnen, 2008; Fratianni, 2008; Fornasari, 2009; Geithner, 2014; Goodhart, 2008; Haldane, 2009; Hubbard, 2009; King, 2016; Marconi, 2010; Masera, 2009; Mishkin, 2011; Reinhart & Rogoff, 2011; Shiller, 2008; Sorkin, 2009; Spaventa, 2010; Stiglitz, 2010; Wolf, 2014).

The trend of the spreads is thus linked to the situation within the various countries and to the perceived credit risk inherent in the sovereign debts as interpreted by the financial markets. Moreover, the trend is also influenced by the overall situation of the euro zone. Progress or worsening of the financial and economic situation within individual countries or involving the euro zone mechanisms leads to positive (reduction) or negative (increase) repercussions on the spreads.

It hardly need be added that speculation undoubtedly influences the fluctuation of the spreads. This makes itself felt not only in definition of the costs of individual public refinancing operations but also in the costs incurred by banks in raising funds, as well as in the costs dictated by the financial markets regarding bank loans to firms. Furthermore, the issue of contagion cannot be ignored, given that the interrelations among states transform the problems of individual states into global problems. This postulate is particularly evident in the context of the euro zone countries, triggering potential contagion among countries viewed as weaker on the financial level and therefore more fragile in the context of speculation.

In the light of the above observations, careful evaluations should be conducted in seeking to devise the best approach for overcoming financial crises and economic crises. More specifically, attention should be paid to identifying the specific problems, estimating the costs and formulating rational choices. Failure to assess these aspects results merely in wasteful use of public resources that provides no solution either for the problems raised by the subprime mortgage financial crisis or for the problems deriving from the sovereign debt crisis. In other words, the complex interactions are not addressed and definitive solutions are basically postponed to an indefinite future (Johnson & Kak, 2008).

It is imperative to examine the main causes, highlighting above all the role played by securitisation and credit derivatives in influencing the extent of credit risk transfer onto loan portfolios and sovereign bond portfolios. This issue is crucial because the repercussions can lead to fluctuations in value, weighing heavily on the losses suffered by financial intermediaries and by operators who invest in mortgages or in financial instruments linked to subprime mortgages or in bonds and financial instruments linked to sovereign states.

One major aspect common to the financial crises discussed here resides in the contraction of liquidity due to the negative fluctuations and losses of value associated with subprime mortgages and the related financial instruments. This phenomenon also impacts on sovereign bond portfolios and the related financial instruments. The repercussions adversely affect the trends concerning the value of bank assets and the assets of financial intermediaries and operators, leading to the need for adjustments and deleveraging processes on various levels.

Such observations underline the importance of correct analysis and evaluation of the credit risk inherent in loan portfolios, asset-backed securities (ABS), credit derivatives, financial instrument portfolios and sovereign bonds. In short, the manner in which the credit risk is manifested, transferred and multiplied on the level of individual financial systems constitutes the basic thread allowing analysis and interpretation of the financial crises that form part of the broader context of the subprime mortgage financial crisis and the sovereign debt crisis.

In the process of credit risk transfer that has characterised international finance essentially since the beginning of the third millennium, it is not easy to identify precisely which repercussions have an impact on the direct circuit as opposed to those that impact on the indirect circuit. Only by exploring the integration between the two processes does it become possible to delineate more clearly the effects of the subprime mortgage financial crisis and the sovereign debt crisis.

Irrational criteria that turn a blind eye to the creation and intensification of credit risk have induced financial intermediaries to engage in unreasonable practices of experimenting with the transfer of credit risk to the financial markets, by means of securitisation and credit derivatives.

This has triggered multiplicative impulses, raising problems concerning medium- and long-term sustainability. Moreover, such practices are suggestive of an original flaw which is of fundamental importance in the evolutionary path of financial systems.

On closer examination, credit risk transfer onto financial markets, where the main figure both in the field of sales and also of purchasing is represented by financial intermediaries, assumes the extended meaning of an increase in the burden of risk weighing upon the financial system, due to the numerous interrelations among financial intermediaries (Shin, 2010). Basically, the problem can be traced partly to unorthodox practices in granting loans to a very poor-quality customer base and partly also to the subsequent experimental practices of risk transfer taken to excessive levels, as well as to failure of the supervisory authorities to exercise proper control.

2.9 Conclusions

Risk identification, measurement and management represent the heart of bank enterprises, and the ability to control them in a situation of asymmetric information is a fundamental bank function for the achievement of economic results.

The typical range of risks includes liquidity, solvency, credit, interest rate and operational. Identification, measurement and management of all risks affecting banking business instruments and business areas are steps to be implemented and carried out. Their evaluation and impact constitute relevant phases which are assigned to the risk management function, thereby underlining its importance and drawing attention to the need for adjustments through time periods.

Therefore risk management is closely related to banking business areas that give rise to implementation and evolution of changes in the overall banking system. In short, it is through risk management that banks acquire heightened awareness of the internal and the external conditions. Building up the risk management function on the level of individual banks is a delicate task, as the appropriate choices depend largely on rational evaluation of every kind of risk involved in the various instruments and business areas. It is necessary to have professional skills and capacity for identification, measurement and management of the entire range of risks and, at the same time, for evaluation of the most appropriate initiatives.

References

Acharya, V., Philippon, T., Richardson, M., & Roubini, N. (2009). The financial crisis of 2007–2009: Causes and remedies. *Financial Markets, Institutions & Instruments, 18*(2), 89–137.

Adrian, T., & Shin, H. S. (2010). The changing nature of financial intermediation and the financial crisis of 2007–2009. *Annual Review of Economics, 2*, 603–618.

Allen, F., & Carletti, E. (2010). An overview of the crisis: Causes, consequences, and solutions. *International Review of Finance, 10*(1), 1–26.

Arrow, K. J. (1951). Alternative approaches to the theory of choice in risk-taking situations. *Econometrica: Journal of the Econometric Society, 19*(4), 404–437.

Bianchi, T. (1992). *I fidi bancari*. Torino: Utet.

Bergendahl, G. (1996). Global ALM in investment banking. In E. Gardener & P. Molineux (Eds.), *Investment banking. Theory and practice*. London: Euromoney Publications.

Bernanke, B. S. (2015). *The courage to act: A memoir of a crisis and its aftermath*. New York: Norton & Company.

Bessis, J. (2015). *Risk management in banking*. New York: Wiley.

Blanchard, O., Dell'Ariccia, G., & Mauro, P. (2010). Rethinking macroeconomic policy. *Journal of Money, Credit and Banking, 42*(s1), 199–215.

Boccuzzi, G. (2011). *Towards a new framework for banking crisis management: The international debate and the Italian model*. Roma: Banca d'Italia.

Bolton, P., & Jeanne, O. (2011). Sovereign default risk and bank fragility in financially integrated economies. *IMF Economic Review, 59*(2), 162–194.

Calabria, M. A. (2009). Did deregulation cause the financial crisis. *Cato Policy Report, 31*(4), 1–8.

Campbell, T. S., & Kracaw, W. A. (1993). *Financial risk management: Fixed income and foreign exchange*. New York: Harper Collins.

Caprara, U. (1954). *L'economia della banca*. Milano: Giuffrè.

Capriglione, F., & Semeraro, G. (2012). *Crisi finanziaria e dei debiti sovrani: l'Unione Europea tra rischi ed opportunità*. Torino: Utet.

Cassidy, J. (2009). *How markets fail: The logic of economic calamities*. New York: Farrar, Straus and Giroux.

Claessens, S., Dell'Ariccia, G., Igan, D., & Laeven, L. (2010). Cross-country experiences and policy implications from the global financial crisis. *Economic Policy, 25*(62), 267–293.

Claessens, S., Ratnovski, L., & Singh, M. M. (2012). *Shadow banking: Economics and policy* (No. 12). International Monetary Fund.

Colombini, F. (1994). *Rischio di saggio di interesse negli intermediari creditizi: analisi dei modelli*. Rassegna Economica. Luglio–Dicembre.

Colombini, F. (1999). Strumenti derivati e intermediari finanziari. *Rivista Bancaria, 55*(1), 111–125.

Colombini, F. (2001). *Intermediari e mercati finanziari: teoria e gestione*. Torino: Utet.
Colombini, F. (2004). Strumenti fuori bilancio negli intermediari bancari. La recente esperienza italiana. *Rivista Bancaria*, 4.
Colombini, F. (2008). *Intermediari, mercati e strumenti finanziari. Economia e integrazione*. Torino: Utet.
Colombini, F. (2011). Crisi finanziarie e risk management. Rilievi critici. *Rivista Trimestrale di Diritto dell'Economia*, 4.
Colombini, F., & Calabrò, A. (2011). *Crisi finanziarie: banche e Stati: l'insostenibilità del rischio di credito*. Torino: Utet.
Crescenzi, A. (2010). *Propagazione ed effetti della crisi finanziaria sull'economia reale. La crisi mondiale. Storia di tre anni difficili*. Roma: Luiss University Press.
Crouhy, M., Galai, D., & Mark, R. (2014). *The essentials of risk management*. New York: McGraw-Hill.
Cucinotta, G., & Moretti, E. (1988). *Strumenti della nuova finanza*. Roma: Nuova Italia Scientifica.
Culp, C. L. (2011). *Risk transfer: Derivatives in theory and practice*. New York: Wiley.
Davies, H. (2010). *The financial crisis: Who is to blame?* Cambridge: Polity Press.
Dell'Amore, G. (1965). *Economia delle aziende di credito*. Milano: Giuffrè.
Dematté, C. (1974). *La valutazione della capacità di credito nelle analisi di fido*. Milano: Vallardi.
Diamond, D. W., & Dybvig, P. H. (1986). Banking theory, deposit insurance, and bank regulation. *The Journal of Business, 59*(1), 55–68.
Dowd, K., & Hutchinson, M. (2010). *Alchemists of loss: How modern finance and government intervention crashed the financial system*. New York: Wiley.
Drago, D. (1998). *Rischio di interesse e gestione bancaria: modelli e tecniche a confronto*. Roma: Bancaria Editrice.
Duffie, D. (2010). *How big banks fail and what to do about it*. Princeton, NJ: Princeton University Press.
Eichengreen, B. (2008). Ten questions about the subprime crisis. Financial Stability Review, 19.
Estrella, A., & Schich, S. (2011). Sovereign and banking sector debt. *OECD Journal: Financial Market Trends, 2011*(2), 21–45.
FCIC. (2011). *The financial crisis inquiry report: Final report of the National Commission on the causes of the financial and economic crisis in the United States. Official Government Edition*. Washington, DC: Government Printing Office.
Flannery, M. J. (1981). Market interest rates and commercial bank profitability: An empirical investigation. *The Journal of Finance, 36*(5), 1085–1101.
Forestieri, G. (1991). *I prestiti bancari nell'economia contemporanea. Tendenze nuove nell' intermediazione finanziaria*. Milano: Egea.

Fornasari, F. (2009). I dati e gli insegnamenti della crisi finanziaria USA. *Economia Italiana, 1*, 53–110.
Franke G., & Krahnen, J. P. (2008). *The future of securitisation.* CFS Working Papers 31.
Fraser, J., & Simkins, B. J. (2010). *Enterprise risk management.* Hoboken, NJ: Wiley.
Fratianni, M. (2008). Financial crises, safety nets and regulation. *Rivista Italiana degli Economisti, 2.*
Freixas, X., & Rochet, J. C. (1997). *Microeconomics of banking.* Cambridge, MA: MIT Press.
Gardner, M. J., & Mills, D. L. (1994). *Managing financial institutions: An asset/liability approach.* Chicago: Dryden Press.
Gatzert, N., Schmeiser, H., & Schuckmann, S. (2008). Enterprise risk management in financial groups: Analysis of risk concentration and default risk. *Financial Markets and Portfolio Management, 22*(3), 241–258.
Geithner, T. F. (2014). *Stress test. Reflections on financial crises.* London: Random House.
Goodhart, C. (2008). The background to the 2007 financial crisis. *International Economics and Economic Policy, 4*(4), 331–346.
Gorton, G., & Metrick, A. (2010). Regulating the shadow banking system. *Brookings Papers on Economic Activity, 2*(Fall), 261–297.
Haldane, A. G. (2009). *Why banks failed the stress test.* London: Bank of England.
Hubbard, D. W. (2009). *The failure of risk management: Why it's broken and how to fix it.* Hoboken, NJ: Wiley.
Hubbard, R. G. (2008). *Money, the financial system and the economy.* Reading, MA: Addison-Wesley.
Johnson, H. J. (1993). *Financial institutions and markets. A global perspective.* New York: McGraw-Hill.
Johnson S., & Kak, J. (2008, September 25). *The price of salvation.* FT.com Economists' Forum.
Kidwell, D. S., Peterson, R. L., & Blackwell, D. W. (1997). *Financial institutions, markets and money.* Orlando: Dryden Press.
King, M. (2016). *The end of alchemy. Money, banking and the future of the global economy.* London: Little Brown.
Knight, F. H. (1921). *Risk, uncertainty, and profit.* Boston: Houghton Mifflin.
Kohn, M. (2004). *Financial institutions and markets.* Oxford: University Press.
Lemma, V. (2016). *The shadow banking system. Creating transparency in the financial markets.* London: Palgrave Macmillan.
Liikanen, E. (2012, October 2). *High-level expert group on reforming the structure of the EU banking sector.* Final Report, Brussels.
Lucas, R. E. (1981). *Studies in business-cycle theory.* Cambridge: MIT Press.

Marconi, F. (2010). *Le origini e la diffusione della crisi finanziaria: evidenze teoriche ed empiriche. La crisi mondiale. Storia di tre anni difficili*. Roma: Luiss University Press.
Masera, R. (2009). *Financial turbulence and the capital standard paradigm: A sequel. The great financial crisis. Economics, regulation and risk*. Roma: Bancaria Editrice.
Masera, R., & Mazzoni, G. (2007). *Una nota sulle attività di risk e capital management di un intermediario bancario*. Quaderno di Ricerca No 62. Roma: Ente Luigi Einaudi.
Mikes, A. (2009). Risk management and calculative cultures. *Management Accounting Research, 20*(1), 18–40.
Mishkin, F. S. (2011). Over the cliff: From the subprime to the global financial crisis. *The Journal of Economic Perspectives, 25*(1), 49–70.
Nocco, B. W., & Stulz, R. M. (2006). Enterprise risk management: Theory and practice. *Journal of Applied Corporate Finance, 18*(4), 8–20.
Oldani, C. (2008). *Governing global derivatives: Challenges and risks*. Aldershot: Ashgate Publishing.
Pozsar, Z., Adrian, T., Ashcraft, A., & Boesky, H. (2012). *Shadow banking*. FRBNY Staff Report No. 458.
Reinhart, C., & Rogoff, K. (2011). *This time is different. Eight centuries of financial folly*. Princeton, NJ: Princeton University Press.
Revell, J. R. S. (1973). *The british financial system*. London: Macmillan.
Revell, J. R. S. (1975). *Solvency and regulation of banks. Bangor occasional papers in economics* (Vol. 5). Cardiff: University of Wales Press.
Ricci, R. (1988). *La banca moderna. Aspetti gestionali e tendenze evolutive*. Torino: Utet.
Richardson, M., Smith, R., & Walter, I. (2010). *Regulating Wall Street: The Dodd-Frank Act and the new architecture of global finance*. New York: New York University Stern School of Business.
Rose, S. (1989). The two faces of AL management. *American Banker*, 1.
Santomero, A. M., & Babbel, D. F. (1997). *Financial markets, instruments, and institutions*. New York: McGraw-Hill.
Saunders, A., & Cornett, M. M. (2008). *Financial institutions management. A modern perspective*. Boston: McGraw-Hill/Irwin.
Savona, P. (2010). *Sugli effetti macroeconomici dei contratti derivati. Dieci lezioni*. Roma: Luiss University Press.
Schroek, G. (2002). *Risk management and value creation in financial institutions*. New York: Wiley.
Shiller, R. J. (2008). *The subprime solution. How today's global financial crisis happened and what to do about it*. Princeton, NJ: Princeton University Press.
Shin, H. S. (2010). *Risk and liquidity*. Oxford: Oxford University Press.

Sinkey, J. F., Jr. (1992). *Commercial bank financial management in the financial-services industry*. New York: Macmillan.
Sorkin, A. R. (2009). *Too big to fail*. New York: Viking.
Spaventa, L. (2010). *Economists and economics: What does the crisis tell us? Global crisis and long term growth: A new capitalism ahead*. Milano: McGraw-Hill.
Stein, J. C. (2010). Securitization, shadow banking, and financial fragility. *Daedalus, 139*(4), 41–51.
Stiglitz, J. E. (2010). *Freefall. America, free markets, and the sinking of the world economy*. New York: Norton.
Toevs, A. L., & Haney, W. C. (1986). Measuring and managing interest rate risk: A guide to asset/liability models used in banks and thrifts. In Platt R. B. (Ed.), *Controlling interest rate risk. New techniques and applications for money management*. New York: Wiley.
van Damme, E. (1994). Banking: A survey of recent microeconomic theory. *Oxford Review of Economic Policy, 10*(4), 14–33.
Wallace, N. (1996). Narrow banking meets the Diamond-Dybvig model. *Federal Reserve Bank of Minneapolis Quarterly Review, 20*(1), 3–13.
Wright, D. M., & Houpt, J. V. (1996). An analysis of commercial bank exposure to interest rate risk. *Federal Reserve Bulletin, 82*, 115–128.
Wolf, M. (2014). *The shifts and the shocks: What we've learned—And have still to learn—From the financial crisis*. London: Penguin.

CHAPTER 3

Credit Risk Management and Banking Business in Europe

Fabiano Colombini

3.1 Introduction

Granting loans to excellent or low-quality enterprises is equally present in bank loan portfolio, with lowering or raising of the credit risk. A complete investigation should be carried out prior to the financing of investment projects, in order to ascertain the extent to which the project has the capacity to produce income. Such an assessment is always regarded as necessary. The temporal horizon and the methodologies used are different in the hypothesis of short-term as compared to medium-term or long-term credit.

These problems can be reduced or eliminated by production of information before and after the granting of financing. The information content produces uncertainty regarding the value of loans and value of assets; this, in turn, causes fluctuations in economic values and capital values. Information production is an important function performed by individual banks and, at the same time, involves an organisational structure. This function tends to produce good quality information as the bank will command greater support for achieving the right choices in the bank business

F. Colombini (✉)
Department of Economics and Management, University of Pisa, Pisa, Italy

F. Colombini (ed.), *Raising Capital or Improving Risk Management and Efficiency?*, https://doi.org/10.1007/978-3-319-71749-4_3

areas. Information quality is particularly important for assessments in granting loans and, at the same time, in loan portfolio composition, which reveals different trends through time periods and economic trends.

This chapter aims to examine bank lending, credit risk and problems and solutions related to non-performing loans (NPLs).

3.2 Bank Lending

Granting loans postulates prior assessment of the credit capacity (Bianchi, 1992; Caprara, 1954; Dell'Amore, 1965; Dematté, 1974; Forestieri, 1991). Such an assessment is always regarded as necessary. The temporal horizon and the methodologies used are different in the hypothesis of short-term as compared to medium-term or long-term credit.

Application of the most modern risk analysis techniques is necessary in order to rationalise choices concerning the granting of credit to clients and, at the same time, to avert problems of adverse selection and moral hazard (Colombini, 2001; Hubbard, 2008; van Damme, 1994).

In an overall perspective, short-term as well as medium- and long-term loans constitute the most important class of bank assets. This is a feature which distinguishes the composition of bank assets with different ratios of total loans to assets from one bank to another and over time. It is important to stress that the loan share in the composition of bank assets bears a relation to costs and revenue and consequently to profits or losses. In the application of the universal model in the European banks, the range of loans partially or entirely includes the following technical forms: short-term loans, medium- and long-term loans, leasing, factoring, consumer credit.

There are differences among the technical forms in which loans are granted, and also in cash flow generation. In short-term loans, monetary flows result from intake of interest payments and from repayment of the entire sum at maturity, the latter often being tacitly renewed. In medium- and long-term loans, on the other hand, repayment arises as a result of the periodic monetary flows from collection of the instalments, which generally include the capital share and the interest share.

Although longer-term loans are associated with greater risk, the resulting cash flow may turn out to be greater and more stable; however, with regard to short-term loans, the implicit and sometimes systematic renewal that is an intrinsic feature of such loans should not be overlooked.

In medium- and long-term loans, the application of fixed rates leads to problems concerning exposure to interest rate risk. This leads to a positive or negative contribution to the profit and loss statement in the event, respectively, of a drop or a rise in market rates.

In the American experience of the 1970s and 1980s of the Savings and Loan Associations specialised in medium- and long-term loans, the growth of fixed rate loans on total assets gave rise to considerable problems, due to the increase in market rates. This led to a contraction of profits and even to cases of losses. Such circumstances caused repeated crises and bankruptcies in the medium- and long-term credit industry, drastically reducing the number of intermediaries present in the industry (Barth, 1991; Kane, 1989; White, 1991).

Some loans are assisted by covenants. In such cases, the debtor is required to obey certain clauses forming part of the loan contract, with particular reference to the following aspects: investment policies, own capital levels, guarantees granted, clarity of information. These clauses make a positive contribution to improvement in the quality of loans (Berlin & Mester, 1992; Rajan & Winton, 1995).

Loans may also be assisted by guarantees. Such guarantees are either personal or collateral. Guarantees create better prospects for recovery of loans in the event of debtor insolvency.

Thus covenants aim to reduce the estimate of exposure in case of insolvency (exposure at default, *EAD*), while guarantees are designed to reduce the percentage loss (loss given default, *LGD*).

Since the class of short-term and medium- and long-term loans is found to be the major component in the structure of a bank's total assets, the relations with cash flow generation and interest earned are immediate and have a considerable impact on monetary repayments and expenses and on the statement of profit and loss.

This shows the importance of the system of interest rates on loan portfolios and the mean return associated with such interest rates. A comparison can thus be drawn with the returns on similar classes of assets, allowing more rational choices concerning composition and recomposition.

It is also important to ensure correct association of the interest rate with the credit risk affecting individual loans, taking into consideration expected losses, unexpected losses and fund-raising costs. This, in turn, presupposes careful investigation of debtors' ability to repay: consequently, the different types of credit risk are classified on the basis of internal ratings (Colquitt, 2007; Jacobson, Lindé, & Roszbach, 2006; Nickell, Perraudin, & Varotto, 2007).

In this context, given equal borrowing and external funding, medium-sized and large enterprises show an increasing or decreasing tendency to have recourse to the market for bond and/or share placement, in order to reduce or increase the demand for bank loans. At the same time, increases or decreases in bank liquidity produce, respectively, positive or negative reflexes on the granting of credit.

3.3 Credit Risk: Measurement and Management

Credit risk is the risk of potential default of borrowers in the repayment of debt as principal and as interest. This is a very powerful risk as it can produce negative impacts and losses which will cause reductions in asset values and write-downs in loans' portfolios and therefore in the level of capital. In this framework, the analysis considers credit risk essentially with application to loans' portfolios.

More generally, credit risk appreciation can be carried out by the analysis of the following parameters: probability of default (*PD)*, loss given default (*LGD*), exposure at default (*EAD*), maturity (*M*).

PD, which is expressed in percentage terms, represents the probability of client insolvency within a year and oscillates between 0 and 1. *LGD* expressed in percentage terms quantifies the loss that would occur in the case of client insolvency. *EAD* measures the level of exposure at the time of client default. *M* concerns the maturity of loans granted to clients. Taking these different parameters into consideration, the bank can formulate precise credit risk assessments on clients' loan portfolio. *PD*, together with *LGD* and *EAD*, constitutes an assessment of the credit risk. Therefore, a rise in credit risk is accompanied by an increase in the credit rate applied.

Credit risk may give rise to expected loss (*EL*) which does not create problems for the bank as appropriate accounting provisions are always made. Therefore, the bank will not undergo any negative impact that would affect future profits. In contrast, if credit risk is unforeseen, this may cause unexpected loss (*UL*) thereby causing problems for the bank.

The distinction between expected loss and unexpected loss is important in consideration of management choices with regard to the following aspects:

- the amounts involved in direct value adjustments and in provisions necessary in order to ensure that expected losses will be covered;

- level of capital in order to cover unexpected losses;
- interest rates that are in line with value adjustments and with provisions designed to cover expected; losses and the cost of capital for unexpected losses.

It follows that it is important to ensure that correct methodologies are used for measurement of expected and unexpected losses (Bessis, 2015; Cirillo, 2005; Lusignani, 2004; Masera, 2005).

Expected loss (*EL*) can be calculated by means of the following product:

$$EL = PD \cdot EAD \cdot LGD$$

Unexpected loss (*UL*) can be identified as arising from volatility of losses around their mean value and, therefore, around expected loss. Unexpected portfolio loss is measured by the standard deviation of the frequency distribution of possible losses affecting the portfolio.

Considering the entire loss probability distribution and a confidence interval of 99.9 per cent on a one-year temporal horizon, the maximum loss level is measured by value at risk (*VaR*) which, after subtracting expected loss (*EL*), expresses unexpected loss (*UL*) and, therefore, the level of capital necessary in order to cover it. The situation is expressed by the following formula:

$$UL = VaR - EL$$

Credit risk can be transferred to other counterparties by means of credit derivatives. This creates cover against the risk of insolvency or deterioration of the debtor's credit quality, even if the credit relationship remains in the hands of the bank (Brandon & Fernandez, 2005; Clark, 1997; Duffee & Zhou, 2001; Moser, 1998; Neal, 1996; Rule, 2001).

Equally, credit risk can be transferred by securitisation, which implies the pooling of loans having similar characteristics and transfer of the pool to external investors; at the same time, asset-backed securities are created.

Asset quality review (AQR) and, at the same time, stress tests by the Banking Supervision of the European Central Bank (ECB) focus on asset values and fluctuation values as the most important problem arising from financial crises in European banks. Deterioration in loan portfolios tends to create non-performing loans (NPLs) which present problems in terms of non-paying interests and non-repaying capital in variable proportions.

3.4 Non-performing Loans: Origins and Solutions

The subprime mortgage financial crisis brings to light the inadequate credit risk management produced by the banking system, which initially gave rise to negative consequences for the financial system and subsequently for the economic system.

Similarly, the sovereign debt crisis highlighted the unbalanced public finance management characterised by the widespread use of debt which, together with the subprime mortgage financial crisis, had a severe impact, as substantial public resources had to be destined to the rescue of banks and financial systems.

Increasing the level of credit risk borne by sovereign states initially generates negative repercussions on public issues and, as a result, on fluctuations in value of financial instruments' portfolios of financial intermediaries.

Readjustments of public accounts cause a tax increase and/or a reduction in public expenditure. In the European context, during the time period between 2007 and 2014, policies for rebalancing the public accounts generated a recessive push economically, essentially implying a loss estimated in several percentage points of gross domestic product (GDP), despite differences among European countries. This is a loss in wealth that is becoming practically irrecoverable, thus underscoring a negative aspect: public accounts rebalancing operations in the context of financial and economic crises imply negative results economically. In Europe, public accounts rebalancing policies generated economic recessions over several years, with a recovery phase which started towards the end of 2013.

Several years of economic recessions gave rise to non-performing loans (NPLs) in a commercial banking context, causing the credit crunch. In Europe, the increase in NPLs is partly attributable to severe economic conditions that leave many customers unable to proceed with the repayment of interest and capital; to some extent, however, the increase in NPLs can also be ascribed to bad selection and monitoring of investment projects and firms. Certain distinctive features of banks and efforts to improve risk management and efficiency exert a positive influence on the evolution of NPLs. Poor management of banks tends to exacerbate the creation of poor-quality loans, negatively influencing efficiency and NPLs (Altunbas, Carbo, Gardener, & Molyneux, 2007; Avgouleas & Goodhart, 2017; Berger & De Young, 1997; Cucinelli, 2015; Duran & Lozano-Vivas, 2015; Kwan & Eisenbeis, 1997; Williams, 2004; Zhang, Cai, Dickinson, & Kutan, 2016). Banks follow some approaches for identification, measurement and management of NPLs and, at the same time, of write-down problems, reducing the level of NPLs and raising negative impact on the profit and loss account.

The introduction of the asset quality review (AQR) and, at the same time, of stress tests by the Banking Supervision of the European Central Bank (ECB) places emphasis on asset values and fluctuation values as the most important problem arising from financial crises in European banks. Deterioration in loan portfolios tends to create non-performing loans (NPLs) which present problems due to non-payment of interest and/or capital, in variable proportions.

The supervision unit at the ECB carries out checks on the level of NPLs in the euro area and, at the same time, on the validity of governance structures, strategies and suitable processes of individual banks for NPL management, taking into consideration the evolution of risk over time.

Considering the high level of NPLs in a number of European banks, it becomes important to set up special units within banks; such units will be dedicated to NPL management and resolution. The definition of strategies over time, with the participation of high level management, is extremely important. Loan classification and underlying guarantees as well as related judicial and non-judicial procedures postulate choices at appropriate times for raising cash and for establishing the number of loan repayments on a regular basis, with the final aim of reducing the new problematic loans. The composition of NPL units requires human resources with high-quality and professional skills, as they have to deal with a delicate and critical issue for evolution of the loan business and for repercussions on costs and revenue of individual banks.

Recovery from non-performing loans can be achieved only in the medium and long period; furthermore, management of such loans requires modernisation with efficient use of information technology to build up an overview of the situation of non-performing loans.

The economic consequences of the credit crunch performed by banks on their customers severely affected the companies' investments, with the logical consequence of sharpening the forces of recession.

Regarding NPL stock, the ECB Banking Supervision published the Guidance to banks on non-performing loans on March 2017, requiring banks with high levels to submit NPL strategies, including targets and reduction plans.

Considering new NPLs, the ECB Banking Supervision published a draft addendum on its Guidance to banks on non-performing loans on October 2017, indicating supervisory expectations for minimum levels of provisions. More specifically, banks are expected to provide full coverage for the unsecured part of new NPLs after two years and for the secured part after seven years. It is worthwhile to stress the supervisory expectations' change every few months which will become *de facto* a restrictive constraint measure on banks' business.

The ECB Banking Supervision will present further policies to address the existing stock of NPLs including transitional arrangements and, at the same time, will evaluate feedback statements from consultation.

In this framework, the creation of bad banks on an internal or external level and NPL divestiture processes seek to reduce the phenomenon of the credit crunch and to promote recovery through better and optimal lending conditions for families and enterprises. The price applied in credit lending divestiture distinguishes between unsecured credit and mortgage credit, the lending rates being lower and higher, respectively.

3.4.1 Bad Bank

A bad bank implies the creation of state-owned or private companies for the use of capital in bad assets purchased from troubled banks, "cleaning up" their balance sheets and assessing the appropriateness of their purchase price. A company set up for bad banking activities implies either a definite public equity presence, feeding the list of public companies, or a definite private equity presence, thus feeding off-balance sheet vehicles.

A bad bank postulates the identification of bad assets and good assets, and a net partition between these two categories, in the sense that bad assets are separated and transferred into the assets of the purpose-established company (the 'bad bank'), whereas good assets remain in the existing company's assets. A clear distinction between bad bank and good bank is thereby introduced (Colombini, 2015; Colombini & Calabrò, 2011).

A bad bank is an intervention that has been repeatedly carried out in countries affected by the effects which have been experienced since the

2007 worldwide financial crisis. Therefore, the intervention establishes clarity and different types of risk management activity, in the context of a recovered bank (good bank) and of a surviving bank (bad bank): the latter now incorporates all the negative and problematic items from the past management.

The activity performed by a bad bank does not represent a sole right for bad banks: in the evolution of financial crises, central banks themselves engage in repeated purchases of government securities and toxic assets in the context of unconventional measures, thus contributing to the placement of government securities and to recovery from the negative situation of bank balance sheets.

These are interventions which cause a considerable increase in the volume of assets; moreover, they cast light and shadows over the central banks from the standpoint, respectively, of a hypothetical value increase or of a hypothetical value reduction due to the presence of financial instruments of high or low quality in their assets.

Taking a closer look, the weakness of many banks makes economic recovery slower and more complex not only for individual countries but also on a European scale. The presence of non-performing loans and, even more so, of toxic securities among banks' assets leads to greater capital absorption, thus comparatively reducing monetary resources allocated for lending to the economy. Rational decision-making in the selection and control of loans to customers is therefore of paramount importance.

On a European level, in order to reinforce economic growth, the creation of a number of bad banks for the ultimate cleaning up of balance sheets in each country is a measure to be pursued. This should recreate more favourable conditions for loans, especially loans to small- and medium-sized enterprises, and therefore as an aid to economic development.

The creation of a pan-European bad bank or asset management company (AMC) has been indicated as a possible solution for NPLs in banks' balance sheets (Arner, Avgouleas, & Gibson, 2017; Avgouleas & Goodhart, 2017; Hellwig, 2017).

The importance of a check-up of European banks' balance sheets needs to be stressed, identifying deteriorated credit levels and toxic securities. The "clean-up" requirements concern both individual countries and also the global level: private or public initiatives should be undertaken for the creation of bad banks and the restoration, by contrast, of good banks.

This fulfils financial stability targets and, in particular, targets for achieving the best conditions that will encourage economic development, as much as good banks will be able to resume their traditional task, that of raising and lending funds to the worthiest enterprises. Even in the worst hypothesis, where, in some cases, it could prove necessary to make use of public resources, the economic outcomes pursued would be far superior to the expenditure of public resources.

Moreover, in past experiments the creation of bad banks—even when using public resources—does not necessarily produce a negative outcome for states. It has been found that the recovery of economic development encourages value readjustments even in bad assets, within bad banks. At the same time, the final net result may, in time, become positive.

3.4.2 *Selling Loans*

In setting up a strategy for NPL reduction, another alternative is represented by the sale of NPLs to specialised companies and funds. However, the crucial question is that the sale price may be very low, thereby creating losses in comparison with the readjusted book values. On the other hand, the loan values are normally reviewed every year in the balance sheet period, thus reducing the value of loans in trouble or NPLs.

A part of these assets can be sold on the market to specialised companies and funds, normally at a discounted price in comparison with the book value. This has a positive impact on the liquidity position of the bank and, at the same time, a negative impact on the profit and loss account.

In this context, variable shares of NPLs and variable decisions to sell such assets give rise to an NPL business that is of considerable importance for European banks and for the specialised companies and funds involved in this business, which are located in various different countries.

An NPL business comprises a range of prices for buying and selling, with differentiated repercussions on bank intermediaries and specialised companies and funds, which belong to various countries. In setting the price, management costs and revenue as well as the final sale price are the essential elements taken into consideration.

Financial crises and economic crises contribute to the expansion of NPLs. Therefore it is important to set a limit on NPLs, expressed as a ratio of total assets. An abnormally high level of NPLs reduces profitability and affects accounting provisions, as it points to the lower availability of liquid resources and, in the worst scenario, it can lead to write-downs of loans in the balance sheet.

In European banks, a higher level of NPLs can be observed in comparison with the banking systems of other countries. The reason lies in the slow recovery from the crisis that has extended over a period of many years and is particularly severe in comparison with the USA. This is and will be an economic gap that will not be recovered over time, as it is very high. It depends to a large extent on political and economic choices that were made and designed in a framework of austerity.

In this context, other routes can be followed. For instance, one possibility is the application of securitisation to risk class loan pools by shifting from the internal side to the external side, thereby reducing the level of NPLs and raising liquidity resources; another alternative involves credit derivatives, reducing the level of the credit risk on loan portfolios by shifting from the internal to the external side.

Pursuing legal action to recover credit losses also can be undertaken, keeping in mind, however, that there will be a variable waiting period. This is particularly true in some southern countries of Europe as compared to other countries where the judicial proceedings are executed more swiftly.

The longer the waiting period for the judicial decision, the more serious the negative impact will be. Keeping a high level of NPLs on the book and, especially, offering a high discount price in comparison with the book value may easily lead to losses in the economic statement of the European banks. This underlines the importance of corrections in efficiency and times of court decisions.

3.5 Conclusions

Granting loans postulates the prior assessment of the credit capacity manifested by customers. Application of the most modern risk analysis techniques is necessary in order to rationalise choices concerning the granting of credit to clients and, at the same time, to avert problems of adverse selection and moral hazard.

Since the class of short-term and medium- and long-term loans is found to be the major component in the structure of a bank's total assets, the relations with cash flow generation and interest earned are immediate and have a considerable impact on monetary repayments and expenses and on the profit and loss statement.

This shows both the importance of the system of interest rates on a loan portfolio and also the role played by the mean return associated with such interest rates. A comparison can thus be drawn with the returns on similar classes of assets that allow more rational choices concerning composition and changes in composition through time periods.

A correct evaluation of the interest rate with the credit risk affecting individual loans, taking into consideration expected losses, unexpected losses and fund-raising costs, is important in order to build premises and rationales for profit.

Credit risk is the risk of potential default of borrowers in the repayment of debt as principal and as interest. It is a potential and severe risk as it can produce a negative impact and losses which will cause reductions in asset values as well as write-downs in loan portfolios and therefore in the level of capital. Thus it is important to ensure that correct methodologies are used for measurement and management of expected and unexpected losses. Credit risk can be transferred by derivatives or by securitisation, contributing to the credit risk reduction. Deterioration in loan portfolios creates non-performing loans (NPLs) which present problems arising from non-payment of interest and failure to repay capital at maturity.

Financial crises, which have been particularly severe in Europe over a prolonged period of time starting in 2007, and related economic crises, have given rise to non-performing loans spreading throughout European banks. This chapter has underlined the need to deal with and to solve the problem in question, which still has negative repercussions on the economic growth of the European Union, above all because it has meant fewer loans to the economy and especially to small- and medium-sized enterprises.

References

Altunbas, Y., Carbo, S., Gardener, E. P., & Molyneux, P. (2007). Examining the relationships between capital, risk and efficiency in European banking. *European Financial Management, 13*(1), 49–70.

Arner, D. W., Avgouleas, E., & Gibson, E. (2017). *Overstating moral hazard: Lessons from two decades of banking crises.* Faculty of Law, University of Hong Kong. Research Paper. No 2017/003.

Avgouleas, E., & Goodhart, C. (2017). Utilizing AMCs to tackle Eurozone's legacy non-performing loans. *European Economy, 1*, 97.

Barth, J. R. (1991). *The great Savings and Loan debacle.* Washington, DC: AEI Press.

Berger, A. N., & DeYoung, R. (1997). Problem loans and cost efficiency in commercial banks. *Journal of Banking & Finance, 21*(6), 849–870.

Berlin, M., & Mester, L. J. (1992). Debt covenants and renegotiation. *Journal of Financial Intermediation, 2*(2), 95–133.

Bessis, J. (2015). *Risk management in banking*. Chichester: Wiley.

Bianchi, T. (1992). *I fidi bancari*. Torino: Utet.

Brandon, K., & Fernandez, F. (2005). Financial innovation and risk management: An introduction to credit derivatives. *Journal of Applied Finance, 15*(1), 12.

Caprara, U. (1954). *L'economia della banca*. Milano: Giuffrè.

Cirillo, A. (2005). *La valutazione probabilistica del rischio di credito*. Roma: Aracne Editrice.

Clark, A. (1997). Derivatives: A regulatory's perspective. *Economic Notes, 2*, 425–440.

Colombini, F. (2001). *Intermediari e mercati finanziari. Teoria e gestione*. Torino: Utet.

Colombini, F. (2015). Risk, regulation, supervision and crises in the European Banking Union. *Law and Economics Yearly Review, 4*(2), 236–273.

Colombini, F., & Calabrò, A. (2011). *Crisi finanziarie. Banche e stati. L'insostenibilità del rischio di credito*. Torino: Utet.

Colquitt, J. (2007). *Credit risk management*. New York: McGraw-Hill.

Cucinelli, D. (2015). The impact of non-performing loans on bank lending behaviour: Evidence from the Italian banking sector. *Eurasian Journal of Business and Economics, 8*(16), 59–71.

Dell'Amore, G. (1965). *Economia delle aziende di credito*. Milano: Giuffrè.

Dematté, C. (1974). *La valutazione della capacità di credito nelle analisi di fido*. Milano: Vallardi.

Duffee, G. R., & Zhou, C. (2001). Credit derivatives in banking: Useful tools for managing risk? *Journal of Monetary Economics, 48*(1), 25–54.

Duran, M. A., & Lozano-Vivas, A. (2015). Moral hazard and the financial structure of banks. *Journal of International Financial Markets, Institutions and Money, 34*, 28–40.

Forestieri, G. (1991). *I prestiti bancari nell'economia contemporanea. Tendenze nuove nell'intermediazione finanziaria*. Milano: Egea.

Hellwig, M. (2017). *Carving out legacy assets: A successful tool for bank restructuring?* (Vol. 3). Bonn: Max Planck Institute for Research on Collective Goods.

Hubbard, R. G. (2008). *Money, the financial system and the economy*. Reading, MA: Addison Wesley.

Jacobson, T., Lindé, J., & Roszbach, K. (2006). Internal ratings systems, implied credit risk and the consistency of banks' risk classification policies. *Journal of Banking & Finance, 30*(7), 1899–1926.

Kane, E. J. (1989). *The S&L insurance mess. How did it happen?* Washington, DC: Urban Institute.

Kwan, S., & Eisenbeis, R. A. (1997). Bank risk, capitalization, and operating efficiency. *Journal of Financial Services Research, 12*(2–3), 117–131.

Lusignani, G. (2004). *La gestione dei rischi nella banca. La banca come impresa.* Bologna: Il Mulino.

Masera, R. (2005). *Rischio, banche, imprese. I nuovi standard di Basilea.* Milano: Il Sole 24 Ore.

Moser, J. T. (1998). *Credit derivatives: Just-in-time provisioning for loan losses.* Economic Perspectives. Federal Reserve Bank of Chicago, Fourth Quarter.

Neal, R. S. (1996). Credit derivatives. New financial instruments for controlling credit risk. *Economic Review. Federal Reserve Bank of Kansas City, 81*(2), 15.

Nickell, P., Perraudin, W., & Varotto, S. (2007). Ratings-based credit risk modelling: An empirical analysis. *International Review of Financial Analysis, 16*(5), 434–451.

Rajan, R., & Winton, A. (1995). Covenants and collateral as incentives to monitor. *The Journal of Finance, 50*(4), 1113–1146.

Rule, D. (2001). The credit derivatives market: Its development and possible implications for financial stability. *Financial Stability Review, 10*, 117–140.

van Damme, E. (1994). Banking: A survey of recent microeconomic theory. *Oxford Review of Economic Policy, 10*(4), 14–33.

White, L. J. (1991). *The S&L debacle: Public policy lessons for bank and thrift regulation.* New York: Oxford University Press.

Williams, J. (2004). Determining management behaviour in European banking. *Journal of Banking & Finance, 28*(10), 2427–2460.

Zhang, D., Cai, J., Dickinson, D. G., & Kutan, A. M. (2016). Non-performing loans, moral hazard and regulation of the Chinese commercial banking system. *Journal of Banking & Finance, 63*, 48–60.

CHAPTER 4

Banking Efficiency in Europe

Fabiano Colombini

4.1 Introduction

The efficiency of financial intermediaries plays an important role in the debate on the validity and appropriacy of regulation, supervision and competition.

Efficiency influences the choice of instruments and business areas, as it affects not only input and output composition but also cost and revenue.

A closer examination shows that the choice of strategy has repercussions on the survival of individual financial intermediaries and also on the associated changes in the number of intermediaries within financial industries.

Efficiency becomes particularly important in the light of the growing financial integration on the European and international level and of the resulting increased presence of financial intermediaries on the individual markets, thereby intensifying competition. Reduction of inefficiencies constitutes a crucial aspect for the survival of individual financial intermediaries.

Efficiency also acts as a reference parameter in mergers and acquisitions among different financial intermediaries. It allows such intermediaries to seek the most rational conditions for resource utilisation and for obtainment of products.

F. Colombini (✉)
Department of Economics and Management, University of Pisa, Pisa, Italy

F. Colombini (ed.), *Raising Capital or Improving Risk Management and Efficiency?*, https://doi.org/10.1007/978-3-319-71749-4_4

A number of differences can be perceived within financial industries. These variations concern the number of intermediaries present within a given industry, as well as the manner of composition of the instruments concerning assets, liabilities and off-balance sheet items (OBSIs). Consequently, differences in the strategies adopted by the various financial intermediaries can be observed. An increase in efficiency leads to a cost reduction and/or an increase in revenue; this, in turn, leads to growth of profit and positive reflexes.

This chapter aims to examine the different concepts of efficiency for their implementation in bank and financial industries.

4.2 X-Efficiency

X-efficiency includes problems of cost minimisation and/or revenue and profit maximisation. This implies problems of production process rationalisation, by optimising input utilisation and/or output obtainment (Blois, 1972; Crew & Rowley, 1971; Leibenstein, 1969). Inefficiency arises when costs, revenue and profits are not in line with the optimum achievable on the efficient frontier.

4.2.1 Cost Efficiency

Cost efficiency implies cost minimisation for a given output level and composition. In the standard approach, technical inefficiencies are considered to arise from higher utilisation of inputs, while allocation inefficiencies are due to deviation from the optimum combination of inputs, with prices considered as exogenous (Berger, Hunter, & Timme, 1993; Farrell, 1957; Kopp & Diewert, 1982; Zieschang, 1983).

Inefficiencies can be measured as higher cost levels and therefore as deviations from the minimum cost (Berger & Humphrey, 1992; Berger & Mester, 1997; Clark, 1996; DeYoung, 1994; Fixler & Zieschang, 1993; Gardner & Grace, 1993; Grabowski, Rangan, & Rezvanian, 1993; Klumpes, 2004; Maudos, Pastor, Perez, & Quesnada, 2002; Mester, 1993; Rogers, 1998).

Cost efficiency refers exclusively to the manner of utilisation and combination of inputs. Thus cost efficiency is achieved by cost minimisation, under equal outputs. Cost efficiency also excludes the economies of scale achievable by reduction and minimisation of average cost whenever output variations occur.

Cost efficiency can be measured by the ratio between the lowest cost $C_{\min}$ of the bank positioned on the efficient frontier and the cost C_i of the bank *i* within the same banking sample, by means of the following indicator:

$$CostEFF_i = \frac{C_{\min}}{C_i}$$

By assigning values contained within the interval (0,1], the best practice bank intermediary is found to be the most efficient when the value is equal to 1. In contrast, the other banks positioned below 1 present inefficiencies measurable as $(1 - CostEFF_i) \cdot C_i$, which indicates the savings that can be achieved. It can easily be shown that with an increase in the indicator towards 1 or a reduction in the indicator towards 0, the respective inefficiencies show a decrease or an increase.

The evolution of technology calls for a revision in the unit cost curve for new and different modes of production factor utilisation and combination (Saunders & Cornett, 2008).

At times, indicators concerning the gap between interest rates on assets and interest rates on liabilities, or rather, the respective weighted averages, are taken into consideration. This measure is still indicative of a financial intermediation cost that is borne by the economy. However, it does not necessarily reflect the different average cost levels and cost efficiency levels of individual banks. Therefore, the above-mentioned indicators constitute in their own right an indirect, or even arbitrary, expression of efficiency levels.

4.2.2 *Revenue Efficiency*

Revenue efficiency implies revenue maximisation for a given input level and composition. The standard approach postulates output prices as given and variations in quantity. The alternative approach postulates input and output quantities as given and price variations, thereby affecting revenue levels. Inefficiencies derive from the lower revenue levels and, consequently, from the gap as compared to maximum revenue (Berger, Humphrey, & Pulley, 1996; Elyasiani & Mehdian, 1990; English, Grosskopf, Hayes, & Yaisawarng, 1993; Rogers, 1998).

Revenue efficiency refers exclusively to the manner in which outputs are obtained, combined and sold. It is pursued by means of revenue maximisation, without change in inputs.

Revenue efficiency can be measured by the ratio between the revenue R_i of the bank intermediary i and the highest revenue R_{max} of the bank situated on the efficient frontier in the same banking sample, using the following indicator:

$$RevEFF_i = \frac{R_i}{R_{max}}$$

Assigning values within the interval (0,1], the best practice bank is found to be the most efficient, obtaining the value of 1. The other banks, situated below 1, present inefficiencies that are measurable as $(1 - RevEFF_i) \cdot R_i$, indicating the achievable increase in revenue. Naturally, it should be underlined that with an increase in the indicator towards 1 or a reduction in the indicator towards 0, inefficiencies show a decrease or an increase, respectively.

4.2.3 *Profit Efficiency*

Profit efficiency concerns maximisation of profit by rationalising costs and revenue. This, in turn, implies maximising the composition and utilisation of inputs as well as the composition and sales of outputs. The standard approach and the alternative approach are both equally applicable, considering, respectively, the hypothesis of given prices and quantity variations and the hypothesis of given quantities and price variations. The inefficiencies concern the lower profit levels and, therefore, deviations from the maximum attainable level (Akhavein, Berger, & Humphrey, 1997; Akhavein, Swamy, Taubman, & Singamsetti, 1997; Berger, Cummins, & Weiss, 1997; Berger, Hancock, & Humphrey, 1993; Berger & Mester, 1997; DeYoung & Hasan, 1998; DeYoung & Nolle, 1996; Humphrey & Pulley, 1997; Klumpes, 2004; Lozano-Vivas, 1997; Maudos, Pastor, Perez, & Quesnada, 2002; Miller & Noulas, 1996; Rogers, 1998).

The efficiency examined here presupposes rational modes of utilisation and combination of inputs. At the same time, it presupposes combination, increase and sale of the output, uniting the information on cost and revenue efficiency.

Profit efficiency can be measured by the ratio between profit π_i of the bank intermediary i and the maximum profit π_{max} of the bank situated on the efficient frontier of the same banking sample. The measurement is carried out using the following indicator:

$$\pi EFF_i = \frac{\pi_i}{\pi_{max}}$$

Assigning values within the interval (0,1], the best practice bank intermediary is found to be the most efficient, obtaining the value of 1. The other banks of the sample, situated below 1, present inefficiencies that are measurable as $(1 - \pi EFF_i)\cdot\pi_i$, indicating the achievable increase in profits. Naturally, with an increase in the indicator towards 1 or a reduction in the indicator towards 0, inefficiencies show a decrease or an increase, respectively.

It should be noted that measuring the technical and allocation inefficiencies only with regard to the cost function leads to their underestimation. This is due to the fact that revenue inefficiencies notably exceed cost inefficiencies (Berger, Hancock, & Humphrey, 1993; Berger & Humphrey, 1997; Berger & Mester, 1997; English, Grosskopf, Hayes, & Yaisawarng, 1993; Rogers, 1998).

Technical and allocational inefficiencies involving cost and revenue tend to exceed diseconomies of scale and scope (Berger & Humphrey, 1991; Berger, Leusner, & Mingo, 1997; Molyneux, Altunbas, & Gardener, 1996). This demonstrates that it is important for such inefficiencies to be correctly identified and eliminated. Deviations from the efficient frontier thus show higher levels as compared to economies of scale and scope, the efficient frontier being hypothesised in terms of econometric estimation.

4.2.4 *Measurement Techniques*

X-efficiency presupposes construction of the efficient frontier by using the cost function in cost efficiency, the revenue function in revenue efficiency or the profit function in profit efficiency, for assessment of deviations that measure inefficiencies. The above-mentioned functions postulate the definition of the production process and, therefore, of the input and output of the bank intermediary.

Measurement of X-efficiency plays a role in non-parametric and parametric techniques (Berger & Humphrey, 1997; Berger, Hunter, & Timme, 1993; Berger & Mester, 1997; Casu, Girardone, & Molyneux, 2004; Fries & Taci, 2005; Molyneux, Altunbas, & Gardener, 1996; Weill, 2004). Non-parametric techniques typically include data envelopment analysis (DEA) and the free disposal hull (FDH), while parametric techniques generally consider the stochastic frontier approach (SFA), the thick frontier approach (TFA) and the distribution-free approach (DFA).

The techniques under discussion here reveal diversities attributable to construction of the efficient frontier and to consideration of the random error. Taken together, these aspects affect the final results and therefore affect assessment of the efficiency level (Berger & Humphrey, 1997; Berger, Hunter, & Timme, 1993).

In the non-parametric techniques, financial intermediaries for which there exist no linear combinations of higher outputs for given levels of input and/or of lower inputs for given levels of output are placed on the efficient frontier.

Parametric techniques, on the other hand, place only the most efficient financial intermediary on the efficient frontier. The necessary information is obtained by utilisation of a particular algebraic form of the cost, revenue or profit function.

The parametric techniques are closer to the above-mentioned concepts of X-efficiency that make a comparison between the cost, revenue or profit levels of a given financial intermediary and the financial intermediary that is considered most efficient and therefore is regarded as best practice. In this case, more restrictions in construction of the efficient frontier are introduced (Berger & Mester, 1997).

Even though the non-parametric techniques calculate deviations from the efficient frontier, they measure inefficiencies without considering random errors (Mester, 1993). In contrast, parametric techniques measure inefficiencies after removal of random errors.

Parametric techniques impose specific hypotheses on the distribution of the probability of random errors. Therefore, there are significant differences in the final results of the estimate.

It follows that non-parametric techniques reveal their typical strong points with regard to the greater ease of calculation and the absence of restrictive hypotheses on the form of the cost, revenue or profit function. Their typical weaknesses concern the failure to identify the best practice financial intermediary in absolute terms and also the failure to separate random error in the calculation of inefficiency.

Parametric techniques, on the other hand, have their strong points in their identification of the best practice financial intermediary and in distinguishing random error in the calculation of inefficiency. The weak points of parametric techniques consist in the rigidity of the hypotheses concerning the cost, revenue or profit function and in the probability distribution of casual error (Berger & Humphrey, 1997).

4.3 Scale Efficiency

The way in which inputs are utilised and combined and, above all, the technological variable greatly influence the classical *U*-shaped trend of the average cost curve. This gives rise to scale efficiency (Bell & Murphy, 1968; Benston, 1972; Benston, Hanweck, & Humphrey, 1982; Berger, Hanweck, & Humphrey, 1987; Clark, 1988; Costagli, 2004; Cummins & Zi, 1998; Forestieri, 1993; Gilligan, Smirlock, & Marshall, 1984; Hardwick, 1989; Humphrey, 1985; Kim, 1986; Lawrence, 1989; Lawrence & Shay, 1986; McAllister & McManus, 1993; Mester, 1987; Molyneux, Altunbas, & Gardener, 1996; Muldur, 1991; Mullineaux, 1978; Murray & White, 1983; Noulas, Ray, & Miller, 1990; Revell, 1987).

Basically, scale efficiency derives from the different growth rate of total costs versus that of production, assuming the same product lines. Although variations in intensity of scale efficiency are observed among the banks involved, as well as differences over time, scale efficiency allows reductions in unit costs.

Economies of scale postulate less than proportional increases in total production costs as compared to the increase achieved in output. We will assume the case of a bank intermediary *i* with total cost $TC_i = TC_i(Q)$ where Q represents the quantity produced, average cost $AC_i = TC_i(Q)/Q$ and marginal cost $MC_i = \partial TC_i(Q)/\partial Q$, and we will bear in mind that in microeconomic theory the average cost decreases as long as marginal cost is lower than average cost; accordingly, economies of scale in the production of a single product are indicated by the following expression:

$$ScaleEFF_i = \frac{AC_i}{MC_i} = \frac{TC_i(Q)}{Q \cdot \left(\frac{\partial TC_i(Q)}{\partial Q} \right)}$$

In the $ScaleEFF_i > 1$ hypothesis, the bank experiences economies of scale, and therefore the bank intermediary's returns increase with increasing output, since marginal cost is lower than average cost. In the $ScaleEFF_i = 1$ hypothesis, the bank *i* experiences neither economies nor diseconomies of scale: the bank thus has constant returns as long as output increases, since marginal cost is equal to average cost. In the $ScaleEFF_i < 1$ hypothesis, the bank intermediary experiences diseconomies of scale and, consequently, decreasing returns whenever output increases, because marginal cost is higher than average cost.

Therefore, even when cost is minimised with respect to individual production volume, the average cost may allow further margins for its reduction in the $ScaleEFF_i > 1$ hypothesis. That is to say, there may be incompletely exploited descending segments of the respective curve and of its classical *U* shape. Output increases obtained by the use of constant price inputs give rise to less than proportional increases in cost, thereby reducing average costs. The problem of the lowering of unit production cost and its minimisation can therefore unproblematically be associated with that of the search for appropriate production volumes, that is, for the optimum size.

When returns rise hand in hand with rising production at individual plants, enterprises or financial industries, this implies scale economies, suggesting that achievement of adequate size is economically advantageous. Estimates tend to underline that economies of scale are more frequently encountered on the level of a given establishment (branches), maintaining the assumption that their number remains unchanged with regard to a given bank or financial intermediary.

The above-mentioned hypotheses are equally applicable to the production of more than one product. The existence of economies of scale creates incentives towards expansion of the entire product range while maintaining the internal composition constant, or towards expansion of the individual product while maintaining the other products unchanged (Baumol, Panzar & Willig, 1982). Under the former hypothesis, the concept of total economies of scale presupposes that the evaluation should be performed totally in order to assess the intensity of a rise in cost resulting from increased production. Under the second hypothesis, the concept of economies of scale with regard to a specific product presupposes consideration of their impact by measuring and isolating the cost increase that arises with an increase in an individual product. The positive effects consisting of the lower increase in cost under equal expansion of global or specific production volumes highlight the economies that can be achieved by means of the ensuing development of production.

Accordingly, exploitation of economies of scale leads to expansion of production volumes in the individual banks, and also to a reduction in the number of such intermediaries, thereby increasing their contractual strength and the market concentration. Their position on the left-hand segment of the *U*-shaped average cost curve rather than at the lowest point tends to prompt merger and acquisition processes that are capable of lowering the unit cost to below the previous values and, in the best hypothesis, of minimising its absolute level. It is worth noting that economies of scale, if considered purely in their own right, do not constitute a sufficient explanation of the concentration processes (Hawawini & Swary, 1990).

4.3.1 Measurement Techniques

The techniques adopted for measurement of economies of scale presuppose fairly complex cost functions. Moreover, the results obtained can be notably diverse, depending on the parameters chosen, the period taken into consideration and, above all, the representation of the production processes.

The econometric estimates typically consider multiproduct functions such as Cobb-Douglas, constant elasticity substitution (CES), translog, hybrid translog and Fourier flexible. The use of Cobb-Douglas or CES functions shows fairly noticeable elements of weakness: this severely restricts the degree of substitutability among inputs and also between the latter and the output.

Recourse to cost functions of the translog or hybrid translog type displays greater flexibility compared to the Cobb-Douglas or CES functions, even though there are further restrictions in the basic hypotheses and in the parameters utilised. This leads to an erroneous specification of the real cost function (McAllister & McManus, 1993).

Cost functions of the Fourier flexible type approximate the real cost function, imposing no special restrictions on the functional form despite the need for an elevated number of observations.

It is important to specify that measurement of economies of scale must be carried out at the efficient frontier, hypothesising full achievement of X-efficiency.

4.4 Scope Efficiency

The downward move of total costs for the extension and combination of *n* product lines as compared to their separate production by *n* enterprises makes it more advantageous to engage in centralised production. This leads to the rise of scope efficiency (Benston, Hanweck, & Humphrey, 1982; Berger, Hanweck, & Humphrey, 1987; Clark, 1988; Forestieri, 1993; Gilligan, Smirlock, & Marshall, 1984; Kim, 1986; Lawrence, 1989; Mester, 1987; Molyneux, Altunbas, & Gardener, 1996; Muldur, 1991; Murray & White, 1983; Revell, 1987).

Scope efficiency originates from a combination and composition of product lines which to a large extent exploit the same production factors (Berger, Hanweck, & Humphrey, 1987; Clark, 1988; Mester, 1987).

Accordingly, assuming the production of two products in the quantities Q_1 and Q_2, to be produced jointly in the bank intermediary *i* and separately in the bank intermediaries *j* and *k*, the existence of economies of scope is linked to the following relation that can be established between the respective cost functions:

$$TC_i\left(Q_{1,}Q_2\right) < TC_j\left(Q_1,0\right) + TC_k\left(0,Q_2\right)$$

Accordingly, the economies of scope achieved by the bank intermediary *i* in the joint production can be calculated by means of the following expression:

$$ScopeEFF_i = \frac{TC_j\left(Q_1,0\right) + TC_k\left(0,Q_2\right)}{TC_i\left(Q_1,Q_2\right)}$$

In the $ScopeEFF_i > 1$ hypothesis, there are economies of scope due to the higher cost of separate production as compared to joint production. In the $ScopeEFF_i = 1$ hypothesis, neither economies nor diseconomies of scope are observed for the same cost level or separate and joint production. The $ScopeEFF_i < 1$ hypothesis shows diseconomies of scope due to the higher cost of joint as compared to separate production.

In industries characterised by the presence of a number of enterprises, the structure is found to be unstable due to the rise of tendencies towards merger processes (Baumol, Panzar, & Willig, 1982).

The existence of economies of scope concerning some products or a specific product motivates, respectively, the production of a set of products or the insertion of a new product.

In the first of these two hypotheses, the concept of total economies of scope presupposes that costs involved in the separate productions are higher than the cost in the joint production for a given level of each product. In the second hypothesis, the concept of economies of scope of a specific product postulates that the cost of the individual product in the separate production mode is higher than the cost of joint production, in reference to the same production combination.

Production diversification reveals differences among the individual types of bank intermediaries, with respect to regulation. The real cost advantages are linked to the extension concerning product lines, distinguished by economies of scope pursued by the joint production.

Product lines set up within bank intermediaries distinguished by economies of scope stimulate processes of reduction of their number in the individual financial industries. Economic calculations in mergers and acquisitions of various banks that have a heterogeneous range of products must also take into account the cost reduction deriving from the extension towards products that were previously established in the separate form. Since the cost level is higher when production concerns the same products in more than one bank as compared to production in only one bank, joint production becomes more advantageous.

4.4.1 *Measurement Techniques*

Similarly to economies of scale, measurement techniques for economies of scope presuppose the definition of cost functions that are basically of the Cobb-Douglas, CES, translog, hybrid translog and Fourier flexible type.

It is worth noting that estimates performed on the cost functions that indicate the existence of economies of scope generally reveal greater uncertainties concerning their real extent as compared to estimates performed on economies of scale. Despite this, the cost function estimates are regarded as important indicators.

Utilisation of these functions for calculation of economies of scope postulates the definition of the production process and, therefore, of inputs and outputs.

It is important to note that measurement of economies of scope must be performed on the efficient frontier, with the hypothesis of full accomplishment of X-efficiency.

4.5 Efficiency and Competition

Achievement of X-efficiency, scale efficiency and scope efficiency often implies an increase in output and sales. The capacity for expansion of production and sales is linked essentially to the form of the demand curve, competitors' reactions and the intensity of price competition. Such circumstances must be correctly evaluated, with attention to the combined reflexes on real changes in cost, revenue and, calculating the difference, profit.

X-efficiency, scale efficiency and scope efficiency tend to have repercussions on the internal set-up of individual financial industries and, above all, on the associated mechanisms of competition. Moreover, the above-mentioned three types of efficiency create strong presuppositions and motives for carrying out more aggressive management policies, aiming to reduce prices by driving competitive pressure. At the same time, such policies will result in crises or bankruptcies of the banks that are structurally and functionally weaker. The presence of X-efficiency, scale efficiency and scope efficiency can lead to monopolistic or oligopolistic types of market, thus reducing the number of enterprises and increasing their price-fixing capacity and achievement of profit.

Restructurings that concern banks, insurance enterprises and other financial intermediaries are a rather frequent occurrence, thereby creating margins of flexibility in evolution of the market. This affects above all the redefinition of the product range, the adaptation and upgrading of the organisational structures and sales channels and also the differentiated utilisation of overall available resources.

When X-efficiency, scale efficiency and scope efficiency are experienced within financial industries, changes can be observed with regard to the manner of utilisation of resources and initiatives in terms of management. Thus various different elements of flexibility and of effects on cost, revenue and profit can be observed (Amel, Barnes, Panetta, & Salleo, 2004; Cummins & Rubio-Misas, 2006; Cummins, Tennyson, & Weiss, 1999; Kapopoulos & Siokis, 2005; Panetta, Schivardi, & Shum, 2004).

Managing their business areas and instruments, banks have the incentive to become closer to best practices, increasing competition, changing bank models and, at the same time, introducing greater risk factors in European banking (Fiordelisi, Marques-Ibanez, & Molyneux, 2011; Kwan & Eisenbeis, 1997; Pastor, 1999).

4.6 Conclusions

Achievement of cost efficiency, revenue efficiency, profit efficiency, scale efficiency and scope efficiency and, accordingly, of total efficiency is of notable importance.

The resulting rationalisation concerning the manner of composition and utilisation of inputs and outputs reflects positively on costs, revenue and profits.

Analysis of market conditions and competition likewise plays a significant role.

Accordingly, X-efficiency, scale efficiency and scope efficiency presuppose joint pursuit of aims and joint evaluation of achievements. These aspects highlight elements of interdependence that directly affect the dynamics and number of enterprises in the individual financial industries. The creation of entry barriers also has effects in terms of limiting the number of new entrants, and at the same time, it can create conditions allowing the formation of oligopolies and monopolies.

European financial markets and financial institutions are moving towards a progressive process of integration. As a result of this integration, there is a strong pressure for improving efficiency in the various forms in the banking sector and in other financial sectors.

Improving risk management and efficiency is very important in order to reinforce structural premises inside banks to offset strong competition and to survive in the evolution of financial markets and financial intermediaries in Europe. A key point is the generation of costs and revenue and, as difference, profits or losses in the economic account, emphasising bank survival conditions in Europe and in the world.

References

Akhavein, J. D., Berger, A. N., & Humphrey, D. B. (1997). The effects of megamergers on efficiency and prices: Evidence from a bank profit function. *Review of Industrial Organization, 12*(1), 95–139.

Akhavein, J. D., Swamy, P. A., Taubman, S. B., & Singamsetti, R. N. (1997). A general method of deriving the inefficiencies of banks from a profit function. *Journal of Productivity Analysis, 8*(1), 71–93.

Amel, D., Barnes, C., Panetta, F., & Salleo, C. (2004). Consolidation and efficiency in the financial sector: A review of the international evidence. *Journal of Banking & Finance, 28*(10), 2493–2519.

Baumol, W. J., Panzar, J. C., & Willig, R. D. (1982). *Contestable markets and the theory of industry structure.* New York: Harcourt Brace Jovanovich.
Bell, F. W., & Murphy, N. B. (1968). Economies of scale and division of labor in commercial banking. *Southern Economic Journal, 35*(2), 131–139.
Benston, G. J. (1972). Economies of scale of financial institutions. *Journal of Money, Credit and Banking, 4*(2), 312–341.
Benston, G. J., Hanweck, G. A., & Humphrey, D. B. (1982). Scale economies in banking: A restructuring and reassessment. *Journal of Money, Credit and Banking, 14*(4), 435–456.
Berger, A. N., Cummins, J. D., & Weiss, M. A. (1997). The coexistence of multiple distribution systems for financial services: The case of property-liability insurance. *The Journal of Business, 70*(4), 515–546.
Berger, A. N., Hancock, D., & Humphrey, D. B. (1993). Bank efficiency derived from the profit function. *Journal of Banking & Finance, 17*(2), 317–347.
Berger, A. N., Hanweck, G. A., & Humphrey, D. B. (1987). Competitive viability in banking: Scale, scope, and product mix economies. *Journal of Monetary Economics, 20*(3), 501–520.
Berger, A. N., & Humphrey, D. B. (1991). The dominance of inefficiencies over scale and product mix economies in banking. *Journal of Monetary Economics, 28*(1), 117–148.
Berger, A. N., & Humphrey, D. B. (1992). Measurement and efficiency issues in commercial banking. In Z. Griliches, T. F. Bresnahan, M. Manser, & E. R. Berndt (Eds.), *Output measurement in the service sectors* (pp. 245–300). Chicago: University of Chicago Press.
Berger, A. N., & Humphrey, D. B. (1997). Efficiency of financial institutions: International survey and directions for future research. *European Journal of Operational Research, 98*(2), 175–212.
Berger, A. N., Humphrey, D. B., & Pulley, L. B. (1996). Do consumers pay for one-stop banking? Evidence from an alternative revenue function. *Journal of Banking & Finance, 20*(9), 1601–1621.
Berger, A. N., Hunter, W. C., & Timme, S. G. (1993). The efficiency of financial institutions: A review and preview of research past, present and future. *Journal of Banking & Finance, 17*(2), 221–249.
Berger, A. N., Leusner, J. H., & Mingo, J. J. (1997). The efficiency of bank branches. *Journal of Monetary Economics, 40*(1), 141–162.
Berger, A. N., & Mester, L. J. (1997). Inside the black box: What explains differences in the efficiencies of financial institutions? *Journal of Banking & Finance, 21*(7), 895–947.
Blois, K. J. (1972). A note on X-efficiency and profit maximization. *The Quarterly Journal of Economics, 86*(2), 310–312.
Casu, B., Girardone, C., & Molyneux, P. (2004). Productivity change in European banking: A comparison of parametric and non-parametric approaches. *Journal of Banking & Finance, 28*(10), 2521–2540.

Clark, J. A. (1988). Economies of scale and scope at depository financial institutions. *Economic Review-Federal Reserve Bank of Kansas City, 73*(8), 16.

Clark, J. A. (1996). Economic cost, scale efficiency, and competitive viability in banking. *Journal of Money, Credit and Banking, 28*(3), 342–364.

Costagli, S. (2004). Economie di scala e di varietà nel settore bancario statunitense. *Giornale degli Economisti e Annali di Economia, 63*(1), 87–137.

Crew, M. A., & Rowley, C. K. (1971). On allocative efficiency, X-efficiency and the measurement of welfare loss. *Economica, 38*(150), 199–203.

Cummins, J. D., & Rubio-Misas, M. (2006). Deregulation, consolidation, and efficiency: Evidence from the Spanish insurance industry. *Journal of Money, Credit, and Banking, 38*(2), 323–355.

Cummins, J. D., Tennyson, S., & Weiss, M. A. (1999). Consolidation and efficiency in the US life insurance industry. *Journal of Banking & Finance, 23*(2), 325–357.

Cummins, J. D., & Zi, H. (1998). Comparison of frontier efficiency methods: An application to the US life insurance industry. *Journal of Productivity Analysis, 10*(2), 131–152.

DeYoung, R. (1994). *Fee-based services and cost efficiency in commercial banks* (Vol. 94, No. 3). Office of the Comptroller of the Currency.

DeYoung, R., & Hasan, I. (1998). The performance of de novo commercial banks: A profit efficiency approach. *Journal of Banking & Finance, 22*(5), 565–587.

DeYoung, R., & Nolle, D. E. (1996). Foreign-owned banks in the United States: Earning market share or buying it? *Journal of Money, Credit and Banking, 28*(4), 622–636.

Elyasiani, E., & Mehdian, S. (1990). Efficiency in the commercial banking industry, a production frontier approach. *Applied Economics, 22*(4), 539–551.

English, M., Grosskopf, S., Hayes, K., & Yaisawarng, S. (1993). Output allocative and technical efficiency of banks. *Journal of Banking & Finance, 17*(2–3), 349–366.

Farrell, M. J. (1957). The measurement of productive efficiency. *Journal of the Royal Statistical Society. Series A (General), 120*(3), 253–290.

Fiordelisi, F., Marques-Ibanez, D., & Molyneux, P. (2011). Efficiency and risk in European banking. *Journal of Banking & Finance, 35*(5), 1315–1326.

Fixler, D. J., & Zieschang, K. D. (1993). An index number approach to measuring bank efficiency: An application to mergers. *Journal of Banking & Finance, 17*(2–3), 437–450.

Forestieri, G. (1993). Economies of scale and scope in the financial services industry: A review of recent literature. In *Financial conglomerates* (pp. 63–124). Paris: OECD.

Fries, S., & Taci, A. (2005). Cost efficiency of banks in transition: Evidence from 289 banks in 15 post-communist countries. *Journal of Banking & Finance, 29*(1), 55–81.

Gardner, L. A., & Grace, M. F. (1993). X-efficiency in the US life insurance industry. *Journal of Banking & Finance, 17*(2–3), 497–510.
Gilligan, T., Smirlock, M., & Marshall, W. (1984). Scale and scope economies in the multi-product banking firm. *Journal of Monetary Economics, 13*(3), 393–405.
Grabowski, R., Rangan, N., & Rezvanian, R. (1993). Organizational forms in banking: An empirical investigation of cost efficiency. *Journal of Banking & Finance, 17*(2–3), 531–538.
Hardwick, P. (1989). Economies of scale in building societies. *Applied Economics, 21*(10), 1291–1304.
Hawawini, G. A., & Swary, I. (1990). *Mergers and acquisitions in the US banking industry: Evidence from the capital markets.* Amsterdam: North Holland.
Humphrey, D. B. (1985). Costs and scale economies in bank intermediation. In *Handbook for banking strategy* (pp. 745–783). New York, NY: Wiley.
Humphrey, D. B., & Pulley, L. B. (1997). Banks' responses to deregulation: Profits, technology, and efficiency. *Journal of Money, Credit, and Banking, 29*, 73–93.
Kapopoulos, P., & Siokis, F. (2005). Market structure, efficiency and rising consolidation of the banking industry in the Euro area. *Bulletin of Economic Research, 57*(1), 67–91.
Kim, H. Y. (1986). Economies of scale and economies of scope in multiproduct financial institutions: Further evidence from credit unions. *Journal of Money, Credit and Banking, 18*(2), 220–226.
Klumpes, P. J. (2004). Performance benchmarking in financial services: Evidence from the UK life insurance industry. *The Journal of Business, 77*(2), 257–273.
Kopp, R. J., & Diewert, W. E. (1982). The decomposition of frontier cost function deviations into measures of technical and allocative efficiency. *Journal of Econometrics, 19*(2–3), 319–331.
Kwan, S., & Eisenbeis, R. A. (1997). Bank risk, capitalization, and operating efficiency. *Journal of Financial Services Research, 12*(2–3), 117–131.
Lawrence, C. (1989). Banking costs, generalized functional forms, and estimation of economies of scale and scope. *Journal of Money, Credit and Banking, 21*(3), 368–379.
Lawrence, C., & Shay, R. (1986). Technology and financial intermediation in a multiproduct banking firm: An econometric study of US banks, 1979–1982. In Lawrence, C., & Shay, R. P. (Eds.), *Technological innovation, regulation and the monetary economy.* Cambridge (Massachusetts): Ballinger.
Leibenstein, H. (1969). Organizational or frictional equilibria, X-efficiency, and the rate of innovation. *The Quarterly Journal of Economics, 83*(4), 600–623.
Lozano-Vivas, A. (1997). Profit efficiency for Spanish savings banks. *European Journal of Operational Research, 98*(2), 381–394.

Maudos, J., Pastor, J. M., Perez, F., & Quesada, J. (2002). Cost and profit efficiency in European banks. *Journal of International Financial Markets, Institutions and Money, 12*(1), 33–58.

McAllister, P. H., & McManus, D. (1993). Resolving the scale efficiency puzzle in banking. *Journal of Banking & Finance, 17*(2–3), 389–405.

Mester, L. J. (1987, January). Efficient production of financial services: Scale and scope economies. *Business Review*, 15–25.

Mester, L. J. (1993). Efficiency in the savings and loan industry. *Journal of Banking & Finance, 17*(2–3), 267–286.

Miller, S. M., & Noulas, A. G. (1996). The technical efficiency of large bank production. *Journal of Banking & Finance, 20*(3), 495–509.

Molyneux, P., Altunbas, Y., & Gardener, E. (1996). *Efficiency in European banking*. Chichester: Wiley.

Muldur, U. (1991). Echelle et gamme dans les marchés bancaires nationaux et globaux. *Revue d'économie financière, 17*, 167–196.

Mullineaux, D. J. (1978). Economies of scale and organizational efficiency in banking: A profit-function approach. *The Journal of Finance, 33*(1), 259–280.

Murray, J. D., & White, R. W. (1983). Economies of scale and economies of scope in multiproduct financial institutions: A study of British Columbia credit unions. *The Journal of Finance, 38*(3), 887–902.

Noulas, A. G., Ray, S. C., & Miller, S. M. (1990). Returns to scale and input substitution for large US banks. *Journal of Money, Credit and Banking, 22*(1), 94–108.

Panetta, F., Schivardi, F., & Shum, M. (2004). *Do mergers improve information? Evidence from the loan market*. Temi di discussione n. 521. Roma: Banca d'Italia.

Pastor, J. M. (1999). Efficiency and risk management in Spanish banking: A method to decompose risk. *Applied Financial Economics, 9*(4), 371–384.

Revell, J. (1987). *Merges and the role of large banks*. Bangor: Institute of European Finance, University College of North Wales.

Rogers, K. E. (1998). Nontraditional activities and the efficiency of US commercial banks. *Journal of Banking & Finance, 22*(4), 467–482.

Saunders, A., & Cornett, M. M. (2008). *Financial institutions management: A risk management approach*. Boston: McGraw-Hill.

Weill, L. (2004). Measuring cost efficiency in European banking: A comparison of frontier techniques. *Journal of Productivity Analysis, 21*(2), 133–152.

Zieschang, K. D. (1983). A note on the decomposition of cost efficiency into technical and allocative components. *Journal of Econometrics, 23*(3), 401–405.

CHAPTER 5

Capital Constraints by Regulation in Europe

Paola Ferretti

5.1 Introduction

In order to ensure that a bank has a sufficient capital to conduct its business, taking into account the risks that weigh on banking institutions, each bank is required to respect the rules imposed by the supervisory authorities concerning capital adequacy. Therefore each bank is required to define the amount extent of its capital as well as the optimal combination of the capital instruments of which the capital itself is made up. Additionally, banks are required to classify and measure and/or assess the various risk types and take into account the relationship between capital and level of risk.

This chapter aims to analyse the evolution of the rules on banking capital adequacy, from Basel I to Basel III, as well as the latest developments on this issue (the forthcoming Basel IV).

5.2 Capital Rules: Nature, Origins and Aims

In general, capital serves as a foundation for a bank's future growth and as a cushion against unexpected losses. Adequately capitalised and well-managed banks are in a good condition to withstand losses and,

P. Ferretti (✉)
Department of Economics and Management, University of Pisa, Pisa, Italy

F. Colombini (ed.), *Raising Capital or Improving Risk Management and Efficiency?*, https://doi.org/10.1007/978-3-319-71749-4_5

furthermore, to provide credit to the economy throughout the business cycle. Adequate levels of capital help to promote public confidence in the banking system. Therefore, from the point of view of the banks and the supervisors, it is crucial to determine how much capital is necessary to serve as a sufficient buffer against unexpected losses. If capital levels are too low, banks may be unable to absorb losses; conversely, if capital levels are too high, banks may not be able to make the most efficient use of their resources, which may constrain their ability to make credit available.

Over the years, the banking industry has become aware of the need to reduce the gap between capital absorbed on the basis of the regulatory requirements and capital estimated internally through risk measurement techniques (Crouhy, Galai, & Mark, 2006). This has led to the need to revise the discipline of international supervision concerning the capital adequacy of banks. The agreements on capital published by the Basel Committee on Banking Supervision (BCBS) since 1988 and up to the present day have undergone an evolution that reflects precisely the above-mentioned question.

Set up in 1974 on the initiative of the Governors of the Central Banks of the G10 in the aftermath of serious disturbances in international currency and banking markets, the BCBS is the primary global standard setter for the prudential regulation of banks and provides a forum for cooperation on banking supervisory matters. Its mandate is to strengthen the regulation, supervision and practices of banks worldwide with the purpose of enhancing financial stability. It possesses no formal supranational authority, and its decisions do not have legal force.

Specifically, the BCBS defines the standards for prudential regulation and bank supervision. These standards are then brought into force and observed by the BCBS members. The BCBS standards constitute the minimum prerequisite, and BCBS members are permitted to adopt more stringent standards. Enactment of the standards defined by the BCBS takes place when they have been transposed within local law through the rule-making process of each jurisdiction, according to terms pre-established by the Committee itself. Apart from a few specific points in the process of transposition, this is the procedure that has been followed so far in Europe with Basel I, Basel II and Basel III.

5.3 Basel I and Basel II

In the early 1980s, the onset of the Latin American debt crisis heightened the BCBS' concerns that the capital ratios of the main international banks were deteriorating at a time of increasing international risks. This prompted the decision to halt the erosion of capital ratios in the various banking systems by adopting an approach of convergence in measurement of capital adequacy. In other words, there was strong recognition within the BCBS of the overriding need for a multinational accord to strengthen the stability of the international banking system and to remove a source of competitive inequality arising from differences in national capital requirements.

All this resulted in the Basel Capital Accord (commonly referred to as Basel I), approved by the G10 Governors and released to banks in July 1988 (BCBS, 1988). The main purposes of the Basel I Accord were to strengthen the soundness and stability of the international banking system and to ensure that rulings would be applied as uniformly as possible on the national level. These objectives were pursued by applying a minimum ratio of capital to risk-weighted assets (RWAs) of 8% (regulatory capital/risk-weighted assets ≥8%). The framework was directed towards assessing capital in relation to credit risk, as the main risk incurred by banks.

In particular, the BCBS chose a weighted risk ratio—in which capital was related to different categories of asset or off-balance sheet exposure, weighted according to broad categories of relative riskiness—as a preferred method for assessing the capital adequacy of banks. The simple weighting structure provided five weights (0, 10, 20, 50 and 100%) depending on the nature of the counterparty (e.g. central governments, banks, firms, etc.), the guarantees received and the possible country risk present in the credit relationship.

The Basel I framework was designed to pursue objectives of great importance, among which one may mention the following: increase in the degree of capitalisation of banks, enhancement of the entrepreneurial independence of the top echelons in the bank within the framework of the close link between risks taken and capital resources and—as already pointed out—harmonisation of the rules in order to create a more uniform competitive context. Finally, the less developed credit systems were required by Basel I to seek to achieve a more efficient and competitive setup, according to a market-oriented logic.

The main critical element, on the other hand, was concerned with the exclusive prudential treatment of the credit risk, although this limit was partly overcome in 1996 when the capital requirements for market risks were defined. Market risks concern the risks of losses in on- and off-balance sheet positions arising from movements in market prices. Originally released in 1996, the Market Risk Amendment was modified first time in 1997 and further in 2005 (BCBS, 2005). Other weaknesses of the Basel I framework concern the unsatisfactory alignment of the weighting coefficients with regard to the risk inherent in the counterparty, as the difference in the creditworthiness of counterparties belonging to the same category was not taken into consideration. For instance, an identical weighting was assigned to enterprises with different risk profiles. Likewise, no attention was paid to the variation in risk associated with different maturities: that is to say, the greater—*ceteris paribus*—risk associated with medium- and long-term credit as compared to short-term credit was disregarded. Furthermore, neither the degree of diversification of assets nor the spread of credit risk mitigation techniques were taken into consideration.

This strengthened the growing conviction that the 1988 Accord should be updated (among others, Lastra, 2004). Such a realisation was further prompted by improvements in internal processes, as well as by the adoption of more advanced risk measurement techniques, and the increasing use of sophisticated risk management instruments and practices (e.g. credit derivatives, securitisation). The latter, in particular, encouraged the spread of practices of regulatory arbitrage, especially in the large banks, thereby making it difficult to define the actual assets of a given bank as well as the correspondence between the effective degree of risk and the regulatory capital requirements.

Accordingly, in order to improve the correlation between capital absorption and the risks undertaken by banks and, finally, to incentivise the adoption of better risk management techniques, the BCBS redefined the prudential treatment of banking risks. This led to the Revised Framework of Capital Standards, the so-called Basel II, of June 2004. This ruling represents the conclusions that emerged from a series of proposals and an intense consultation process on the international level. The resulting statement set out the rules for measurement of capital and of the capital ratios that banks had to respect (BCBS, 2006). This framework was transposed into the European framework by European Parliament Directives 2006/48 and 49 of 14 June 2006.

Immediately appearing more complex compared to the relatively simple nature of the previous accord, Basel II was therefore intended to reduce the gap between prudential rules and market rules, encouraging interaction among these and seeking greater coherence between the regulatory and economic capital (Garside & Bech, 2003). The economic capital expresses the amount of capital that is necessary for the performance of business versus the assumption of a certain level of risk independent of standard regulations.

Basel II was built upon three pillars, namely, (1) calculation of minimum capital requirements, (2) evaluation of risk control systems and capital adequacy policies by the supervisory authorities and (3) efficient use of market discipline aiming to implement transparency and promote sound banking management policies. The intention of the supervisors was to exercise control over the banking risk through the joint operation of these three pillars (Decamps, Rochet, & Roger, 2004).

The first pillar established a specific capital requirement to cover the risks associated with banking and financial instruments (credit risk, counterparty risk, market risk and operational risk). Therefore, as compared to Basel I, the range of risks taken into consideration was enlarged. For the purposes of quantification of capital requirements, alternative methodologies were envisaged, characterised by different levels of complexity with regard both to risk measurement and also to the organisational and control requirements. Banks were called upon to respect, constantly, a capital endowment no lower than the overall capital requirement, which is given by the sum of the capital requirements that would be needed to face the above-described risks; the total capital ratio was to be no lower than 8% (total regulatory capital/RWAs ≥8%).

Box 5.1 gives a diagrammatic representation of the quantification methods concerning the capital requirements for Pillar 1 risks, as laid down first by Basel II and to a large extent reiterated by the framework currently in force—Basel III (see Sect. 5.4).

Box 5.1 Methodologies for calculating capital requirements—First Pillar of Basel II

Credit risk, as a possible loss due to default of the debtors. The alternative methodologies are the standard method (among others, Van Roy, 2005) and that of internal ratings—Internal Rating Based, IRB (Allen & Overy, 2014). The first constitutes an evolution of the method of Basel I, since it introduces greater segmentation of portfolios and recourse to ratings expressed by agencies recognised by the control authorities (Export Credit Agencies (ECA) or specialised agencies, External Credit Assessment Institutions (ECAI)). In contrast, IRB, distinguished into basic IRB and advanced IRB, specifies that the risk weightings must be a function of the evaluation that banks carry out internally with regard to debtors (or regarding operations).

Counterparty risk, as a special case of credit risk, represents the risk that the counterparty of a transaction dealing with financial tools may prove to be in default before the transaction itself is settled. This results in a loss if the transactions undertaken with a counterparty have positive value at the moment of insolvency. In contrast to the credit risk deriving from a loan, for which the probability of loss is unilateral—i.e. it affects only the bank that granted the loan—the counterparty risk can generate a bilateral loss. This is due to the fact that the market value of the transaction may be positive or negative for both counterparties. The intermediaries can choose between a variety of methodologies for quantifying the value of exposures (allocation either in the banking book or in the trading book). The associated capital requirement is determined, substantially, by recourse to weighting factors for the counterparty, as provided for by the rules concerning credit risk.

Market risk. The capital requirement in this case aims to cover losses deriving from the operations carried out in connection with financial instruments, currencies and commodities. The rules identify and provide binding norms for the treatment of different risk typologies, in reference to the trading book for supervisory purposes (position risk, concentration risk) and in reference to the entire balance sheet of the bank (settlement risk, exchange risk, commodity risk). The methodology adopted for the calculation can be standard or advanced. The standard methodology is based on the building-block approach, according to which the overall requirement is obtained as a sum of the "blocks" of capital requirements pertaining to the different individual risk typologies mentioned above. The advanced methodology is defined by means of internal models, based on daily checking of the risk exposure. The risk exposure itself is calculated by means of the "Value at Risk" (VaR) approach, which is to be integrated with other forms of risk measurement and control.

Operational risk. The introduction ex novo of a structure of operational risk requirements was designed to address the losses due to the inadequacy or dysfunction of procedures, human resources and internal systems or to exogenous events. This purpose-designed capital requirement can be explained by the increased exposure of banks to the risk typology in question, as well as by the need to avoid forms of competitive inequality among intermediaries specialised in different fields of operativeness, and also by the desire to increase the modes and circumstances allowing management and control of the intermediaries (Birindelli & Ferretti, 2017). Three methods have been set up for determination of the capital requirement: basic, standard and advanced. The basic indicator approach establishes that the requirement should be achieved by applying 15% to the average of the last three observations of the indicator of the volume of banking activity, which is identified as the gross income. The standardised method establishes that after having divided up banking activity into eight business lines (corporate finance, trading and sales, retail banking, commercial banking, payment and settlement, agency services, asset management, retail brokerage), the capital requirement should be obtained as an average of the last three observations of the sum of the gross income of each business line, weighted on the basis of regulatory coefficients (ranging from 12 to 18%). Finally, the advanced measurement approach specifies that the capital requirement should be determined on the basis of operational losses and other elements collected and analysed by the bank. Utilisation of the advanced method must be authorised by the supervisory authorities; furthermore, in order to make use of the method in question, the intermediary must conform to qualitative and quantitative suitability criteria, with reference to the operational risk measurement and management system. Exclusively with regard to this approach, it may be considered suitable to lower the capital requirement on the basis of provisions, correlation estimates and recourse to risk transfer procedures (e.g. insurance cover).

Pillar 2 was expressed as the Internal Capital Adequacy Assessment Process (ICAAP), namely, the evaluation process carried out by individual banks to assess their capital adequacy in relation to overall risk exposure. ICAAP was integrated by the verification procedures enacted by the supervisory authorities, which conducted the Supervisory Review and Evaluation Process (SREP) and were required to formulate an overall judgement on the intermediary and, if necessary, to call for corrective measures.

Thus, on the basis of the ICAAP, every bank was required to determine what should be the adequate level of capital, in terms of amount and composition, that would enable the bank to cope with any risk type in the framework of an independent evaluation of its risk exposure, both current and prospective, considering the strategies adopted and the evolution of the reference context. With regard to the types of risk to be considered, suggestions were usually put forward by the supervisory authorities; the task of identifying potential additional and different risk factors related to the bank's specific operativeness was generally left up to prudent assessment by the banks themselves.

The banks were also required to perform the task of defining which type of risks should be addressed by means of quantitative methodologies for determination of capital, and which risks could, instead, be dealt with more appropriately in combination or as an alternative by adopting risk control or mitigation measures. The implementation of the ICAAP process was to be founded on banking systems that were appropriate for risk management and organisation, with clearly defined lines of responsibility and effective internal control systems. Responsibility for the ICAAP process was assigned to institution's bodies, which had the responsibility for enacting and updating the process, in order to ensure its constant correspondence to the bank's operating characteristics and to the strategies adopted. Finally, the ICAAP process was to be documented, known and shared by the banking structures and subjected to internal control.

By virtue of SREP, on the other hand, the supervisory authority was required to analyse the bank's risk profile and assess its governance system, the functionality of its bodies, the organisational structure and the internal control system, and also to check that prudential rules were properly enforced. This activity was based on interaction with intermediaries and utilisation of systems of analysis and assessment of the institutions supervised. If anomalous profiles emerged, the supervision authority could call for appropriate corrective measures of an organisational and capital-related nature. Any action undertaken was commensurate with the severity of the problems observed. In general, an additional capital requirement was imposed if application of the organisational measures did not appear to be capable of ensuring removal of the abnormality within an appropriate lapse of time.

Finally, the third pillar involved the obligation to provide the market with information concerning the capital adequacy, risk exposure and the associated management and control systems. The aim of this pillar was to enable market operators to obtain a more accurate picture of the capital solidity and risk exposure of the banks. For this reason, summary tables were drawn up in order to classify the quantitative and qualitative information that intermediaries were required to disclose. This procedure was designed to increase data transparency and comparability and to guarantee better conditions of a level playing field for competition. Finally, rules were introduced concerning the manner and frequency of the publication of the aforesaid information, the possible derogations and the checks to be carried out on the information destined to be made public.

5.4 Basel III

In later years following the international subprime mortgage financial crisis of 2007 and the sovereign debt crisis in Europe, the supervisory authorities felt the need to rethink the prudential rules in order to ensure greater stability, solidity and transparency in the banking system. This effort gave birth to the regulatory framework known as Basel III, adopted in Europe by the Capital Requirements Regulation (CRR—Regulation No 575/2013 of the European Parliament and of the Council of 26 June 2013 on prudential requirements for credit institutions and investment firms) and by the Capital Requirements Directive IV (CRD IV—Directive 2013/36 of the European Parliament and of the Council of 26 June 2013 on access to credit institutions and supervision of credit institutions and investment firms).

The review of the previous regulation (Basel II) was prompted not only by financial crises but also by certain limits inherent in the framework itself. Among these, it is worth mentioning the inadequately supervised (or totally neglected) profiles of banking activity, such as the following: the degree of leverage of the intermediaries; the unbalanced quali-quantitative composition of the regulatory capital of banks; the insufficient liquidity endowment of banks, in terms of resources and governance methodologies; the inappropriate prudential treatment of market risks and counterparty risk.

To these should be added the effects of pro-cyclicality, that is, the amplification of the fluctuations of the economic cycle, given that the capital requirements necessary to deal with the credit risk may be based on internal ratings and therefore may tend to decrease during growth phases and increase during recessions. While pro-cyclicality has accentuated the shock over time, the interconnection among the institutions in the international financial scenario has amplified the shock in a spatial dimension, thereby generating the conditions for a veritable contagion and consequently for the appearance of systemic risk.

Basically, the introduction of Basel III recalls links that are reminiscent of financial crises, their manifestations and the inability of banks to deal adequately with the consequences. This has been mainly due to operational distortions that have come to characterise the banking business in recent years. In particular, the banking sectors of many countries had built up excessive on- and off-balance sheet leverage; this was accompanied by a gradual erosion of the level and quality of the capital base. At the same time, many banks were holding insufficient liquidity buffers. The banking system was therefore unable to absorb trading and credit losses. This was further amplified by a pro-cyclical deleveraging process and by the interconnection of systemic institutions through an array of complex transactions.

Basel III is a comprehensive set of reform measures, developed by the BCBS with the objective of strengthening the regulation, supervision and risk management of the banking sector (BCBS, 2011, 2013a, 2014b). The overall aims of the reform measures are (1) to improve the banking sector's ability to absorb shocks arising from financial and economic stress, thus reducing the risk of spillover from the financial sector to the real economy, (2) to improve risk management and governance and (3) to strengthen banks' transparency and disclosures. Basel III defines bank-level regulation (microprudential approach), in order to strengthen the resilience of individual banking institutions during periods of stress. Furthermore, it considers system-wide risks that can build up across the banking sector as well as the pro-cyclical amplification of these risks over time (macroprudential approach). These two approaches to supervision are complementary as greater resilience at the individual bank level reduces the risk of system-wide shocks. Although the formal starting point of the new regulatory system coincided with 2014, many requirements will be introduced gradually up to the beginning of 2019, within which all the prudential measures are planned to be fully operational (gradual approach).

The approach of Basel II, based on three pillars, is maintained by Basel III, which integrates and reinforces it in order to increase the quantity and quality of capital endowment, also introducing anti-cyclical measures as well as rules on liquidity risk management and on containment of the leverage. A condensed overview of content of the three pillars is given in Box 5.2.

Box 5.2 The three pillars of Basel III

First Pillar: This pillar is reinforced by a more harmonised definition of capital and higher capital requirements. Stricter capital requirements are introduced in order to reflect more clearly the genuine risk associated with certain activities (e.g. securitisation and trading book); a qualitatively more elevated definition of capital is given, which is essentially centred on Common Equity. Additional capital buffers are imposed with a function of conservation of capital and with an anti-cyclical function; specific capital buffers are imposed also for the systemically important financial institutions. A leverage ratio is introduced; it is designed to protect the risk-based capital requirement and also to contain growth of leverage on the system level. Additionally, the first pillar introduces requirements and supervision systems for the liquidity risk; the focus is on a standard of short-term liquidity (liquidity coverage ratio, LCR), on a longer-term standard for a structural balance (net stable funding ratio, NSFR) and also on principles for management and supervision of the liquidity risk both in individual banks and on the systemic level.

Second Pillar: Increasing attention is devoted to the structure of corporate governance and to internal control systems, as a crucial factor for stability of the individual banks and for the financial system as a whole. The regulatory requirements concerning the role, qualification and composition of the governing bodies are strengthened; furthermore, the governing bodies as well as top management are required to be aware of the organisational setup and of the risks a bank may face. Stricter rules concern the control functions (with particular regard to the following aspects: independence of those who are in charge of the function, detection of any risk involving off-balance sheet activities and securitisations, assessment of the assets and performance of the stress tests) and the remuneration and incentive systems. Finally, the list of risks to be evaluated is amplified, and new types of risks are taken into consideration, including—among others—the leverage risk: this is defined as the risk that a particularly elevated leverage in comparison to the bank's own capital renders the bank vulnerable, making it necessary to adopt corrective measures in the context of the bank's industrial plan.

Third Pillar: This pillar was revised so as to introduce transparency requirements concerning exposure to securitisations, greater information on the composition of regulatory capital and on the manner in which the bank calculates capital ratios.

In the following section, we outline the main areas of intervention of the current framework.

Own Funds. Given that a marked erosion of the level and quality of capital became evident during financial crises, revealing that the capital held by financial intermediaries was basically unable to absorb losses (Demirguc-Kunt, Detragiache, & Merrouche, 2010), the supervisory authorities decided to take action with regard to the quantity and composition of capital, in the framework of an overall greater harmonisation of capital aggregates (Kato, Kobayashi, & Saita, 2010). The rationale of these interventions is to promote stability of the capital aggregate and thus to strengthen the capacity to absorb losses while maintaining continuity of business. This aim is pursued by means of rules designed not only to achieve a significant increase in the incidence of Common Equity Tier 1 (which is composed essentially of common shares and retained earnings) but also to establish more stringent computation requirements for the other capital instruments. The rule also provides for simplification of the structure of aggregates, for example, by eliminating the configuration of Tier 3 capital, which was previously required in order to cover market risks. In other words, it is now considered appropriate to make use of prime quality capital to cover risks of this kind. As far as Tier 2 is concerned, its composition must be such as to have the capacity to absorb losses if the bank were to be placed in run-off management or subjected to some similar procedure. As far as the level of own funds is concerned, while the total capital ratio (total capital/RWAs) remains set at 8%, the common equity ratio (common equity/RWAs) and the Tier 1 ratio (Tier 1/RWAs) are fixed at 4.5 and 6%, respectively.

Capital Buffers. Capital requirements based on the use of ratings tend to decrease during economic growth phases and to increase during recessions. Clearly, this is due to the increase in the risks faced by banks during recessions. One need only think of the increase in the credit risk: during an economic downturn, firms that have been granted a loan by a bank face greater difficulty in honouring their repayments. It follows that in such circumstances banks not only have to carry out greater value adjustments for loans, but they also tend to grant less credit.

This leads to distortions in the relation between banks and firms (customers) and, more generally, in the bank-market relation. It therefore becomes clear that there is a need to reinforce the solidity of banks with respect to pro-cyclical trends. Accordingly, the supervisory authorities made the decision to impose a capital conservation buffer and a countercyclical buffer. These two reserves are thus introduced—in addition to the other requirements in terms of own funds mentioned earlier—as a means of assuring that during economic growth periods a sufficient capital base is accumulated that will be capable of covering losses during recessions.

The capital conservation buffer consists of common equity and is equivalent to 2.5% of RWAs. It is designed to make sure that during positive economic periods, the banks will accumulate capital reserves—in an amount exceeding the minimum requirements—on which they will be able to draw during negative phases. Therefore, this measure implies that during positive economic periods, the banks will be required to accumulate high-quality capital up to 7% of RWAs. It will be possible to use this reserve—up to the limit of 4.5%—to cover losses suffered during adverse economic phases. The aim is to ensure the continuing availability of a further buffer during periods of financial and economic stress in order to withstand losses. Different characteristics but similar aims of counteracting pro-cyclicality can be observed in the countercyclical buffer. This is a further requirement of additional capital, which can be as much as 2.50% of RWAs. It is set up with the use of common equity. The aim it pursues is to inhibit the growth of bank credit if a tendency that differs significantly from the long period trend is noticed. Its introduction is not compulsory and is left up to the decision of the individual national authorities, which are therefore free to decide in favour or against its application, regardless of the credit trend.

A financial intermediary that fails to abide by the combined capital buffer requirements can be subjected to measures designed to achieve prompt reconstitution of the level of own funds. The reference is to limits on distribution of profit, including payment of dividends and of the variable components of the remuneration of the bank's management.

Leverage ratio. As mentioned above, one of the distinctive features that contributed to financial crises resided in the fact that banks had accumulated an excessive degree of leverage. In particular, it became clear that banks could no longer continue to take on debts to a fairly elevated extent if this did not reflect the outcome of a stable funding among the bank's customers. The liquidity crisis forced banks to decrease their leverage; in order to do so, they were compelled to reduce a part of their assets (typically, financial assets and loans). This further depressed the price of the assets sold on the market, thereby intensifying the interconnected downturn involving losses, erosion of capital and decline in availability of credit (Colombini, 2013; Pezzuto, 2013). Consequently, a limit (equal to 3%) was imposed on bank indebtedness: the leverage ratio. This measures the maximum level of indebtedness that an individual bank can have. The leverage ratio is set up in immediately perceivable terms: as a ratio between Tier 1 and total assets, including both on- and off-balance sheet exposures.

The introduction of this minimum requirement aims to set a limit on growth of assets, or rather, to limit their growth for the part financed by debts. Thus a clear and evident limit is set on the expansion of credit-related and financial intermediation that banks can undertake when they have recourse to the growth of debts. In actual fact, a limit that has the same aims is already in force, in the form of the minimum capital requirement designed to cope with the risks of various types that the bank takes on. It is commensurate with the credit, market and operational risks, but it is a limit of a different nature: the amount is fixed by the risks that have been taken on and by how they are measured. In contrast, the limit on leverage is based on the risks arising from an indebtedness that is regarded as excessive. Precisely this characteristic makes the leverage ratio into an additional—and different—rule as compared to the usual risk-based constraints (Tutino, 2011). The difference is important both for choices concerning management of the bank and also for the system stability demanded by the regulators. If a risk-based limit is exceeded, the bank can find a solution by modifying the composition of its assets in such a manner as to reduce assets that are subject to risk and replace them with others that are exposed to lesser risks.

Therefore, it is not always necessary to reduce the total amount of current assets, the intermediated volumes can remain unchanged (or even increase, provided that they are sufficiently adequately substituted with assets that carry a lower risk). By contrast, if the maximum leverage level is exceeded, the assets must be reduced by the amount that is over the limit, independently of the risks that may concern the assets in question.

Risk protection. The financial crises in European banks have made it clear that the counterparty riskiness associated with over-the-counter (OTC) derivatives had been severely underestimated. Accordingly, the new rules on counterparty risks require an increase in capital endowment as a specific cover against such risks; they also seek to reduce the pro-cyclical nature of counterparty risks and to provide incentives in order to promote the settlement of over-the-counter contracts by means of central counterparties. The aim is thus to help decrease systemic risk on financial markets. To this end, an ad hoc capital requirement has been introduced, designed to cover losses deriving from adjustments to market value of OTC derivatives after variations in the credit merit of the individual counterparties; additionally, a specific treatment has been introduced for exposure towards central counterparties.

In accordance with proposals put forward in July 2009 (BCBS, 2009), the prudential treatment of market risks is likewise reinforced, in order to lessen the weaknesses revealed by financial crises. In this context, higher capital requirements are imposed in order to capture the credit risk of complex trading instruments; furthermore, a stressed value-at-risk (VaR) requirement is included, which may help dampen the cyclicality of the minimum regulatory capital framework.

Liquidity standards. The widespread inadequacy, as revealed by financial crises, of the rationales on which management of the liquidity risk was based, has led the supervisory authorities to introduce two requisites with regard to liquidity: a short-term indicator and a structural indicator, designated respectively as the liquidity coverage ratio (LCR) and the net stable funding ratio (NSFR). Briefly, in order to respect the liquidity coverage ratio, banks must hold liquid assets that will be capable of covering—in certain conditions and at least for a specified length of time—the outflow of liquidity minus the inflow of liquidity. The aim is to guarantee that the bank has availability of liquid reserves that would be adequate to cope with a potential imbalance between inflows and outflows during a phase of extreme stress for a period of 30 days. Naturally, during periods of stress, the bank can reduce liquid—or liquidable—assets in order to use them as a means of covering the higher than usual net outflows.

Therefore, the bank must have availability of liquid—or liquidable—"high-quality" reserves in order to respond to cash flow requirements on a short-term basis during particularly complex situations or market tensions. Such reserves may be composed, for instance, of cash held at the central bank or of financial assets that can be sold on the market without suffering excessive loss of value. On the other hand, the net stable funding ratio is an indicator of financial structure. However, the bank must make a choice among types of indebtedness—by source and counterparties, operational types and maturities—that will be able to provide adequate support over time, in terms of stability on the financial point of view, for the choices concerning the assets which the bank records on the balance sheet. Accordingly, the NSFR is a constraint that guides the composition of the financial structure: the "stable" sources of funding must be greater than the "stable" assets. The "stable" sources include own funds and the stable sources of funding that have the characteristic of "stability", while the "stable" assets concern assets that require prolonged coverage over time. Typically, these are non-short-term assets. Thus the constraint is built up as a ratio to be respected: the sources of funding are in the nominator, the assets in the denominator.

5.5 Rationales for Basel IV

Despite the recent enactment of the Basel III framework (although it is not yet fully in force), the BCBS is introducing further refinements of the post-crisis reforms. Specifically, it is working to finalise its reform that aims to eliminate shortcomings highlighted by financial crises, in order to make banks safer and more resilient. The changes focus, above all, on the circumstance whereby banks use their own internal risk measurement models and examine the impact this has on risk reduction. In this regard, it should be borne in mind that the financial crises revealed a certain degree of unreliability of the RWAs of banks, above all when the RWAs are determined by means of advanced models. A debate thus arose concerning the extent of their effectiveness in terms of risk measurement; the debate is still ongoing.

It is known that the introduction of advanced models, which formed part of Basel II, attempted to grant banks the option of carrying out risk measurement as an internal procedure for regulatory purposes as well.

However, the growing complexity of risk management and measurement techniques, in addition to the related discretional aspect of such procedures—which is recognised by the regulatory framework—has weakened the reliability of these risk measurement procedures. To this should be added the difficulty of making a comparative assessment of the RWAs among different institutions, especially if they belong to different jurisdictions; consequently, the capacity of the RWAs to flag problematic aspects is further weakened. This is a cause of worry among the supervisory authorities, who are concerned that the prudential measurement metrics may not succeed in giving a precise evaluation of the overall risk exposure of banks, partly also because of the operations of RWAs optimisation. Further doubts are raised with regard to the possibility that the levels of capitalisation may prove to be inadequate to deal with the risks that have effectively been taken on. From the point of view of the banks, the main worry involves the eventuality of unequal treatment among players operating in different jurisdictions, in case where divergences among RWAs are not justified by a genuine distinction in the risk level of the assets (Ledo, 2011).

The answer that has been given by the supervisory authorities with regard to these problems is both intense and clearly structured. Thus on the one hand, the rules for calculating the RWAs have been revised, and a leverage ratio has been introduced. These modifications, as is known, have been included in the framework of Basel III and are designed to give a clearer and more immediate picture of the risks implicit in the different segments of the banking activity. On the other hand, the question has been included in the list of reforms to be examined and dealt with (BCBS, 2014c): in fact it has already been on this list for several years. The rationale of the refinement process springs from the need to increase the capacity of banks to withstand strains and stresses while endeavouring at the same time to attenuate recourse to a single capital adequacy coefficient as a tool for ensuring solidity and soundness. Over the years, the quest for greater sensitivity of risk has led to the complexity of the capital adequacy framework (Haldane & Madorous, 2012), with particular regard to RWAs calculation. This, in turn, has increased the danger of a lack of balance between the objectives of risk sensitivity, simplicity and comparability. In other words, the regulatory systems have little by little accumulated complexity as the rules became more fine-tuned in order to counter arbitrage and take into account the various innovations. Thus the quest for greater risk sensitivity has encouraged the use of complex mathematical statistical formulas in risk models. Consequently, the regulatory framework has amplified its complexity in order to keep abreast with the increasing sophistication of the risk measurement techniques. But the crucial point today is to try to reduce the complexity of the scheme without impairing its rigorous approach. Simplifications of the adequacy coefficients have already been carried out in the numerator: it now remains to be ascertained whether removal of the complexities of the RWAs will increase the effectiveness of the system (BCBS, 2013b). In this context, the BCBS has examined some aspects of the situation in greater depth and has confirmed that there are material variances in banks' regulatory capital ratios arising from factors other than differences in the riskiness of banks' portfolios. These variances undermine confidence in capital ratios. In response to these difficulties, the BCBS has initiated a number of policy and supervisory actions to address excessive variability in risk-weighted assets that are based on a bank's internal models and to harmonise capital calculations (BCBS, 2014c). In Box 5.3 we summarise the main initiatives put forward as part of the Basel IV framework.

Box 5.3 Basel IV: Key regulatory initiatives

- Market risk: a revised internal model approach (IMA), a revised standardised approach (SA), a shift from VaR to an expected shortfall measure of risk under stress, incorporation of the risk of market illiquidity, a revised boundary between the trading book and banking book (BCBS, 2016a)
- Credit risk: a revised standardised approach (BCBS, 2015), constraints on the use of internal model approaches (BCBS, 2016b)
- Operational risk: removal of advanced measurement approach, application of standardised measurement approach (SMA) (BCBS, 2016c)
- Interest rate risk in the banking book: focus on stress testing, model validation, disclosure, review by the supervisor (BCBS, 2016d)
- Large exposures: focus on measurement, aggregation and control of single-name concentration risk across jurisdictions (BCBS, 2014a)
- Disclosure: consolidation of the existing requirements, updates to reflect ongoing reforms (total loss-absorbing capacity (TLAC) regime for globally systemically important banks, market risk and operational frameworks; BCBS, 2017)

The actions undertaken, which in many cases have not yet been completed, aim to achieve multiple objectives, among which we may mention an improvement in informational transparency and an increase in the risk sensitivity of the standardised approaches, as well as the related quest for a balance between complexity and simplicity. Extensive reliance on internal models for the determination of capital levels, coupled with a lack of transparency, presents some drawbacks: for example, market participants may not be able to gauge the risk of banks; with several internal model methods, the senior management of banks may find it hard to judge and steer the level of risk of their respective banks. On the other hand, an overreliance on simplified approaches lacks risk sensitivity and does not capitalise on advances in risk management. Therefore, ideally, new Basel regulations should offer the risk sensitivity of Basel II and III while striving for the simplicity of Basel I (Capgemini, 2015).

Such aims are not easily achievable, especially considering the impact they may have on bank management (Amorello, 2016; KPMG, 2016). Banks will not only have to face greater severity with regard to capital requirements, but they will also be required to engage in mitigating actions, such as an increase in RWAs accuracy and improvement of the regulatory capital, an increase in the capital efficiency and profitability mix and adjustment of the business model to the new regulatory environment (McKinsey & Company, 2017). Moreover, these actions will take place in a context of marked instability and fairly low economic growth of the European system, above all in comparison with the situation of the United States, which may result in additional competitive disadvantage for Europe. This explains the proposal of the BCBS to differentiate the standards as a function of geographic areas; however, the propensity towards a standardised global approach still seems to be considered as an attractive approach, although the extent of the complex of reforms seems to point towards a fairly lengthy timescale for all the measures to come into full force. This precaution is in the interest of the financial and economic system (Tutino, 2016).

5.6 Conclusions

In the light of the above considerations, there is no broad industry consensus on what the future regulatory scenario and its impact will look like. However, the aim of stability of the economic and financial system remains a central goal. Equally central is the question of growth, which should be capable of generating stability to a greater extent than could derive from reinforcement of capital by the banks. In particular, while not disregarding the importance of the presence of capital and its solidity, there is a need to identify and make best use of all the drivers capable of ensuring the solidity of the individual institution as well as of the system as a whole. In other words, it is necessary to reinforce healthy and prudent management, identify the strategic risks and set in motion courageous supervision, focusing not merely on capital and limits but also on operational prohibitions that will prevent risk-taking beyond levels that could not be reasonably sustained by an individual bank.

References

Allen & Overy. (2014, January). *Capital requirements directive IV framework.* Internal Ratings Based Approach to Credit Risk in the Banking Book.

Amorello, L. (2016). Beyond the horizon of banking regulation: What to expect from Basel IV. *Harvard International Law Journal, 58*, 18.

BCBS—Basel Committee on Banking and Supervision. (1988, July). *International convergence of capital measurement and capital standards.*

BCBS—Basel Committee on Banking and Supervision. (2005, November). *Amendment to the capital accord to incorporate market risks.*

BCBS—Basel Committee on Banking and Supervision. (2006, June). *Basel II: International convergence of capital measurement and capital standards: A revised framework.* Comprehensive version.

BCBS—Basel Committee on Banking and Supervision. (2009, July). *Guidelines for computing capital for incremental risk in the trading book.*

BCBS—Basel Committee on Banking and Supervision. (2011, June). *Basel III: A global regulatory framework for more resilient banks and banking systems.* Revised version.

BCBS—Basel Committee on Banking and Supervision. (2013a, January). *Basel III: The liquidity coverage ratio and liquidity risk monitoring tools.*

BCBS—Basel Committee on Banking and Supervision. (2013b, July). *The regulatory framework: Balancing risk sensitivity, simplicity and comparability.*

BCBS—Basel Committee on Banking and Supervision. (2014a, April). *Supervisory framework for measuring and controlling large exposures—Final standard.*

BCBS—Basel Committee on Banking and Supervision. (2014b, October). *Basel III: The net stable funding ratio.*

BCBS—Basel Committee on Banking and Supervision. (2014c, November). *Reducing excessive variability in banks' regulatory capital ratios.*

BCBS—Basel Committee on Banking and Supervision. (2015, December). *Revisions to the standardised approach for credit risk—Second consultative document.*

BCBS—Basel Committee on Banking and Supervision. (2016a, January). *Minimum capital requirements for market risk.*

BCBS—Basel Committee on Banking and Supervision. (2016b, March). *Reducing variation in credit risk-weighted assets—Constraints on the use of internal model approaches—Consultative document.*

BCBS—Basel Committee on Banking and Supervision. (2016c, March). *Standardised measurement approach for operational risk—Consultative document.*

BCBS—Basel Committee on Banking and Supervision. (2016d, April). *Interest rate in the banking book.*

BCBS—Basel Committee on Banking and Supervision. (2017, January). *Pillar 3 disclosure requirements—Consolidated and enhanced framework.*

Birindelli, G., & Ferretti, P. (2017). *Operational risk management in banks. Regulatory, organizational and strategic issues.* London: Palgrave Macmillan.

Capgemini. (2015). *Basel IV, changing the regulatory landscape of banks.*

Colombini, F. (2013). Interview. In I. Pezzuto (Ed.), *"Predictable and avoidable. Repairing economic dislocation and preventing the recurrence of crisis", experts' insights for improved governance.* Farnham: Gower.

Crouhy, M., Galai, D., & Mark, R. (2006). *The essentials of risk management.* New York: McGraw-Hill.

Decamps, J.-P., Rochet, J.-C., & Roger, B. (2004). The three pillars of Basel II: Optimizing the mix. *Journal of Financial Intermediation, 13*(2), 132–155.

Demirguc-Kunt, A., Detragiache, E., & Merrouche, O. (2010). *Bank capital: Lessons from the financial crisis.* Policy Research Working Paper Series 5473. The World Bank.

Garside, T., & Bech, J. (2003). Dealing with Basel II: The impact of the New Basel Capital Accord. *Balance Sheet, 11*(4), 26–31.

Haldane A. G., & Madouros, V. (2012, August 31). *The dog and the Frisbee, Speech at the Federal Reserve Bank of Kansas City's 366th economic policy symposium.* The changing policy landscape, Jackson Hole, Wyoming.

Kato, R., Kobayashi, S., & Saita, Y. (2010, May). *Calibrating the level of capital: The way we see it.* Bank of Japan Working Paper, 10-E-6.

KPMG. (2016, December). *The world awaits: Basel IV nears completion.*

Lastra, R. M. (2004). Risk-based capital requirements and their impact upon the banking industry: Basel II and CAD III. *Journal of Financial Regulation and Compliance, 12*(3), 225–239.

Ledo, M. (2011). Towards more consistent, albeit diverse, risk-weighted assets across banks. *Estabilidad Financiera, 21*(11), 41–61.

McKinsey & Company. (2017, April). *Basel IV: What's next for banks?*

Pezzuto, I. (2013). *Predictable and avoidable. Repairing economic dislocation and preventing the recurrence of crisis.* Farnham: Gower.

Tutino, F. (2011). Raccolta, liquidità, patrimonio in Basilea III: impatti su strategie e gestione delle banche. In F. Tutino, G. Birindelli, & P. Ferretti (Eds.), *Basilea III. Gli impatti sulle banche* (pp. 361–394). Milano: Egea.

Tutino, F. (2016). Fiducia nelle banche, bail-in, tutela del risparmio: un approccio sistemico di lungo periodo. *Rivista Bancaria, 4–5*, 191–200.
Van Roy, P. (2005, August). *Credit ratings and the standardised approach to credit risk in Basel II*. ECB Working Paper, Number 517.

CHAPTER 6

Capital Constraints by Supervision in Europe

Fabiano Colombini

6.1 Introduction

The Single Supervisory Mechanism (SSM) aims to ensure the soundness and stability of European banks both individually and as a system, distinguishing between significant banks and less significant banks established respectively under the supervision of the European Central Bank (ECB) and the supervision of national competent authorities (NCAs).

The Single Supervisory Mechanism is carried out by an integration between a supranational authority, the European Central Bank and national competent authorities of individual countries of the European Union (EU), essentially applying a uniform set of standards.

The Single Supervisory Mechanism postulates control over bank capital ratios on the basis of Basel III and forthcoming Basel IV regulations and over economic, financial and capital trends of individual banks identifying problems and eventually adopting discretional measures.

The Supervisory Board takes meetings to discuss, plan and carry out the supervision over European banks. Hence the structure of the ECB between the conduct of monetary policy and supervision reveals separate units which sometimes provide indications which do not conform particularly closely.

F. Colombini (✉)
Department of Economics and Management, University of Pisa, Pisa, Italy

F. Colombini (ed.), *Raising Capital or Improving Risk Management and Efficiency?*, https://doi.org/10.1007/978-3-319-71749-4_6

This chapter aims to analyse supervision issues considering recent developments and implementation in the context of the evolution of the banking business in the euro area.

6.2 Setting Up the Single Supervisory Mechanism

The creation of the banking union in Europe, applying uniform criteria for supervision over banks through the Single Supervisory Mechanism (SSM) as well as uniform criteria for bank crisis resolution through the Single Resolution Mechanism (SRM), is introduced in a single and reinforced supervision perspective (Angeloni, 2015; Barba Navaretti, Calzolari, & Pozzolo, 2015; Schoenmaker, 2011; Trentinaglia, 2015).

Supervision needs a strong and level regulatory base aiming to harmonise the rule book and encourage greater reliance on EU regulations that can be directly applied in all member states, creating the base for bank competition on a level playing field (Lautenschlager, 2017). European supervisors will be able to make a broad-based cross-border comparison among banks, assessing problems by means of the same main tool, namely, SREP (Nouy, 2017).

The Single Supervisory Mechanism has become necessary because the recent financial and banking crises in Europe have shown that simple coordination between central banks has not proved to be satisfactory in the light of operations across national borders. Hence there is the need to apply common evaluation standards in Europe and, at the same time, to ensure financial stability.

The SSM was created jointly with the SRM; it is managed by the Single Resolution Board (SRB) and the Single Resolution Fund (SRF), fed by the banks and the projected single scheme for deposit guarantee.

Supervision over European banks is characterised essentially by gathering and processing information on banking business and economic trends on both a central and decentralised level. The ECB directly supervises around 120 significant banks of the participating countries; these banks hold almost 82% of banking assets in the euro area. The NCAs supervise around 3,500 less significant banks in the euro area.

Setting up the SSM implies the transferring of supervisory responsibility from individual authorities to a central and supranational authority. The ECB performs its own supervisory task but also considers information on banks produced by NCAs. A slow or inept information-gathering process by the NCAs may adversely influence the supervisory process.

Supervision is a delicate and complicate task that requires a large quantity of up-to-date and top-quality information in order to assess bank economic, financial and capital conditions and their evolution. Planning on-site inspections and monitoring of European banks are very important both in terms of bank selection and in terms of time frame. In particular, there is a need to set up a plan of on-site inspections for investigations of weak banks at given times in order to engage in early remedial action that will avert critical situations and crises. This process requires professional skills and capacity in order to monitor and, where necessary, intervene in the procedures over European banks. It is important to improve and increase the number of AQR, stress tests and on-site inspections and their frequency in the context of European banks, so that critical situations can be rapidly identified and prompt remedial measures set in place.

The SSM implies cooperation among different bodies in gathering and processing information. To date, the results in terms of efficiency do not appear very satisfactory. The cleaning up of bank balance sheets in the European context is far from being fully achieved: economic recovery is still under way though some benefits to banks are beginning to appear.

In this context, it is vital to enhance the skills, professional capacity and quality of inspectors dedicated to monitoring and identification of critical banking situations. These supervisory tasks can be applied to ECB for significant banks and to NCAs for less significant banks throughout Europe.

The level playing field can be achieved through the rule harmonisation and uniform application of supervisory methodologies by the Banking Supervision of the ECB and by the NCAs in different European countries. Sets of information and data built up within the central bank and within the national competent authorities can be used for the operations in question.

In this framework, the substantial novelty in bank crisis management is represented by the bail-in (Boccuzzi, 2016; Colombini, 2015; Joosen, 2015; Sommer, 2014). This implies the aid of shareholders and bank creditors, including subordinated and straight bonds for coverage of serious losses and the rescue of the bank in question. In the event of severe economic, financial and capital instability, account holders could run the risk of losing their deposits which exceed 100,000 euros, although this is a rather remote hypothesis. States can intervene with their financial aid only in an extreme and residual hypothesis.

It needs to be emphasised that, in the case of a crisis affecting a very large cross-border bank or in the event of a systemic crisis, a bail-in will not remove the need for public support of funds (Avgouleas & Goodhart, 2014).

The bail-in presents critical aspects from different standpoints in the EU banking context. First of all, it is rather problematic, even for the most careful saver, to obtain the right indications to assess and correctly follow the bank's economic, financial and capital evolution, there being an issue of informative asymmetry which is not resolvable (Colombini, 2008).

Secondly, a confidence crisis severely affects savers in the event of a crisis and bank failure. The repercussions can become difficult to control, with negative knock-on effects (Avgouleas & Goodhart, 2014).

In the third place, it is conceivable that the bail-in and the onset of a crisis and bank failure may induce a contraction of the channel of banking bonds for fund raising. This, in turn, may cause significant damage to the extent of monetary resources flowing to the bank with medium- to long-term maturity and, therefore, used typically for medium- to long-term loans towards investments for EU small- and medium-sized enterprises.

Finally, the drying up of the channel of banking bonds has negative repercussions on the bank's financial balance, due to the resulting lack of medium- to long-term monetary resources.

For the above reasons, the bail-in seeks not to burden the cost of the crises and bank failures on state budgets; however, it tends to introduce aspects of financial instability.

For these reasons, the bail-in constitutes a set of rules which must be changed radically. The basic impression is that the critical aspects of the bail-in have been neither assessed nor simulated. It is enough to point out that, in the event of a confidence crisis on the part of savers hit by the failure of a bank of significant size, the spread and extension to other banks could carry serious implications for bank intermediaries and financial markets. This, in turn, could raise the issue of state intervention.

In the drafting of the bail-in, there are economic and financial elements which seem to have been ignored. Thus in the event of crisis—or worse, of bank failure—the most immediate aspect, which, on the basis of what has been concluded above, is of fundamental importance, leads to irrational choices by the management, in particular, by risk management. More specifically, there have been from the start, and there will remain over time, informative asymmetries towards shareholders and bank creditors, impeding an accurate appreciation of the economic, financial and capital conditions of the bank in question.

6.3 Additional Capital Requirements by Supervision in Europe

The Basel approach to capital requirements has been adjusted through time by imposition of risk-weighted assets (RWAs) which leads to more capital with respect to the increasing level of assets and risk. The percentage system for calculation has no scientific base: rather, it has evolved over time with the evolution of the real situation.

Every bank in the world will start the business with an amount of capital and will add capital over time as bank business and risk increase. The imposition of capital requirements by regulatory authorities can be considered a capital constraint. The imposition of capital requirements by supervisory authorities can be viewed as an additional capital constraint. Banks tend to hold capital in excess of regulatory minimum requirements as a tool against adverse shocks (Wagner, 2014).

The logic of the Basel approach is the prudential criterion; the logic of supervision is the discretional criterion. The two criteria stand at opposite poles and therefore are in contrast with each other. This leads to the need for adjustments in the capital level. Such adjustments can create bank problems in the case of a sudden change in the amount of capital for running the business.

Reducing leverage and increasing capital buffers seek to improve the bank's financial structure, with the aim of ensuring that the bank would be able to cope with possible losses incurred and capital reductions. Additional capital requirements imposed by supervision can be viewed as discretional measures. This overlapping creates uncertainty and instability for bank management.

What is more worrying is the length of time required in making decisions for bank solutions, as delays tend to increase the cost of implementing any solution. It is known that the cost of distress increases in highly critical situations.

Supervision measures inspired by discretion contribute to the shape of the banking system, leading to and increasing the demand for capital, addressed to financial markets.

In this framework, the mixture of regulatory requirements and supervisory requirements reveals contradictions, sudden manifestations and uncertainty. Two different views on capital can be perceived: one approach prescribes low leverage for the bank and high capital levels of 20–30% and 40–50% and still more of its total assets (Admati & Hellwig, 2013; Fama, 2010); another approach suggests maintaining high leverage for the bank and provision of liquidity to the economy (DeAngelo & Stulz, 2015; Gorton & Ordonez, 2013). There are no scientific arguments nor quantitative analysis to indicate high capital levels (Rochet, 2015) of 20–30% or of 40–50% and still more: along this line there is a distortion in the banking system as it underlines an evolution of the bank model towards the mutual fund model, perfectly matched in the hypothetical case of capital equal to a 100% of assets (Kotlikoff, 2010). This view moves towards a bank model which has no capacity to provide liquidity to the economy; moreover, it is a model that misses the financial transformation. The other view tends to maintain the presence of high leverage and good conditions of financial transformation, thereby providing liquidity to the economy.

All indications on high percentages of capital level miss a very important point: it is not the high level of capital at a given time that is capable of maintaining the safety and soundness of the individual bank; rather, it is the quality of its management, which should be able to take the right decisions in order to create economic conditions between revenue and costs that will enable banks and banking systems to improve and survive over time. Capital is merely a factor which is important for solvency risk at a given time. The situation of capital can change suddenly because of negative events and bad management: for instance, financial crises have been caused by poor screening and monitoring of loans and by deterioration in public finances for state interventions.

The development of the Supervisory Review and Evaluation Process (SREP) consists of a tool built up by the SSM for evaluating individual banks. The SREP assessment considers and evaluates business model, governance, risk management, risks to capital and risks to liquidity. The overall SREP score reflects the supervisor's assessment of the bank's viability. SREP can be considered as a sort of final indicator at the base of an evaluation process on an individual bank which can draw advantage from on-site inspections.

The SREP results can induce supervisory authorities to prompt individual banks to increase their capital. Estimation for additional capital is a delicate task which includes a real and accurate analysis of the bank in question, in order to indicate the need and to estimate the level of new capital. Delays in the process are very frequent, and they lead to increasing the impact of bad news on the additional level of capital. This is a point that needs to be corrected and improved in order to avoid increases in the need for capital.

6.4 Supervisory Performance

Supervisory authorities carry out the supervisory task over time, with particular attention to economic and financial trends and their development and impact on financial industries. Financial crises and economic crises in Europe in recent times have created a range of banking problems with state interventions and increases in public budgets. Individual banks, especially large banks, have come under pressure several times, due to liquidity and solvency problems. Many banks were found to be in critical conditions and received state aid to assist their recovery and to reshape not only their business models but also their financial and economic structures.

Supervision is a delicate task which involves heavy responsibilities. The actual task of supervision is split between the Banking Supervision of the ECB at a central level over the significant banks and the NCAs at a national level over the less significant banks in collaboration with the ECB. In this framework, decisions taken and interventions should consider uniform criteria for evaluation and resolution among different European banks which have the head office in European countries. The main indicator for supervisory decisions to build up, estimate and consult is the SREP based on quantitative and qualitative tools related to individual banks.

It is important to bear in mind that crises are likely to differ over time and place: it implies that different levels of capital raising are likely to be imposed for recovery of troubled banks, especially if the bank will stand alone in the recovery process. The main problem is the estimation as there is a trade-off between the required level for increasing capital and the bank's capacity for restructuring while still doing business in the presence of market pressure and competition.

This is a very important and delicate exercise: if the capital requirement is set too high, the bank may encounter difficulty in raising the required funds; on the other hand, setting a capital requirement too low may make it impossible for the bank to recreate suitable conditions for bank management viability.

The macro-critical point is capital raising for individual banks: which effects will lead in the future to survival of different banks? Will additional capital suffice or will the critical situation recur in the future?

In the European banking landscape, there are situations where banks are affected by temporary problems, and others where banks are in critical conditions: supervisory authorities have the task of investigating and distinguishing between different problems. Capital requirement is usually the measure implemented by the Banking Supervision of ECB for the banks' survival on the market. This recurrent request, which obliges individual banks to provide additional capital, can at times be a problem of incorrect estimation made by supervisory authorities or a problem of bad management during periods following the raising of capital. There may also be a problem of "wasting capital" for the individual bank where capital increases are repeated: in such circumstances, bank conditions will deteriorate within a short or medium time frame. It will be necessary to monitor the bank management and gather information concerning ongoing bank recovery and still going in trouble on a European scale. In seeking to assess the recovery of banks, attention should focus on such aspect as the times of additional capital constraints, economic trends in costs and revenue, evolution of assets and liabilities and experiment of once again additional capital for the same banks will be quite important for eventual identification of wasting capital.

Supervision timing and decision timing are very crucial, especially in case of intervention for bank critical situations. Supervisory decisions imply a sort of collaboration among the Supervisory Board of the ECB, the European Banking Authority (EBA), the European Commission and NCAs; though the collaboration is necessary, it contributes to time delays for the solution. It can also be argued that supervisory interventions based simply on capital will provide a weak performance in recreating best premises for the future survival.

In this framework, a panel of data for banks in crisis and bank failures can be drawn up, outlining individual years, duration periods and explaining the relation between capital requirements on a discretional basis by supervisory authorities and the future of banks involved. This will be an exercise of transparency and will show the real effects from repetition of capital raising as a usual measure.

Supervisory performance can be investigated essentially considering banks which have been assessed providing suggestions and measures' implementation under the ECB direct supervision or under the NCA supervision. It can be done by looking and evaluating banking reinforcement and banking performance in the going-on of typical business areas. Considering the analysis carried out throughout this book, better results will be difficult to achieve without radical changes aiming at improving risk management and efficiency of individual banks.

6.5 Conclusions

Supervisors perform the task of monitoring the real situation and the real evolution of individual banks distinguishing between significant and less significant banks. The systemic banks are under control of the Banking Supervision of the ECB, and the nonsystemic banks are under control of NCAs in coordination with the ECB.

Supervision is carried out by using information, on-site inspections, AQR and stress testing and therefore evaluating SREP results which constitute the standard for the type and timing of initiatives on European banks.

Imposing additional capital requirements by supervision, at the same time, tends to increase compliance costs, leading to the need to make a comparison between costs and benefits from the point of view of a micro and macro perspective.

The balance postulates the correct evaluation of costs which tend to increase as the complexity of rules is going up and the benefits essentially in terms of financial stability.

Supervision is carried out by the Banking Supervision of the ECB over large banks and by the NCAs over small- and medium-sized banks. This leads to a problem of collection, analysis and evaluation of a substantial range of information on the viability of banks operating typically in several different countries or in individual countries. The NCAs gathered and produced sets of information through a supervisory experience built up over many years; in contrast, the Supervision Unit of the ECB collected and evaluated information through a supervisory task that has been active for the last few years.

References

Admati, A., & Hellwig, M. (2013). *The bankers' new clothes: What's wrong with banking and what to do about it.* Princeton, NJ: Princeton University Press.

Angeloni, I. (2015). The single supervisory mechanism. *European Economy, 1*(3), 43–55.

Avgouleas, E., & Goodhart, C. (2014, July). *A critical evaluation of bail-in as a bank recapitalisation mechanism.* Discussion Paper 10065. CEPR.

Barba Navaretti, G. B., Calzolari, G., & Pozzolo, A. F. (2015). Sand in the wheels: Implementing the single supervisory mechanism and multinational banking in Europe. *European Economy, 1*(3), 9–23.

Boccuzzi, G. (2016). *The European Banking Union: Supervision and resolution.* London: Palgrave.

Colombini, F. (2008). *Intermediari, mercati e strumenti finanziari. Economia e integrazione.* Torino: Utet.

Colombini, F. (2015). Risk, regulation, supervision and crises in the European Banking Union. *Law and Economics Yearly Review, 4*(2), 236–273.

DeAngelo, H., & Stulz, R. M. (2015). Liquid-claim production, risk management, and bank capital structure: Why high leverage is optimal for banks. *Journal of Financial Economics, 116*(2), 219–236.

Fama, E. (2010, May). *Interview.* CNBC.

Gorton, G. B., & Ordonez, G. (2013). *The supply and demand for safe assets* (No. w18732). National Bureau of Economic Research.

Joosen, B. (2015, March). *Regulatory capital requirements and bail in mechanisms.* Working Paper, University of Amsterdam—Faculty of Law, European Banking Institute.

Kotlikoff, L. J. (2010). *Jimmy Stuart is dead: Ending the world's financial plague before it strikes again.* Hoboken, NJ: Wiley.

Lautenschlager S.(2017, September 28). Speech, ESE conference 2017, Vienna.

Nouy, D. (2017, September 29). Statement, single resolution board conference, Brussels.

Rochet, J. C. (2015). The bank capital controversy. *European Economy, 1*, 39–46.

Schoenmaker, D. (2011). The financial trilemma. *Economics Letters, 111*(1), 57–59.

Sommer, J. H. (2014). Why bail-in? And how! *Economic Policy Review, 20*(2), 207–228. Federal Reserve Bank of New York.

Trentinaglia, M. T. (2015). Institutions. *European Economy, 1*(3), 31–34.

Wagner, W. (2014). Unintended consequences of macroprudential policies. In *Macroprudentialism* (pp. 105–113). London: CEPR Press.

CHAPTER 7

Banking Regulation and Supervision in Europe

Antonella Cappiello

7.1 Introduction

Financial crises which started in 2007 led policy makers to rethink the financial architecture in the light of its gaps and inability to react promptly to systemic shocks. The vast extent of the subprime mortgage financial crisis and the sovereign debt crisis indicated causes and highlighted the need to adopt structural preventive measures, above all in order to avert a repetition of the phenomenon.

The steps undertaken in this regard, namely, the Dodd-Frank Act introduced in the United States, and the creation of the European System of Financial Supervision (ESFS), set up a new architecture for the regulation and supervision of financial markets. This led to a new and incisive role for the central banks.

In this context, the development of the project of a European Banking Union specifies the structure of the planned Union and reinforces the regulatory architecture and supervision on the supranational level. The aims pursued by the European Banking Union thus concern the establishment of an integrated framework designed to safeguard financial stability.

A. Cappiello (✉)
Department of Economics and Management, University of Pisa, Pisa, Italy

F. Colombini (ed.), *Raising Capital or Improving Risk Management and Efficiency?*, https://doi.org/10.1007/978-3-319-71749-4_7

The European Banking Union has a twofold dimension, both banking-related and monetary, as the reforms it has introduced concern not only the objectives pertaining to the banking market, but also the requirements of the euro monetary system, with specific reference to the aim of price stability. In this context, the establishment of a European Banking Union would represent, first and foremost, an essential step towards completion of the European Monetary Union Project; additionally, it would provide an effective response to the disruption of the 2007 financial crises. It is also designed to pursue several objectives; specifically, it must eliminate the association between sovereign risk and banking risk, mitigate the fragmentation of the EU market, and ensure that supervision is updated in order to adapt to changes in the banking system in which financial intermediaries with Europe-wide extension have begun to appear.

This chapter aims to analyse the new Europe-wide regulatory and supervisory structure, describing the project of an European Banking Union and the relative three pillars that are being gradually introduced, with a critical focus on the new resolution rules to be applied in cases of bank crises.

7.2 Bank Regulation in Europe

During the financial crises, the inadequacy of the regulatory and supervisory system in the EU became stronger. It was still firmly anchored to the national level and based on the principle of mutual recognition; consequently, it impaired the integrity of the internal market creating problems in crises management (Acharya, 2009).

In June 2009, the leaders of European governments reached an agreement on a new model for supervision of the financial markets. Consisting of a series of legislative projects presented by the European Commission, it led to the creation of new supervisory bodies. Thus in addition to traditional supervision on the national level, the European System of Financial Supervision (ESFS) was set up, designed to harmonise the rules and coherence of supervisory practices both on the European level and also among contiguous sectors (Mottura, 2011).

The European System of Financial Supervision consists of an integrated network of national and European supervision. The scheme is based on two levels:

1. Macro supervision, entrusted to the European Systemic Risk Board (ESRB). This organism, which is a genuine innovation within the European framework, has competence with regard to macro policies, that is, policies concerning the conditions which can contribute to reinforcing financial stability on the systemic level. Its task is to assess and evaluate risk for the stability of the overall financial system and, if necessary, to issue a preventive alert concerning the possible evolution of systemic risks. Additionally, it is required to provide the micro level supervisory authorities with recommendations concerning the measures to be adopted in order to avert such risks.
2. Micro supervision, entrusted to the European Supervisory Authorities (ESAs): European Banking Authority (EBA), European Insurance and Occupational Pensions Authority (EIOPA), and European Securities and Markets Authority (ESMA) to supervise banks, insurances, and securities and markets, respectively. Each of the three authorities interacts and cooperates with the European Systemic Risk Board (ESRB) as far as macroprudential policies are concerned, and with the Joint Committee of the ESAs, the European Central Bank (ECB) and the Member States' national competent authorities (NCAs).

In this framework, the ESAs enjoy considerable independence. They improve the functioning of the internal market by providing pan-EU regulation and harmonising supervisory practices in the EU. The task of the ESAs, on the one hand, is to ensure uniform rules and common supervisory approaches across the eurozone and, on the other, to implement the binding laws of the European Union. In actual fact, the powers vested in the ESAs belong almost exclusively to the sphere of rule-making, with reference to technical rules, without implying any strategic decisions or political choices. The EBA performs regulatory tasks and aims at increasing the quality and consistency of supervision across the EU.

The European banking legislation was previously based on directives that left room for significant divergences in national rules. This has led to different interpretations of the rules in question and to legal uncertainty, enabling banks to exploit regulatory loopholes, distorting competition, and making it burdensome to operate across the single market. Despite the existence of common rules, divergent supervisory practices and outcomes pose a potential risk to the effective supervision of cross-border groups and hinder the development of a level playing field in financial services. Moreover, the financial crises have shown that in integrated financial markets, these divergences can have very disruptive effects. Once risks have materialised that were generated under the curtain of minimum harmonisation, the impact often cannot be contained within national boundaries but is spread across the EU single market.

Among the tasks assigned to EBA by the Regulation with which it was set up, one of the most significant is the creation of a Single Rulebook for financial services. It aims to address the aforementioned shortcomings in order to move towards a more resilient, more transparent, and more efficient European banking sector; it ensures that the prudential safeguards are applied across the EU and not limited to individual Member States, as the crisis has highlighted the extent to which Member States' economies are interconnected. By providing the regulatory framework for the integrity and efficiency of banking in the EU, the EBA also contributes to financial stability across the Union.

The financial crisis demonstrated that the opaqueness of regulatory requirements in different Member States was a major cause of financial instability. A Single Rulebook ensures that institutions' overall financial situation is more transparent and comparable across the EU for supervisors, deposit-holders and investors.

Additionally, the EBA is assigned a key role in ensuring uniform application of the Basel III framework in all Member States. It will close regulatory loopholes and will thus contribute to a more effective functioning of the single market. It is, therefore, crucial to use exactly the same definition of regulatory aggregates and the same methodologies for the calculation of key requirements, such as capital ratios and liquidity standards.

The EBA is mandated to produce a large number of Binding Technical Standards (BTS), guidelines and reports for implementation of the CRD IV/CRR package, the BRRD, and the DGSD (EBA, 2015). Finally, as part of its contribution to a common supervisory culture across the EU, the EBA will review the application of all BTS adopted by the European Commission and will propose amendments where appropriate (European Commission, 2016a).

In order to assess the impact of the full implementation of the Basel III framework on the European banking system, the EBA conducts, on a semi-annual basis, a monitoring exercise on a sample of EU banks.

Although the Single Rulebook is a key for Europe, it is true that the new regulatory framework has to be shaped in such a way as to leave a certain degree of national flexibility in the activation of macroprudential tools, given that credit and economic cycles are not synchronised across the EU. In any case, the rules in the Single Rulebook remove a large number of national options and discretions and allow Member States to apply different requirements only where these are justified through a process which ensures input from EU bodies including the EBA.

However, each Member State is responsible for adjusting, for example, the level of its countercyclical buffer to its economic situation and should protect its economy/banking sector from any other structural variables that can pose a threat to financial stability. Furthermore, Member States would naturally retain current powers under Pillar 2, that is, the ability to impose additional requirements on a specific bank following the Supervisory Review and Evaluation Process (SREP).

The EBA is also mandated to assess risk vulnerability in the EU banking sector through, in particular, regular risk assessment reports and pan-European stress tests, in close cooperation with the ECB. It also conducts the yearly EU-wide transparency exercise, which is part of EBA's efforts to foster market discipline, improves the understanding of the EU banking system, and ensures both a detailed snap shot and consistent time series.

Finally, it should be underlined that EBA cannot be defined as an independent regulatory authority *stricto sensu*. In contrast to the initial impression it may convey, it is not empowered to pass laws under its own initiative; it thus differs notably from the models of the regulatory sectorial authorities (Pisaneschi, 2016).

The power to create rules, which constitutes the essence of regulation, is vested in the European Commission. The role of the EBA as compared to that of the European Commission consists basically in providing technical assistance. However, it can be noted that in recent years, EBA, possibly influenced by the economic downturn, has not directed its efforts so much towards the main activity of coordination and harmonisation of the rules and supervision as, rather, to the exercise of its few powers of direct intervention. Such powers include the formulation of stress tests and the ensuing recommendations to the national authorities, which would have the task of ensuring supervision of banks, insurances, and securities and markets. So far, however, we do not yet have a unified body of supervisory rules on the European level (see the report of the European Commission concerning the new proposals for a regulation) (European Commission, 2016b).

7.3 Bank Supervision in Europe

The financial crisis has clearly highlighted the need to bridge the gap represented by the lack, on the institutional level, of a banking union (Carmassi, Di Noia, & Micossi, 2012; Van Rompuy, 2012). The project of a European Banking Union is aimed to reinforce the regulatory architecture and supervision on the supranational level (Berglöf, De Haas, & Zettelmeyer, 2012; Colliard, 2015; Constâncio, 2014; Goyal et al., 2013; Véron, 2015), establishing an integrated framework designed to safeguard financial stability and to reduce the cost of bank defaults (Maloney, 2014).

It follows that the Banking Union is designed to pursue several objectives such as to eliminate the association between sovereign risk and banking risk, mitigate the fragmentation of the EU market, and ensure that supervision is updated in order to adapt to changes in the banking system in which financial intermediaries with Europe-wide extension and activities have begun to appear.

Effectively, the sectorial literature explains the Banking Union as a step which is, in a sense, indispensable as a means to solve the contradiction of the financial trilemma (Schoenmaker, 2013). In his analysis, the overall picture is perfectly represented by the situation of European financial policy, with great intermediaries operating on transnational markets but a supervisory system under national responsibility (Acharya, 2009; Ferrarini & Chiodini, 2012).

The European Banking Union currently applies to all 28 Member States; additionally, countries not belonging to the euro area may become members, although no non-euro area country has done so yet.

The foundation of the Banking Union relies on the implementation of the Single Rulebook, which includes provisions for capital regulation, deposit protection, and for banks' recovery and resolution.

To implement the Banking Union, three pillars are being gradually introduced:

1. The first pillar is represented by the Single Supervisory Mechanism (SSM): a new European system of banking supervision, set up with a purpose-designed EU Regulation in October 2013, which came into effect as from November 2014. The SSM, which according to the intentions of the European Council represents the first step towards Banking Union, is composed of the European Central Bank (ECB) and the national supervisories of the participating countries.

It is headed by a Supervisory Board which oversees the task of supervision and has responsibility for the function of proposal for final decisions by the board of the ECB.

2. The second pillar concerns the Single Resolution Mechanism (SRM), which pursues the main aim of efficient resolution of distressed banks, containing to the greatest possible degree the burden of costs for tax-payers and the real economy.
3. The third pillar concerns the proposal to establish the European Deposit Insurance Scheme (EDIS), namely, a fund created by the banks that will be used to cover the expenses of rescuing the intermediaries themselves who are contributing to the scheme. The proposal pertaining to harmonisation of the national systems for the guaranteeing of deposits includes procedures designed to ensure that national deposit guarantee systems are set up in each Member State. Such systems need to be solid enough to limit any repercussions associated with the flight of deposits between institutes or countries. Furthermore, guarantees must also be established to ensure an adequate level of protection of depositors in the European Union.

7.4 The Single Supervisory Mechanism

The genesis of the SSM implies the loss of sovereignty of EU member countries that results from banking supervision on a supranational level, and also the partial loss control over the system regulating credit and financial markets (Calzolari & Loranth, 2011).

The establishment of the SSM, which in the intentions of the Council of Europe was intended to represent the first step towards Banking Union, has redesigned banking supervision in Europe. In this new perspective, the ECB stands as the focal point of the prudential micro (and also macro, with regard to some aspects) supervision system, as the central supervisor, ultimately responsible for financial stability and supervision-related tasks. The text of Article 4.2.18 of the 2012 Council Proposal states that the ECB "will be exclusively competent for key supervisory tasks which are indispensable to detect risks for banks' viability and require them to take the necessary action".

In the new setup of supervisory functions assigned to banks in the Member States, the ECB takes on exclusive tasks and power of supervision, never previously attributed to a supranational authority within the framework of the European juridical system (Ferrarini & Recine, 2015;

Singh, 2016). In the earlier systems, banking supervision was carried out by the NCAs, not endowed with supranational power of supervision, despite the creation of the EBA in 2011.

The aim pursued by the introduction of SSM is to reinforce the homogeneous application of the prudential rules and to establish genuine surveillance on cross-border banking markets. In short, SSM deals with supervision of all credit institutions in the participating Member States and ensures that EU policy is carried out in a coherent and effective manner by means of best practice in supervision, applied to all the intermediaries of the system.

The main aims of SSM can be summarised in three points: (1) ensure the security and solidity of the European banking system; (2) increase integration and financial stability; (3) guarantee coherent supervision, pursuing not only the fundamental principles required for effective banking supervision drawn up by the Basel Committee but also the rules pertaining to supervision drawn up by EBA, which constitute a solid basis both for regulating and also for carrying out supervision and ensuring proper governance as well as risk management in the banking sector.

The SSM introduces a consolidated supervision system, in which the ECB has a leading role, as its functions include the role of ensuring effective and coherent functioning of the SSM, in cooperation with the competent national authorities of the Member States of the eurozone; it may also, at times, cooperate with the national authorities of States that have not yet adopted the common currency, but which nevertheless wish to establish some form of close cooperation within the SSM.

All the tasks not explicitly attributed to the ECB remain under the power of the NCAs. This includes responsibility for consumer protection and the prevention of money laundering, and it also covers supervision of credit institutions of third countries that open branches or offer cross-border services in the Member State.

To ensure efficient supervision, the respective supervisory roles and responsibilities of the ECB and the NCAs are allocated on the basis of the significance of the supervised banks. The significance is identified on the basis of the following criteria: size, importance for the economy of the European Union or for a Member State, volume of cross-border activity, request—or absence of request—for aid from the ESM (see Box 7.1).

It follows that the ECB is directly in charge of monitoring the largest banks that are classified as significant, whereas the NCAs continue to conduct the direct supervision of less significant, while assuring, however, close collaboration between the central authority (ECB) and the national authorities.

Box 7.1 Classification of institutions as significant or less significant
To determine whether or not a credit institution is significant, the SSM conducts a regular review: all credit institutions authorised within the participating Member States are assessed to determine whether they fulfil the criteria for significance. A credit institution will be considered significant if any one of the following conditions is met:

- the total value of its assets exceeds €30 billion or—unless the total value of its assets is below €5 billion—exceeds 20% of national GDP;
- it is one of the three most significant credit institutions established in a Member State;
- it is a recipient of direct assistance from the European Stability Mechanism;
- the total value of its assets exceeds €5 billion and the ratio of its cross-border assets/liabilities in more than one other participating Member State to its total assets/liabilities is above 20%.

Notwithstanding the fulfilment of these criteria, the SSM may declare an institution significant to ensure the consistent application of high-quality supervisory standards. The ECB or the NCAs may ask for certain information to be submitted (or resubmitted) to help facilitate the decision.

Through normal business activity or due to exceptional occurrences (e.g. a merger or acquisition), the status of credit institutions may change. If a group or a credit institution that is considered less significant meets any of the relevant criteria for the first time, it is declared significant and the NCA takes responsibility for its direct supervision to the ECB. Conversely, a credit institution may no longer be significant, in which case the supervisory responsibility for it returns to the relevant NCAs. In both cases, the ECB and the NCAs involved carefully review and discuss the issue and, unless particular circumstances exist, plan and implement the transfer of supervisory responsibilities so as to allow for a continued and effective supervision. To avoid rapid or repeated alternations of supervisory responsibilities between NCAs and the ECB (e.g. if a credit institution's assets fluctuate at around €30 billion), the classification has a moderation mechanism: whereas the shift in status from less significant to significant is triggered if just one criterion is met in any one year, a significant group or credit institution will only qualify for a reclassification as less significant if the relevant criteria have not been met over three consecutive calendar years.

Institutions are notified immediately of the SSM's decision to transfer supervisory responsibilities from the NCAs to the ECB, or vice versa: prior to the adoption of the decision, the ECB gives the institution the opportunity to provide written comments. During the transition, institutions receive regular updates as needed and are introduced to their new team of supervisors. Once the transition is complete, a formal handover meeting is organised for representatives from the supervised institution and the outgoing and incoming supervisors.

The ECB can also take on the direct supervision of less significant institutions if this is necessary to ensure the consistent application of high supervisory standards. The ECB is also involved in the supervision of cross-border institutions and groups, either as a home supervisor or a host supervisor in Colleges of Supervisors. Moreover, the ECB participates in the supplementary supervision of financial conglomerates in relation to the credit institutions included in a conglomerate; it assumes the responsibilities of the coordinator referred to in the Financial Conglomerates Directive.

The important duties and powers attributed to the ECB imply that this authority plays a fundamental role for correct implementation of the integrated supervision system, which is fully distinct from any concerns of an exclusively national relevance.

As far as doctrinal analysis is concerned, some criticisms of the SSM have been raised. It has been objected that the current system does not allow sufficient separation between the supervision function and European monetary policy functions, although on paper such functions are very carefully distinguished. This is due above all to the consideration that decisions concerning supervision are taken by the ECB's Governing Council, which could lead to a conflict of interests (Buch, Körner, & Weigert, 2014). On the other hand, numerous other analysts argue that potential synergies arise from the exercise, at one and the same time, of supervision powers and monetary policy (Troger, 2015).

The ECB finds itself, for the first time, being called upon to play an operative role of politically sensitive supervision, but at the same time it is also required to account for its actions systematically in the framework of the SSM. The ideal design suggested by the de Larosière Report, concerning a supervision function that is totally independent of the political powers but also, at the very same time, completely transparent in vis-à-vis such powers, will probably require a certain length of time in the case of the complex system of the SSM.

It should also be underlined that the SSM covers a limited part of the financial sector, given that the legislative definition appears to exclude intermediaries that are exclusively concerned with investments. However, such intermediaries do play a key role in the stability of the financial system. Their supervision will remain at the national level, with the result that, for instance, the part of a credit institution which deals with insurance could be subject to supervision on the national level while its banking branch could, instead, be covered by supervision on the SSM level, leading to the associated challenges of coordination of the two types of task.

The criterion of significance has been used as a watershed distinguishing the tasks of the ECB versus NCAs. However, this distinction remains critical, not only because small banks can, under certain circumstances, create systemic effects but also because the importance of the institute may affect the overall situation in a markedly different manner, depending on the banking system of the individual member country. Furthermore, the definition of "significant institution" according to the wording of Article 6 (4) of Reg. 1024/2013 allows a certain degree of discretion for points 2 and 3, where reference is made to the relative importance of the national context.

The SSM presupposes that the national authorities have some flexibility in terms of their capacity to adapt, but this cannot be taken for granted. And even if this were the case, there remains the problem of action by the ECB and the national authorities in the potential "grey areas". The system of "mixed administration" with supervisory powers shared between ECB and NCAs is particularly complex, inasmuch as the ECB and NCAs are responsible both on the national and the European level, sometimes on both levels at the same time.

It should be noted, finally, that SSM applies to Member States whose currency is the Euro or to Member States that have established a close cooperation, in accordance with Article 7 of Reg. 1024/201352. Therefore, the question arises of whether Member States whose currency is not the Euro will have to decide whether or not to apply SSM within their territory. The decision will be taken on the basis of political considerations (for instance, the United Kingdom is not expected to apply SSM) but, considering that non-Euro countries have a limited say within the ECB, the incentives for participation would appear to be rather limited.

It is thus clear that establishment of the Single Supervisory Mechanism is by no means a final arrival point, but rather a starting point. As doctrinal evidence has clearly highlighted, it remains to be seen, on specific points, how the new system will function in actual practice and to what extent the institutions, both European and national, will be capable of cooperating in this complex balance of powers and responsibilities.

7.5 The Single Resolution Mechanism

Prior to the 2007–2008 economic-financial crisis, the majority of the Member States had no resolution mechanisms appropriate for managing banking crises. Similarly, there was a total lack of institutional mechanisms capable of dealing with crises that affected transnational subjects (Dermine, 2016). In order to harmonise resolution processes at the national level, on the basis of common principles and tools, in May 2014 the European Parliament and the EU Council adopted the Bank Recovery and Resolution Directive (BRRD) (Directive 2014/59/EU), which introduced principles, procedures and resolution tools for common resolution of crises.

Subsequently, to overcome the inefficiencies associated with the national dimension of bank crisis management, the Single Resolution Mechanism (SRM) was set up for the euro area countries. The SRM introduces a centralised decision-making process on the supranational level, to be utilised together with the tools and principles contained in the BRRD.

The SRM, which has been operative as from 1st January 2016, represents an essential component of the European Banking Union, as a complement to the Single Supervision Mechanism. It is composed of a centralised authority, the Single Resolution Board (SRB), and the Single Resolution Fund (SRF). The Board is responsible for effective and coherent functioning of the SRM; in particular, it is responsible for devising the resolution plans (Article 8, Regulation 806/2014/EU) and for adopting all the decisions concerning the resolution (Article 28, c.1 Regulation 806/2014/EU). The supranational discipline also assigns additional powers to the Board, such as the power of investigation, inspection, and sanctioning (SRB, 2016).

The second constitutive element of the SRM is the Single Resolution Fund (SRF), established on the supranational level; the fund is owned by the Board, which is also in charge of management of the aforesaid fund.

The SRF, financed by contributions from the banking system and by some investment enterprises set up in the Member States that participate in the banking union, will be set up gradually over a ten-year transition period. It will be created by the gradual mutualisation of the individual resolution funds (national sectors) of each participating country. When the ten-year implementation phase is finally accomplished, there will be roughly 55 bln, or 1% of covered deposits in member countries, certainly insufficient to face a large systemic crisis.

The primary function of the SRF is that of financing the implementation of resolution measures. However, if further actions were to be necessary in order to avert the risk of contagion, the fund will have the capacity, within certain limits, to absorb losses, thereby reducing the amount of the bail-in. Additionally, individual member countries have entered into an intergovernmental Loan Facility Agreement (LFA) to grant an advance on such funds in case of need while the fund is being built up. But after the transition period, no further fiscal backstop is envisaged as a means of integrating the fund's monetary availability by granting an advance with "bridge loans" or loans guaranteed with public money (Mayers, Kendrick, Tornese, & Darvas, 2014).

The delay in setting up the Single Resolution Mechanism as compared to the Single Supervision Mechanism has a number of causes. For instance, mention should be made of the necessary adjustments of the regulatory setup of the Union and the Member States, as well as the various obstacles and problematic issues raised by some participants concerning the manner of collection and utilisation of the resources becoming available to the SRF (Gordon & Ringe, 2015). However, it should also be noted these difficulties have been partly solved by the current discipline of Regulation 806/2014/EU. A preliminary condition for access to the SRF is the application of the bail-in rules and of the principles laid down by the BRRD and by the resolution mechanism.

For banks defined as significant and for cross-border groups, the Board is assigned the task of identifying the best manner to address the crisis, most appropriate way of managing it in concrete terms by adopting a resolution programme. It is then the task of the national resolution authorities to implement the programme, exercising the powers attributed to them by the European rules and the national laws. Furthermore, the programme must be submitted to the European Commission and, in some cases, to the Council as well. This distribution of tasks is also applied in the case of small banks, whenever the intervention of the Single Resolution Fund is required for management of the crisis. In the other cases, the national resolution authorities maintain responsibility for crisis planning and management, according to the guidelines and orientations defined by the committee, and rating as decentralised authorities endowed with supranational function.

7.6 Banking Crises: Bail-in or Bail-out?

Since the beginning of the financial crisis and until quite recently, state aid in support of distressed banks has reached extremely elevated levels, pursuing the objective of averting a chain reaction of disastrous bankruptcies. The losses of the banking sector thus become collective, thereby preventing the risk of contagion on a system level (Acharya, Drechsler, & Schnabl, 2014; Bolton & Jeanne, 2011; Honohan & Klingebiel, 2003; Schoenmaker, 2016).

The by now recurrent European experiences show that a number of States, especially those that are relatively small, have not independently saved their own banks which have systemic relevance. Rather, they have had to ask for international support, and this has been granted under very severe conditions imposed by the competent organisms. This has meant that the enormous burden of the bail-out has indirectly been offloaded onto the tax-payers, by means of the increase in the public debt/GDP ratio (Avgouleas & Goodhart, 2015; Guynn, 2012).

It would be pointless to mention that until the accounts of the struggling States are once more "balanced", the latter will be unable to commit any further resources that could be needed in order to rescue hypothetical failing banks. The latter will therefore inevitably be doomed to collapse and the States in question will face the inevitable consequences on a systemic level. Furthermore, if a distressed bank is so large that it would have to be considered "too big to save", the bail-out plans adopted in recent years could not be applied even in the most virtuous countries, due to insufficient amount of public resources.

The unsustainability of the bail-out system is due to the risk that the State could fail, or in any case find itself on the verge of bankruptcy as a result of the enormous outlay involved in preventing the crash of a bank (sovereign debt crisis). Moreover, the socialisation of losses encourages moral hazard behaviour by the banks, which allow themselves to be encouraged by the State's implicit guarantees concerning irresponsible and excessive risk exposure (Gornika & Zoican, 2016).

In this sense the Bank Recovery and Resolution Directive, and the subsequent establishment of the SRM, has sought to devise a remedy for the critical points of the old system of bank crisis management, by guaranteeing, at least insofar as intentions are concerned, the principle according to which the cost of bank crises must be kept within the financial sector and must not affect the tax-payer (Faia & Weder di Mauro, 2016; Singh, 2016).

Thus harmonised rules have been introduced on the European level to prevent and manage critical situations. Basically, the rules subdivide the resolution procedure into three phases, which do not necessarily follow one another in order stated here: (1) adoption of recovery plans, (2) utilisation of early interventions, and (3) adoption of resolution procedure in the strict sense.

The latter phase, which concerns a situation that does not admit of a preventive remedy, initiates a restructuring process characterised by an elevated number of actors: Supervision Unit of ECB, Single Resolution Board, European Commission, Council of Europe, Competition Committee, national resolution authority. The actors enter into play to a varying degree and with a difference in role and importance. By means of techniques and powers allowed by the directive, the procedure aims to avoid interruptions in the supply of essential services (such as deposit and payment services) and to restore conditions of economic sustainability of the healthy part of the bank and to liquidate the remaining parts by means of: (1) sale of part of the assets; (2) temporary transfer of assets and liabilities to a bridge bank, that is, to an organism that has been set up specifically to enable the most important functions to continue, with a view to subsequent transfer to the market; (3) transfer of deteriorated assets to a bad bank, which will be in charge of the liquidation; (4) recourse to the bail-in mechanism, that is, an internal rescue procedure consisting of devaluation of the shares and credits, in order to absorb losses and allow recapitalisation of the bank in stress (or of a new entity that will continue the bank's essential functions).

In the latter case, the bank's shareholders are the first to be called upon to cover the losses; therefore their investment is wiped out. Next in line after the shareholders come the subordinate bond-holders.

If these actions were to prove to be insufficient, the senior bond-holders would be raided, and finally, deposits in excess of 100,000 euros. This procedure would be undertaken up to a value of 8% of the bank's total liabilities, beyond which the Resolution Fund is called upon to intervene.

The European regulation permits the provision of governmental assistance to ailing banks only in exceptional circumstances. The norms in question also insist on the principle of extensive burden-sharing by (certain) stakeholders as a prerequisite (Micossi, Bruzzone, & Cassella, 2016).

The logic of the bail-in resides in the intention not only to ensure that the weight of losses incurred by banks is not borne by the entire collective community, but also to avert forms of behaviour that include moral hazard on the part of the banks (Calello & Ervin, 2010; Goodhart & Avgouleas, 2014). While BRRD is certainly a good start as far as the prohibition against use of public funds to salvage banks is concerned, doubts may still be raised with regard to its genuine effectiveness in preventing "moral hazard".

Finally, it should be borne in mind that during phases of strong market turbulence, the panic that undermines trust in the banks results in a situation whereby the bail-in no longer protects the tax-payer and the State: rather, it may aggravate the systemic banking risk, thereby adversely affecting both the economy and growth. As is the case of a bank failure, a bail-in could likewise trigger a bank run among holders of non-guaranteed financial instruments issued by potentially risky intermediaries.

Thus it cannot be taken for granted that recourse to a bail-in will always be successful. Since the markets do not always find the right balance independently, it may prove to be necessary, when contagion risks arise, to have recourse to public intervention, above all in the case of a supra-national union such as the European Union (Avgouleas & Goodhart, 2015).

7.7 Bail-in Worrying and Bail-out Applying

The aim pursued on the European level by regulations concerning banking crises is certainly ambitious and can definitely be shared. It seeks to provide assurances that resolution costs in the banking system will weigh primarily on the private sector, by fostering an increase in market discipline and reducing to a minimum the residual costs of bank failures that weigh on tax-payers.

However, a number of misgivings remain, and criticisms with regard to the offloading of rescue costs onto savers show no signs of abating.

On the European level, two alternatives have been considered: the possibility of setting up an ad hoc authority for solution of bank crises or the proposal of invoking an already existing authority. The first solution has prevailed, although the composition of the Single Resolution Board, the central role of the European Commission and, in a few special cases, also of the Council in the decision-making process make the Board into something resembling a network of national authorities. This is far from the original proposal of a strong and to all effects supranational resolution authority (Gordon & Ringe, 2015), endowed with the necessary independence to achieve effective resolutions and at minimum cost.

Moreover, there remain numerous limits, involving first and foremost the functional complexity of the resolution mechanism. This is more elevated than the SSM, partly due, as mentioned above, to the involvement of various authorities—national, supranational, and intergovernmental—both in the decision-making process and in the phase of implementation of resolution decisions. Consequently, delays may arise in adoption of the resolution schemes, as can be noted with reference to the more recent crisis events. Such delays contrast with the basic assumption that rapid intervention is an essential factor of the resolution process. As is evident, the cost of resolution is reduced whenever early and rapid interventions contribute to safeguarding the economic value of the entity with regard to which the crisis must be resolved (Enria, 2016).

It should also be borne in mind that joint participation of many authorities in the decision-making process, each of which represents different public interests, may be justifiable in terms of the need to assure that the decisions benefit from greater accountability. On the other hand, this procedure may generate compromises, leading to solutions that are poorly effective.

The involvement of the Commission can be justified by the intention to balance any national interests that could prevail within the Single Resolution Board; on the other hand, the role of the Council, which is a political organ, appears more debatable in the framework of a technical procedure. This is in line with the tendency to reinforce the intergovernmental element. As shown by the United States example, the assumption that the resolution organ acts independently of the political situation should be a condition capable of guaranteeing effective management of the resolution.

Although BRRD has already been in force for over a year, an assessment of recent banking crises in Europe shows that the new rules have failed so far. Whether it is a question of trying to distribute bank losses among the bank's competitors, or whether complex legal exceptions are invoked, or whether political indications arrive from on high, almost all the protagonists focus their anxieties on one particular issue: the aim of preventing the European law from being fully applied. From Austria to Germany, Denmark, Italy, Portugal, Greece, or Slovenia, everywhere the BRRD has been *de facto* ignored, circumvented, or has produced more financial, political, and constitutional problems than it has solved.

Basically, this is a paradox. All the European governments and citizens agree to offload part of the financial woes onto the investors, thereby protecting the tax-payers who would have to finance the entire rescue operations. Yet the rules are not working, and each country requests exceptions to the bail-in as a means of preventing the rescue operations of failing banks from affecting bond-holders and depositors (Benczur, Cannas, Cariboni, Di Girolamo, Maccaferri, & Giudici, 2016).

Apart from Cyprus, which in 2013 provided the example of full application of the bail-in to bank deposits, Italy is the only country in the euro area to have experienced the resolution procedure, in the case of the collapse of the regional banks, namely, Banca Etruria, CariChieti, Cariferrara, and Banca Marche. During the period when the complicated dialogue with the European Commission was under way, the situation of the four banks inevitably deteriorated. Thus in the end their resolution was the only possible solution, although it came with additional costs, both for the banks and the subordinate creditors. The resolution of the four banks—during which, it should be noted, no depositor was sacrificed—appears to have resulted in a loss of deposits of the commercial banks, to the advantage of other intermediaries. The loss is estimated at around 50 billion. The effect has been that of loss of trust in the banking system as an overall concept, regardless of the individual situation. In the formalisation of the bail-in mechanism, certain elements do not appear to have been carefully assessed. If a bank is in distress or enters into a crisis, the elements in question may lead to irrational choices by investors with regard to risk management, as well as to propagation of the contagion effect with repercussions on the cost of funding.

Accordingly, the assumption that liabilities subject to bail-in should include the component of deposits—which is a major item among the funding sources of the banking balance sheet—does not seem to respond either to criteria of justice in sharing out the burden of the difficulties or to objectives of financial stability. Therefore it would be desirable to extend the guarantee on deposits up to a far higher level than the current 100,000 euros, or indeed guarantee them entirely, leaving other liabilities to be subject to bail-in.

In this perspective, it is vital for work on the definition of a common European-level deposit protection network to proceed rapidly. The priority is to complete the Banking Union with implementation of the third pillar, consisting of an integrated deposit insurance system. This would provide greater impetus for the European Deposit Insurance Scheme (EDIS), which aims to create a mutualistic deposit insurance scheme on the European level (Avgouleas & Goodhart, 2016, Loranth & Morrison, 2007). Such a scheme would help to reduce the competition distortions arising from the difference in forms of protection and manner of functioning of the national schemes. To date, the latter are guaranteed by funds the European Commission requires the States to create, independently, in order to cover deposits below 100,000 euros.

EDIS is designed to create, progressively, a single deposit guarantee fund within 2024, in three phases: (1) reinsurance of the national guarantee systems, (2) coinsurance period, (3) progressive mutualisation designed to be completed with the creation of a single guarantee fund managed by the SRB.

It has been pointed out, in this connection, that since EDIS allows more extensive risk-sharing, it would strengthen the resilience of the Banking Union against future crises; furthermore, it would consolidate financial stability, sustain depositors' confidence with regard to the national banking system, achieve equal competition on the internal market, and equalise the funding costs. However, the private burden-sharing uniquely contemplated for the EDIS may again make it not fully credible even when considered at its final completion phase in 2024.

Implementation of the Single Deposit Guarantee System is hampered by objections from countries that are unwilling to join the project unless there is genuine equalisation of the credit risk, which is particularly high in some banking systems of the eurozone.

In the overall context of bank regulation, criticism has been voiced concerning the excessive and unbalanced weight of credit risk for purposes of calculating the capital requirement, in comparison to other risks such as operational and legal risks. These latter categories have weighed very heavily on many European Union banks. Thus it would seem to be necessary to harmonise risk-weighted assets (RWAs), a move that would also help to ensure a level playing field of competition. Such a development is expected to be achieved as the outcome of the revision work recently undertaken by the banking authorities (EBA and ECB) to reduce unwarranted variability in RWAs across banks (ECB, 2017).

7.8 Conclusions

The implementation of a project of a European Banking Union represents, first and foremost, an essential step towards the completion of the European Monetary Union Project; furthermore, it is the response to the disruption of financial crises starting in 2007. The project sets itself several objectives: it aims to sever the connection between sovereign and banking risk, to mitigate the fragmentation of the market in the EU, and to assure that supervision is brought into line with ongoing changes in the banking system, which has seen the rise of intermediaries whose size and range of action have a Europe-wide dimension.

The foregoing observations clearly show that the first two pillars of the Banking Union—namely, the Single Supervision Mechanism and the Single Resolution Mechanism—can in no way be considered as the final arrival point: rather, they are a starting point. That is to say, although the overall framework is comprehensive and well advanced, it remains incomplete, and a number of challenges are still to be overcome. First, it should be noted that the European Deposit Insurance Scheme, despite having been recognised as an integral part of the Banking Union, is not yet in existence, and in any case its complete implementation is unlikely to be achieved in the short term. There is, however, general recognition that this further step is necessary to complete and harmonise the Single Resolution Mechanism (SRM) in the euro area.

Given the way in which SRF and EDIS are configured, they will in any case have a target endowment of a limited sum as compared to the potential need during a systemic crisis. One need only reflect that capital injections in large banks during the crisis have been in the order of the hundreds of billion. It is necessary to create new and different tools or refine the existing mechanisms, first and foremost all the voluntary systems for deposit protection on the national level, which should be free to intervene without becoming entangled in the controversial prohibition of State aid. On the European level, however, credibility of such funds would effectively require a fiscal backstop which may conflict with the diabolical loop of some of the sovereign debts, unless it is based on solid mutualisation.

In any case, adaptive interpretations and possible regulatory revisions and careful supervision call for a joint and responsible community-level effort, in the urgent search for flexible solutions capable of guaranteeing a proper balance between protecting the market versus competition, safeguarding the functionality of the system versus guaranteeing the rights of investors. To accomplish this result, it will be necessary to overcome the opposition of States that are averse to the prospect of greater risk-sharing.

Finally, some issues remain for banks and supervisors in connection with regulatory changes. The legislative framework, which underpins banking supervision, allows several elements of flexibility, available to supervisors or Member States. Moreover, the need for transposition into national legislation opens the door to legislative differences between countries and prevents achievement of a truly level playing field within the banking union. It remains to be seen, when the specific aspects are brought into action, how the new system will actually function and to what extent both the European and the national institutions will succeed in cooperating within the framework of this complex balancing act of powers and responsibilities.

References

Acharya, V. (2009). A theory of systemic risk and design of prudential bank regulation. *Journal of Financial Stability, 5*(3), 224–255.

Acharya, V., Drechsler, I., & Schnabl, P. (2014). A pyrrhic victory? Bank bailouts and sovereign credit risk. *The Journal of Finance, 69*(6), 2689–2739.

Avgouleas, E., & Goodhart, C. (2015). Critical reflections on bank bail-ins. *Journal of Financial Regulation, 1*, 3–29.

Avgouleas, E., & Goodhart, C. (2016). An anatomy of bank bail-ins why the Eurozone needs a fiscal backstop for the banking sector. *European Economy, Banks, Regulation and the Real Sector, 16*(2), 75–90.

Benczur, P., Cannas, G., Cariboni, J., Di Girolamo, F., Maccaferri, S., & Giudici, M. P. (2016). Evaluating the effectiveness of the new EU bank regulatory framework: A farewell to bailout? *Journal of Financial Stability*. https://doi.org/10.1016/j.jfs.2016.03.001.

Berglöf, E., De Haas, R., & Zettelmeyer, J. (2012). Banking union: The view from emerging Europe. In T. Beck (Ed.), *Banking union for Europe: Risks and challenges*. London: Centre for Economic Policy Research (CEPR).

Bolton, P., & Jeanne, O. (2011). Sovereign default risk and bank fragility in financially integrated economies. *IMF Economic Review, 59*(2), 162–194.

Buch, C., Körner, T., & Weigert, B. (2014). Towards deeper financial integration in Europe: What the Banking Union can contribute. *Credit and Capital Markets, 48*(1), 11–49.

Calello, P., & Ervin, W. (2010, January 28). Economic focus: From bail-out to bail-in. *The Economist*.

Calzolari, G., & Loranth, G. (2011). Regulation of multinational banks: a theoretical inquiry. *Journal of Financial Intermediation, 20*, 178–198

Carmassi, J., Di Noia, C., & Micossi, S. (2012, September). *Banking Union: A federal model for the European Union with prompt corrective action*. In CEPS Policy Briefs, n. 282.

Colliard, J. E. (2015, April). *Optimal supervisory architecture and financial integration in a banking union*. ECB Working Paper, No. 1786.

Constâncio, V. (2014). *Banking Union and European integration*. Speech at the OeNB Economics Conference, Vienna (Vol. 12).

Dermine, J. (2016). *The single resolution mechanism in the European Union: Good intentions and unintended evil*. Insead, Working Paper, Singapore.

EBA. (2015). *EBA final draft regulatory technical standards*. London: European Banking Authority.

ECB—European Central Bank. (2017). Targeted review of internal models (TRIM), Media briefing conference call, February Commission (2010), An EU Framework for Crisis Management in the Financial Sector, Brussels.

Enria, A. (2016). *From bank bail-outs to bail-in: Progress and open issues*. Speech given at Regent's University, London.

European Commission. (2016a). Proposal for a directive amending directive 2014/59/EU of the European parliament and the council on loss absorption and recapitalisation capacity of credit institutions and investment firms, COM (2016) 852.

European Commission. (2016b). Proposal for a directive amending directive 2014/59/EU of the European parliament and the council as regards the ranking of unsecured debt instruments in insolvency hierarchy, COM (2016) 853.

Faia, E., & Weder di Mauro, B. (2016). *Cross-border resolution of global banks: Bail-in under single point of entry versus multiple points of entry*. CEPR Discussion Paper No 11171.

Ferrarini, G., & Chiodini, F. (2012). Nationally fragmented supervision over multinational banks as a source of global systemic risk: A critical analysis of recent EU reforms. In E. Wymeersch, K. J. Hopt, & G. Ferrarini (Eds.), *Financial regulation: A post crisis analysis* (pp. 193–231). Oxford: Oxford University Press.

Ferrarini, G., & Recine, F. (2015). The single rulebook and the SSM: Should the ECB have more say in prudential rule-making? In D. Busch & G. Ferrarini (Eds.), *European Banking Union* (pp. 118–154). Oxford: Oxford University Press.

Goodhart, C. A., & Avgouleas, E. (2014, July). *A critical evaluation of bail-in as bank recapitalization mechanisms*. Discussion Paper 10065. Centre for Economic Policy Research.

Gordon, J. N., & Ringe, W. G. (2015). *Bank resolution in the European Banking Union: A transatlantic perspective on what it would take*. Columbia Law Review, 115.

Gornika, L. A., & Zoican, M. A. (2016). Too-international-to-fail? Supranational bank resolution and market discipline. *Journal of Banking and Finance, 65*, 41–58.

Goyal, R., Brooks, P. K., Pradhan, M., Tressel, M. T., Dell'Ariccia, M. G., & Pazarbasioglu, C. (2013). *A banking union for the Euro area*. International Monetary Fund Staff Discussion Notes No. 13/1.

Guynn. (2012). Are bailouts inevitable? *Yale Journal on Regulation, 121*, 137–140.

Honohan, P., & Klingebiel, D. (2003). The fiscal cost implications of an accommodating approach to banking crises. *Journal of Banking and Finance, 27*, 1539–1560.

Loranth, G., & Morrison, A. (2007). Deposit insurance, capital regulation and financial contagion in multinational banks. *Journal of Business Finance & Accounting, 34*, 917–949.

Maloney, N. (2014). European Banking Union: Assessing its risks and resilience. *Common Market Law Review, 51*(6), 1609–1670.

Mayers, D.G., Kendrick, R., Tornese, E., & Darvas, Z. (2014, December). *The funding of bank resolution in Europe: Will the new framework meet expectations?* Finance and Financial Regulation.

Micossi, S., Bruzzone, G., & Cassella, M. (2016, April). *Fine-tuning the use of bail-in to promote a stronger EU financial system*. CEPS Special Report No 136.

Mottura, P. (2011). Rischio sistemico. Serve una regolamentazione strutturale? *Bancaria*, 6.

Pisaneschi, A. (2016). La regolamentazione Bancaria multilivello e l'art.47 della Costituzione. In M. P. Chiti e V. Santoro (Eds.). L'Unione Bancaria Europea, Pacini giuridica.

Schoenmaker, D. (2013). *Governance of international banking: The financial trilemma*. New York: Oxford University Press.

Schoenmaker, D. (2016). *Resolution of international banks: Can smaller countries cope?* CEPR working paper.

Singh, D. (2016). The centralisation of European financial regulation and supervision: Is there a need for a single enforcement handbook? *European Business Organization Law Review, 16*, 439–465.

SRB—Single Resolution Board. (2016). *The single resolution mechanism-introduction to resolution planning*.

Troger, T. (2015). The single supervisory mechanism—panacea or quack banking regulation? Preliminary assessment of the new regime for prudential supervision of banks with ECB involvement. *European Business Organisation Law Review, 15*(4), 464.

Van Rompuy, H. (2012). *Towards a genuine economic and monetary union*. Report presented at the December 2012 European Council.

Véron, N. (2015). The economic consequences of Europe's Banking Union. In D. Busch & G. Ferrarini (Eds.), *European Banking Union* (pp. 33–55). Oxford: Oxford University Press.

CHAPTER 8

Monetary Policy, Banking Supervisory Policy, and Economic Growth in Europe

Antonella Cappiello

8.1 Introduction

Maintaining price stability is the primary purpose of the monetary policy pursued by the ECB in the euro area. It is widely known that price stability contributes to increasing the economic welfare and growth potential of the economy. Central banks face a complex system of economic interactions; in fact, several channels that convey the stimulus of monetary policy to the real economy may be contemporarily involved and have distinct influences on price developments.

At the same time, by ensuring an orderly functioning of the transmission mechanism of monetary policy, financial stability helps a central bank to foster price stability. In the short term, financial stability and price stability may not always go hand in hand. However, from a long-term perspective, financial stability and price stability could mutually reinforce the objectives of the policy.

From the perspective of economic growth, it is important to know the real ability of the financial system to transmit monetary policy impulses to the economy. In the euro area, this transmission mechanism has been impeded in the past, initially by an increase in risk premia, due to doubts

A. Cappiello (✉)
Department of Economics and Management, University of Pisa, Pisa, Italy

F. Colombini (ed.), *Raising Capital or Improving Risk Management and Efficiency?*, https://doi.org/10.1007/978-3-319-71749-4_8

on the survival of the euro area and, later, by the widespread bank deleveraging. In this respect, it is necessary to discuss and evaluate the consequences of restrictive banking regulation and supervisory policy in relation to the capital adequacy framework. The supervisory policy would need to go beyond the capital and liquidity regulatory frameworks to support and not delay the effectiveness of the monetary policy measures.

This chapter aims to analyse how the monetary policy, on the one hand, and the bank regulation and supervision, on the other, can mutually affect the economic growth in the euro area, focusing on the role of the banking channel.

8.2 Monetary Policy in Europe

On January 1, 1999, the European Central Bank (ECB) assumed responsibility for the monetary policy decision-making in the euro area. The transfer of this responsibility from the national competent authorities (NCAs) to a new supranational institution represented a milestone in a long and complex process of integration among the European countries.

Maintaining price stability, as the primary objective of monetary policy in the euro area, is a necessary condition to support the general policies of the European Union, aimed at achieving balanced economic growth. This purpose is pursued through the definition of intermediate objectives (interest rate, exchange rate, and amount of money) and appropriate instruments defined by the ECB, respecting the principles of market freedom, efficient allocation of resources, and an equal treatment of the counterparties (ECB, 2011).

The purpose of price stability, which is to be exercised in the medium term, is to maintain the inflation rate at lower values, but close to two per cent. The monetary policy strategy is based on a two-pillar framework for the analysis of the risks of price stability, which represent two complementary perspectives on the determinants of price developments. The first perspective, referred to as economic analysis, intends to access in the short to medium term the determinants of price developments, focusing on real activity and cost factors driving prices over those horizons. It takes into account the fact that short- to medium-term price developments are influenced by the interplay of supply and demand in the goods, services, and market factors. Therefore, the second perspective, referred to as monetary analysis, is based on the relationship between money growth and inflation, over the medium to long-term outlook and exploits the fact that monetary trends lead to inflationary trends (ECB, 2011).

By virtue of the monopolistic supplier of the monetary base, the central bank is able to influence money market conditions and steer short-term interest rates. In the short run, a change in money market interest rates induced by the central bank sets in motion a number of mechanisms and actions by economic agents, ultimately influencing developments in economic variables such as output or prices. This process—also known as the monetary policy transmission mechanism—is complex and, while its broad features are understood, there is no single and uncontested view on all aspects involved. This mechanism is characterised by long, variable, and uncertain time lags and is influenced by exogenous shocks. In the end, changes in the credit supply will affect the general price level, but not the level of real income or employment. The latter, in the long run, are determined by real (supply side) factors such as technology, population growth, preferences of economic agents, and all aspects of the institutional framework of the economy (Ciccarelli, Maddaloni, & Peydró, 2013; Mishkin, 1995; Rabin & Jeager, 1997).

It is widely acknowledged that price stability contributes to increase the economic welfare and the potential growth of the economy. Central banks face a complex situation of economic interactions. In fact, several channels that transmit the stimuli of monetary policy to the real economy may be involved, while at the same time, influencing price developments.

The monetary policy strategy and the operational framework have a specific role in the implementation of monetary policy. The strategy determines the level of money market interest rates required to maintain the price stability in the medium term, whereas the operational framework determines the means to achieve this interest rate level using the available monetary policy instruments and procedures (see Table 8.1).

In order to achieve its primary purpose of maintaining price stability for the euro area, the Eurosystem—composed by the ECB and the central banks of the Member States whose currency is the euro—uses two types of standard (also named conventional) operations: open market operations and standing facilities. The most important operations are the open market operations. This is the term used for operations conducted by the ECB, usually in the money market, where the maturity of transaction is less than one year.

Open market operations include main refinancing operations (MROs), longer-term refinancing operations (LTROs), fine-tuning operations

Table 8.1 Eurosystem monetary policy operations

Monetary policy operations	*Type of transaction*		*Maturity*	*Frequency*
	Liquidity providing	*Liquidity absorbing*		
Open market operations				
Main refinancing operations	• Reverse transactions	–	One week	Weekly
Longer-term refinancing operations	• Reverse transactions	–	Three months	Monthly
Fine-tuning operations	• Reverse transactions • Foreign exchange swaps	• Reverse transactions • Collection of fixed-term deposits • Foreign exchange swaps	Non-standardised	Non-regular
Structural operations	• Reverse transactions • Outright purchases	• Issuance of ECB debt certificates • Outright sales	Standardised/ non-standardised –	Regular and non-regular Non-regular
Standing facilities				
Marginal lending facility	• Reverse transactions	–	Overnight	Access at the discretion of counterparties
Deposit facility	–	• Deposits	Overnight	Access at the discretion of counterparties

Source: ECB (2011)

(FTOs), and structural operations. These operations play an important role in steering interest rates, signalling the stance of monetary policy and managing liquidity conditions for the banking sector in the euro area. Furthermore, the ECB requires banks in the euro area to hold compulsory deposits on accounts with the NCBs, the so-called minimum reserves. The amount of reserves to be held by each institution is determined by the elements of its balance sheet. The first key function of the minimum reserve system is to stabilise interest rates in the money market. This function is performed by the averaging provision. The averaging provision allows banks to soften daily liquidity fluctuations, since temporary reserve imbalances can be offset by opposing reserve imbalances generated during the same maintenance period.

The smooth transmission of monetary policy intentions to money market rates depends on the behaviour of banks and their availability to entertain the regular exchange of liquidity in the interbank market. Dysfunctional money markets may weaken the ability of monetary policy to influence the prospects of price stability only through interest rate adjustments.

Recent events have demonstrated that the orderly transmission of monetary policy can be hampered when massive financial turbulences occur. In order to keep the transmission mechanism fully operational and ensure the maintenance of price stability in the medium term, the central bank may need to introduce non-standard policy measures, that is, liquidity interventions aimed at facilitating the transmission of the interest rate policy and enhancing the flows of credit to the general economy (see Box 8.1).

When the financial turmoil turned into a crisis, the ECB responded with standard and non-standard measures, the latter to support the effec-

Box 8.1 Non-standard measures: The ECB's asset purchase programme (APP)

The asset purchases are non-standard measures, which the ECB uses to cope with the risks associated with a prolonged period of low inflation and to bring inflation down to below two per cent in the medium term. As part of the expanded programme of purchase of assets (APP), the ECB acquires a series of financial instruments such as government securities issued by European supranational institutions, corporate bonds, securities resulting from guaranteed securitisations, and bonds at a rate of 60 billion euros per month. Purchases influence the most general financial conditions and, ultimately, the economic growth and inflation through three main channels: direct transmission, portfolio rebalance, and signalling effect. Both channels of direct transmission and the rebalancing of portfolios improve the overall financial conditions for households and enterprises in the euro area. By reducing the financing costs, the asset purchases can stimulate consumption and investment. Ultimately, a more dynamic demand by enterprises and consumers will contribute to the return of inflation rates below but close to two per cent in the medium term.

Targeted Longer-Term Refinancing Operations (TLTROs)

Together with the other policies of the ECB, the TLTROs support the transmission of monetary policy to the real economy and help to achieve the main objective of price stability, by maintaining inflation rates at levels below but close to two per cent over the medium term. The first TLTRO series was launched in 2014. The second one, introduced in March 2016, is called TLTRO II. In conventional terms, liquidity for banks is available for a short period (up to three months). Through TLTROs, the Central Bank provides long-term loans (with maturity of four years) to banks and offers them an incentive to increase their lending to businesses and consumers in the euro area. Unlike in usual monetary policy operations, the amount of money that the banks can obtain through TLTRO-II and the cost of borrowing depend on the amount of loans they provide to the real economy. Banks participating in the TLTRO-II can lend up to 30 per cent of their outstanding loans to businesses and consumers. This means that banks that lend more to the real economy will be able to borrow more and at a lower interest rate than the ECB usually offers.

In 2016 and in the first part of the current year, the Eurosystem continued to offer liquidity to banks through fixed rate auctions with the full allocation of the required amounts in the main refinancing operations and in the longer-term refinancing operations. The liquidity provided in the refinancing operations lasting up to three months decreased by 120 billion (to 20 at the end of April); the one provided through targeted refinancing operations in the longer term has increased by 344 billion (to 762). As part of the PAA, the Eurosystem has acquired financial assets for 1,834 billion at the end of April, of which 24 were asset-backed securities, 216 of guaranteed bank bonds, 82 of non-bank bonds, and 1,512 of public securities. On the same date, the average remaining life of the PSPP portfolio was eight years, the average remaining life of the sub-fund of Italian government bonds of about eight years and eight months. The purchase methods have been such as not to impair the normal functioning of markets. Cash held by banks with the Eurosystem, in excess of reserve requirements increased, mainly as a result of purchases of government bonds as part of the PAA and the liquidity provided through TLTRO2; in early May was approximately 1.6 trillion.

The size of the Eurosystem's balance sheet has grown by 50 per cent, reaching record highs (about 4.15 trillion at the end of last April, at around 40 per cent of euro area GDP).

tive transmission of interest rate decisions to a broader economic area in the Euro zone, in a weakened context within some segments of the market and the financial system.

At times of heightened stress and uncertainty, the ECB used its liquidity operations in a pragmatic manner. In addition to reducing conventional interest rates to historically low levels, the ECB decided to adopt non-standard (also named unconventional) measures—comprising Enhanced Credit Support and the Securities Markets Programme—to restore the transmission mechanism of monetary policy.

Overall, the measures implemented by the Eurosystem in response to the financial crisis helped to sustain the financial intermediation in the euro area, by safeguarding the financing of solvent banks and restoring confidence among financial market participants. In turn, preserving the viability of the banking system and important segments of the financial market was instrumental to keep credit available to households and enterprises at accessible rates and, ultimately, to maintain price stability (ECB, 2017b).

According to the data provided by the European Central Bank on the Eurosystem's Bank Lending Survey regarding the relation to the supply of credit in the euro area, in 2016 non-standard measures of quantitative easing (QE) helped to loosen bank lending conditions and terms, supporting credit for the economy. In general, the policies of loan supply to enterprises and households have stabilised, and demand has increased due to the low level of interest rates (ECB, 2017a).

Some studies recently found a new focus on the role of the credit supply in the transmission of monetary policy, due to the prominent role of credit development in the financial crisis (Bernanke & Blinder, 1988; Boeckx, de Sola Perea, & Peersman, 2016). The analysis of the transmission of both conventional and unconventional monetary policies shows a *positive* relation between the level of regulatory capital and conventional monetary policy pass-through and a *negative* relation with unconventional policy (Altavilla, Canova, & Ciccarelli, 2016). The focus on the transmission of the ECB credit easing policies (i.e. the subset of measures designed to provide ample liquidity for banks and increase lending) highlights that these policies had a greater impact on small banks, banks with less liquid balance sheets and banks more reliant on wholesale funding (Boeckx, de Sola Perea, & Peersman, 2016).

The capital role is ambiguous and interacts with other characteristics of the bank. Overall, the response of more capitalised banks to the credit easing policies was more pronounced, largely reflecting the impact of higher capital on the effects related to size, funding structure, and balance sheet liquidity. Studying the transmission of conventional and unconventional monetary policies in the euro area through the shift in the credit supply, it was found that the bank lending channel works for both types of measures, although its functioning differs (Albertazzi, Nobili, & Signoretti, 2016). For standard operations, the transmission is weaker for banks with more capital and a solid funding structure, in line with an important role of asymmetric information. However, for non-standard operations, the credit supply expands by more to banks with stronger capital and funding positions, suggesting a crucial role for regulatory and economic constraints. The transmission of unconventional measures is attenuated by the negative effect of the regulatory constraint, and it may be considered more restrictive for banks characterised by a higher incidence of traditional intermediation activities. The results also suggest that large sovereign exposures mute the response of lending rates to conventional policy, but amplify the transmission of unconventional measures (Crockett, 2000).

8.3 Monetary Policy and Financial Stability

The financial crisis that started in the summer of 2007 has led to a series of financial regulation and supervision reforms aimed at promoting financial stability, in line with the thesis that the absence of authorities with this specific mandate contributed to the origin of the crisis (de Larosière, 2009).

With the entry into force of the Single Supervisory Mechanism (SSM), the ECB has been equipped with macro-prudential instruments to deal with the emergence of potential systemic risks in the financial system (Angelini, 2014). The responsibility for decisions on macro-prudential measures in the euro area is shared between the ECB and the national competent authorities (NCAs). NCAs retain the power to apply macro-prudential measures, while the ECB has the right to supplement the measures taken by national authorities for macro-prudential instruments conferred on it by the European legislation. This asymmetry of power reflects the role that the ECB has to play to overcome any inertia at national level. The ECB may establish, in place of the national authorities, higher capital requirements than those applied locally, and stronger measures to tackle systemic or macro-prudential risks, subject to the procedures laid down by the relevant EU legislation (Hanson, Kashyap, & Stein, 2011). For example, after notifying the national competent authorities, the ECB may impose on banks stronger or additional obligations concerning (1) countercyclical capital reserves, (2) capital reserves against systemic risk, (3) capital requirements for banks of systemic relevance, (4) the risk weights for exposures in the real estate market and in the financial sector, and (5) the limits of large exposures.

The ECB mainly operates on two fronts in the financial stability area. Together with other central banks of the Eurosystem, it keeps under observation structural and cyclical trends in the banking and other financial sub-sectors. Moreover, to analyse the potential impact of systemic risks regarding the stability and resilience of the financial system, it uses quantitative instruments and modelling techniques.

The systemic risk, already difficult to define (see Box 8.2), is also difficult to measure and, especially, to predict. Although monetary policy objectives

Box 8.2 The systemic risk

Systemic risk is defined by the IMF-BIS-CSF (2009) as the risk of a disturbance in the supply of financial services with the potential to have serious negative consequences on the real economy. Other sources give complementary definitions, putting more emphasis on pro-cyclicality. For example, the Bank of England (2009) argues that macro-prudential policies should ensure the stable provision of financial intermediation services to the economy while avoiding the explosive growth cycles and subsequent sharp contraction that tend to characterise the credit dynamics. A common element to the various systemic risk definitions, although not explicitly mentioned, is the concept of negative externalities—mechanisms that determine costs for which financial operators or the individual supervisory authorities do not take into account but which, at the aggregate level, can destabilise the financial system.

are tested and known as imperfect measures available, such as inflation rates, measures of economic activity and systemic risk are at a much less advanced stage. This is mainly due to the elusive nature of the phenomenon. In financial terms, systemic risk may arise and spread within a given class of financial institutions, between companies in different sectors, markets, geographical areas, and market infrastructures (Angelini, 2015).

Forecasting the causes of financial instability is therefore very difficult, and research in terms of leading indicators has not yet provided conclusive results. Based on the assumption that there is a relationship between the excessive credit growth and financial crises (Borio & Drehmann, 2009; Kannan, Rabanal, & Scott, 2011; Reinhart & Rogoff, 2008; Taylor, 2015), the Basel Committee chose to propose the relationship between credit and GDP as a guide to the activation of the countercyclical capital reserve (Panetta, Angelini, Albertazzi, Columba, Cornacchia, & Di Cesare, 2009).

There are several macro-prudential instruments, many of which have been introduced in Europe by the Fourth Capital Requirements Directive and the related regulation (CRD4-CRR) (ESRB, 2014, 2015), which in early 2014 adopted the Basel 3 Regulatory Framework. Other tools, not provided in the CRD4-CRR package, contain overheating episodes of the real estate sector, directly affecting loan demand: for example, the loan-to-value limit, the loan-to-income limit, or finally the debt service-to-income limit (see Table 8.2).

Table 8.2 Main macro-prudential instruments

		Article
CRD4	Countercyclical capital buffer	130, 135–140
	Other systemically important institutions buffer	131
	Systemic risk buffer	133,134
	Pillar II requirements	103
CRR	Own founds conservation buffer/leverage ratio/ sectorial requirements	458
	Higher risk weight/stricter criteria for exposures secured by mortgages on immovable property	124
	Increasing the LGD floor	164
Not included in CRD4-CRR	Loan-to value/loan-to-income/debt service-to-income caps	National law

It should be noted that there is no clear allocation of competences between the different authorities responsible for the use of such instruments, so there is ample room for discretion, leaving sometimes a lack of coordination and consolidated guidelines (Lim, Columba, Costa, Kongsamut, Otani, & Saiyid, 2011; Yellen, 2011).

The mechanisms of interaction and potential conflict between macro-/micro-prudential policies and monetary policy are complex and not always easy to understand. In fact, even empirical observations show that the risk of a potential conflict between micro- and macro-prudential policies seems limited to negative cyclical phases and situations of high capitalisation of the banking system: when capitalisation is low, it is difficult for the macro-prudential authority to propose a relieve, although it is desirable (Diamond & Rajan, 2009).

On the other hand, important interactions between macro-prudential policies and monetary policy are noted, though not fully understood, where it is difficult to incorporate into a single model all the multiple forms of systemic risk (Angelini, Neri, & Panetta, 2014; Cecchetti & Kohler, 2012). There are several uncertain areas on the transmission mechanism of these policies regarding their effectiveness in the presence of specific macroeconomic shocks or the potential unwanted effects and the unexpected reactions by financial intermediaries that can undermine the impact of these measures.

Monetary policies that are also aimed at counteracting financial tensions appear to be preferable to traditional ones, which pursue only inflation targets and economic growth (Angelini, Nicoletti-Altimari, & Visco, 2012). These considerations suggest that although the two objectives—price stability and financial stability—combine the two instruments—monetary and macro-prudential—in the new institutional configuration, a strict separation of the two policies does not seem desirable. There is now a consensus on the view that monetary policy has a role in the fight against the development of financial imbalances, and not only in mitigating ex post consequences (Brunnermeier & Schnabel, 2014; White, 2009), even if it is not easy to define in concrete terms, how this should be done.

In the euro area, structural factors make monetary and macro-prudential policies more complementary than elsewhere, and macro-prudential instruments are, in principle, more powerful and therefore more important (Carosio, 2010; Ciccarelli, Maddaloni, & Peydró, 2013; Panetta, 2014). This is firstly due to the fact that the macro-prudential instruments used so far are predominantly of the banking type and that banks play an important role in financing the economy of the euro area. Secondly, the area consists of economies characterised by economic and real estate cycles relatively heterogeneous. In a context where monetary policy cannot take into account these differences, single framework per country can be effectively used to avoid real financial imbalances. It is evident that if two coordinated policies are not sufficiently connected, two policies with such strong interactions can easily come into conflict (MAG, 2010; Roger & Vitek, 2012). This potential conflict requires institutional arrangements that favour coordination and cooperation between the two policies. It is not by chance that the current macro-prudential policy framework is under review in the EU, with the aim of increasing its effectiveness and simplifying its procedures.

8.4 Capital Requirements, Bank Lending, and Economic Growth

All capital requirements and loss absorption measures, under several circumstances, may hinder growth. It follows that specific provisions and the design of these measures must be evaluated and understood with care and steadiness (Aiyar, Calomiris, & Wieladek, 2015; IIF, 2011). Especially crucial is the discussion on total loss absorption capacity (TLAC), given that its regulatory framework is still under definition and that this is a considerable measure supposed to have a major impact on the structure of banks' liabilities. In this regard there is no unitary judgement in theoretical studies about the role of capital requirements in the regulatory and governance framework of banks and their critical interaction with other regulatory rules, while empirical studies would suggest that there is a trade-off between banks' leverage, growth, and systemic risk (Beck, 2015; Clerc, 2015; Cohen & Scatigna, 2014, Den Haan, Sumner, & Yamashiro, 2007; Rochet, 2015). To a first approximation, it is argued that a higher capital charge imposed on banks or, similarly, a lower leverage or a tightening limit on the provision of bank loans increases systemic stability because it allows banks to absorb greater losses. On the other hand, these measures negatively affect growth because they restrict lending to the economy.

In response to an increase in regulatory capital requirements, banks gradually increase their capital ratios to rebuild the buffers they initially held above the regulatory minimum (Aiyar, Calomiris, & Wieladek, 2015; Bridges, Gregory, Nielsen, Pezzini, Radia, & Spaltro, 2014; Ediz, Michael, & Perraudin, 1998; Francis & Osborne, 2009). There would not be a reduction in lending if additional funding could be raised on the market or through the reduction of dividends and share repurchases. However, in the case of most European banks, this boosting of capital ratios has been achieved through the reduction in lending or the change in the risk profile of asset holdings, given that raising capital in the market is not attractive in the current circumstances. However, in the long term, higher capital buffers might imply stronger reliance on external funding rather than retained earnings, if the banking system grows, involving therefore higher costs (Calomiris, 2013).

Results vary across sectors, but in response to an increase in capital requirements, lending growth typically falls in the year following regulatory changes and recovers within three years (Capgemini, 2014). Regulatory requirements tend to permanently affect capital ratios and temporarily affect credit supply (Bridges, Gregory, Nielsen, Pezzini, Radia, & Spaltro, 2014). The banks' reactions vary depending on the bank size, capital buffers held, business cycle, and the direction of the change in capital requirements. During the transition to higher global regulatory standards, the effects of changes in capital requirements may be different. For example, increasing capital requirements might augment rather than reduce lending for initially undercapitalised banks if confidence effects boost their resilience and capacity to lend. Finally, macro-prudential regulators are often required to consider the wider implications of changing capital requirements, which could include any adverse impact on lending.

It is important to differentiate between transitional and long-term effects of higher capital requirements. As some of the current adjustments come during the recession and through the lending cycle, the transitional effects might be stronger than the long-term effects. Although the two short-term dimensions—stability and growth—are conflicting, in the long run, if the capital ratio is not arbitrarily high, there is a possibility of reconciling them. Indeed, it is possible to strike a balance where the economy is more stable and grows at a higher rate because people have greater trust in the stability of the banking sector (Aiyar, Calomiris, & Wieladek, 2015; Bridges, Gregory, Nielsen, Pezzini, Radia, & Spaltro, 2014).

The increase in capital requirements is one of the many regulatory reforms so that a stand-alone assessment might be difficult. The discussion on the optimal level of capital requirements has been too limited to stabilise concerns, ignoring other roles and functions of capital in the bank funding mix. However, even with the reduction of the fragility risk, capital buffers assumed additional functions, including the ones of macro-prudential instruments (Beck, 2015).

Based on the results of the Bank Lending Survey, starting at the end of 2011, the growth of bank credit to enterprises has gradually slowed down in Europe, and then showed the first negative signs in the summer of 2012, as a result of the low demand and the restriction of the banking supply (ECB, 2013). The latter was driven, in peripheral countries, by increasing the risk of borrowers, with the consequent deterioration in the quality of the bank's loan portfolio. Credit supply was also affected by the need to be compliant with new and more stringent capital rules that have made banks more aware of the absorption of different assets. There was a restriction on the criteria of offering to corporate credit, particularly related to higher loans, while the effect on loans to households was lower (ECB, 2014).

Faced with the risk of deflation and a new recession, the ECB intervened with a series of unconventional measures to counteract the transmission system's dysfunctions caused by the banks' leverage to ensure a uniform transmission of monetary policy decisions. Consequently, the banks reduced lending rates on average and loosened lending conditions and terms in the wake of monetary policy measures (ECB, 2016).

To address any side effects of monetary policy, macro-prudential policy has been aimed at mitigating the risk-taking channel of monetary policy transmission, where low interest rates could have pushed for greater yields, encouraging banks to loosen their credit standard, with a consequent increase in the volume and average risk of the loans granted (Borio & Zhu, 2012; Jiménez, Ongena, Peydró, & Saurina, 2014; Maddaloni & Peydró, 2011).

Supervisory authorities have reached decisions on the identification of financial institutions of systemic relevance that were required to hold additional capital. They have also made decisions regarding the calibration of systemic risk and countercyclical capital reserves, as well as the specific capital requirements for real state and housing sectors (ECB, 2017a). It should be noted that in this area, national macro-prudential authorities are also quite active; many countries in the euro area have introduced prudential measures, for example, by imposing limits on the ratio between credit and the value of the collateral, to counter emerging risks (Constâncio, 2017).

The new framework is intended to support the implementation of monetary policy and, at the same time, strengthen the financial capacity of the financial system. Unconventional monetary policy measures and improvements to institutional and regulatory architecture have strengthened the ability of the euro area banking system to send the ECB's stimulus to households and enterprises. According to the Bank Lending Survey, the latest easing phase of the ECB (2017a) has coincided with a strong rebound in demand for consumer credit to purchase durable goods, while the demands for fixed investment loans were gradually established. At the same time, lower borrowing costs reduced interest payment charges and facilitated deleveraging. That's one of the reasons for the first time since 1999, spending increased while the debt decreased.

However many issues are still left: among them is the increasingly cumbersome burden of bad loans, that is, credits on insolvent or near insolvent parties (see Chap. 3).

A bad loan may be the result of economic misfortune, but it is more than just an indicator of a debtor's inability (or unwillingness) to pay. A non-performing loan (NPL) is a burden for both the lender and the borrower. For a debtor, a non-performing loan traps valuable collateral, and the unresolved debt makes it more difficult to obtain new funding and make investments (Bernanke, Gertler, & Gilchrist, 1999; Myers, 1977). At the same time, the lender has to meet the costs of the bad loan, including the write-down costs.

High levels of non-performing loans involve high capital absorption and, by increasing the vulnerability of banks to external shocks, they can increase financing costs and modify their propensity to take risks. An increase of exposures classified as non-performing, especially if unexpectedly, also leads to an increase in hedging provisions, which squeeze the banks' profitability and impair their assets, reducing the ability to lend funding. There is a broad consensus on the view that non-physiological levels of NPLs ultimately contract credit supply, distort allocation of credit, worsen market confidence, and slow economic growth (Caballero, Hoshi, & Kashyap, 2008; Cucinelli, 2015; Kwan & Eisenbeis, 1995; Peek & Rosengren, 2000). The deliberate and sustainable reduction of NPLs in the banks' balance sheets is beneficial to the economy. At the same time, it is acknowledged that economic recovery is also an important enabler of bad loan resolution.

The global financial crisis turned the NPL problem once again relevant for the countries in the euro area. Across the European Union, the stock of NPLs relative to the GDP doubled between 2009 and the end of 2014 (IMF, 2016). After reaching a minimum of 2.5 % at the end of 2007, the NPL share on total loans to the euro area as a whole reached a peak of 7.7 % at the end of 2013, then dropped to 6.7 % in mid-2016 thanks to the concrete action of several countries (in particular

Ireland, Slovenia and Spain) and the slight improvement in the macroeconomic environment. Nonetheless, in some parts of the euro area, banks still have large exposures to NPLs on their balance sheets. The share of NPLs is persistently high in some countries such as Cyprus (47.0 %), Greece (37.0 %), Italy (17.5 %), and Portugal (12.7 %). The deterioration in the quality of bank assets in the euro area mainly concerns the business sector, especially small and medium-sized enterprises (SMEs), and the commercial real estate sector (ECB, 2017a).

In the years before the financial crisis, many countries recorded a high growth of credit and indebtedness of the private sector, often accompanied by an increase in real estate prices, which made the effects of the financial crisis even more pronounced (Colombini & Calabrò, 2011). In addition to these cyclical components, however, high NPL shares and their persistence reflect various structural factors in different countries. High corporate leverage, low productivity and low external competitiveness hinder investment and business expansion, while public finance weakness increases the country's risk premium (Ahamad, Guohui, Ali, & Rehman, 2016; Cucinelli, 2015). At the same time, the sluggishness of labour market reforms—aimed at reducing segmentation and increasing flexibility—and the dynamics of real estate collateral markets in some countries hinder NPL reduction in the retail segment. Finally, the gaps in the legal framework, in particular the ineffectiveness of foreclosure and insolvency legislation, together with the limited sharing of data between creditors and the tax treatment of write-downs, prevent efficient disposal of NPLs.

The fragility of banks' balance sheets could propagate to the real economy, where banks with a high share of NPLs have lower lending growth and apply higher interest rates. A reduction in the NPLs in the euro area would therefore improve economic growth. The estimates in this regard indicate that the reduction in NPLs could increase GDP growth by up to two percentage points per year (Balgova, Nies, & Plekhanov, 2016; IMF, 2016).

Faced with a possible moderate economic recovery and high levels of public and private debt (ECB, 2017a), NPLs are unlikely to decline significantly in the medium term in the absence of further measures. Reduction of NPLs requires a broad-based strategy focusing on their structural determinants (Fell, Grodzicki, Martin, & O'Brien, 2016). An analysis of historical data shows that banks that have simultaneously undertaken timely policy actions on budget items and off-balance sheet items, focusing specifically on targeted portfolio segments considered to be the main determinants of NPLs, have recorded a substantial decrease of the latter: it refers to Ireland, Slovenia and Spain, where the share of NPLs dropped by 16.7, 5.3, and 3.3 percentage points respectively between 2013 and mid-2016 (ECB, 2017a).

So far, the progress in reducing the level of NPLs has been slow. Despite some improvement in overall asset quality metrics, progress in reducing high NPLs to manageable levels remains insufficient in some countries (ECB, 2017b).

Large stocks of non-performing loans in the bank's balance sheets in the euro area continue to offer risks to financial stability. The resolution of the NPL problem, however, cannot be left to banks and supervisors alone. Fast policy measures must be implemented to eliminate the structural barriers that prevent banks to work out and sale bad loans. The actions in this area should be directed to improve the legal and judicial systems, in particular regarding the access to guarantees, duration of recovery procedures and, in general, the legal framework for debt restructuring and the removal of tax disincentives. It is also necessary to develop a primary and secondary market for impaired loans, possibly in the form of secure and transparent securitisation, at the euro zone level and at national level. In this regard, initiatives will also be needed to promote the development of a specialised NPL servicing sector, improve quality and access to data, and eliminate possible tax and legal impediments.

The price of NPLs depends mostly on whether these structures are effective and efficient. Significant legal and administrative reforms have been undertaken over recent years in countries with high levels of NPLs to streamline insolvency proceedings and maximise the recovery of amounts of NPLs. However, the market continues to provide low valuations of NPLs that result in large bid-ask spreads, thus preventing large-scale sales. This special feature highlights the potential role and benefits of co-investment strategies between the private sector and the state concerning NPLs. These co-investment strategies may reduce information asymmetries between buyers and sellers, thereby enabling transactions that might otherwise not occur, or facilitate sales at higher prices. In addition, the schemes proposed are quoted at market levels and may therefore be free of state aid (Fell, Grodzicki, Martin, & O'Brien, 2016).

8.5 Conclusions

In a monetary union consisting of several countries with segmented financial markets, such as the euro area, monetary policy measures are inevitably more difficult to calibrate, more complex to implement, and more exposed to the risk of producing undesirable side effects.

Structural factors amplify the constraints of complementarity between monetary policy and the micro- and macro-prudential policy, boosting the role of the latter. This is due primarily to the fact that the macro-prudential instruments used so far are predominantly of banking type and that banks play a very important role in financing the economy of the euro area. Secondly, the area is composed of economies with economic and real estate cycles still relatively heterogeneous. In a context in which monetary policy cannot take into account this diversity, specific macro-prudential measures for each country can be used to prevent financial imbalances. It is evident that, if not properly coordinated, two policies with such strong interactions can easily come into conflict. This potential conflict requires institutional arrangements that favour coordination and cooperation between the two policies. It is evident that if two coordinated policies are not sufficiently interconnected, they can easily come into conflict. This potential conflict requires institutional arrangements that foster coordination and cooperation between the two policies.

During the crisis, monetary policy reacted to economic and financial shocks with the appropriate medium-term orientation to ensure a solid anchoring of inflation expectations in line with the goal of keeping inflation rates below, but close to, two per cent in the medium term. This medium-term orientation implied that monetary policy had to look beyond short-term movements in prices and remedy the monetary transmission mechanism. To do so, the ECB has used standard and non-standard measures—between those are the Enhanced Credit Support and the Securities Markets Programme—to restore the transmission mechanism of monetary policy.

The role of credit supply in the monetary policy transmission has recently found new focus due to the prominent role of credit development in the financial crisis.

There is no unitary judgement in the theoretical studies about the critical interaction of capital requirements with other supervisory rules, while empirical studies suggest that there is a trade-off between banks' leverage, growth, and systemic risk. All capital requirements and loss absorption measures are necessary, but they are also imperfect tools for achieving financial stability, and under some circumstances, they may have important repercussions for lending costs, lending volumes, and ultimately investment and economic growth. It follows that the specific provisions and the design of these measures must be evaluated and understood with care and balance.

In this regard, the main international regulatory initiatives are under way, such as the expected reform of prudential requirements, the introduction of the Minimum Requirement for own funds and Eligible Liabilities (MRELs), and the entry into force in 2018 of the new accounting standard on the valuation of financial instruments (IFRS 9). In the implementation of these measures, in addition to long-term expected benefits, their short-term costs must also be taken into account.

In Europe, supervisory and political authorities felt that the answer to the crisis was to increase the capital strength of the banks. Despite the significant results obtained, it is evident that the recapitalisation was a necessary condition, but not sufficient to solve the other problems that remain open—first, the one relating to the management of non-performing loans—requiring adequate structural responses geared to real recovery and economic growth.

References

Ahamad, M., Guohui, W., Ali, R., & Rehman, R. (2016, October). Non-Performing Loans and Economic Growth. *Journal of Economics, Business and Management, 3*, 584–586.

Aiyar, S., Calomiris, C. W., & Wieladek, T. (2015). How to strengthen the regulation of bank capital: Theory, evidence, and a proposal. *Journal of Applied Corporate Finance, 27*(1), 27–36.

Albertazzi, U., Nobili, A., & Signoretti, F. M. (2016, December). *The bank lending channel of conventional and unconventional monetary policy.* Working Paper No. 1094, Banca d'Italia.

Altavilla, C., Canova, F., & Ciccarelli, M. (2016). *Mending the broken link: Heterogenous bank lending and monetary policy pass-through.* CEPR Discussion Papers 11584.

Angelini, P. (2014). The European framework for financial stability: A bird's eye view. In E. Barucci & M. Messori (Eds.), *Towards the European Banking Union.* Firenze: Passigli.

Angelini, P. (2015, June). *Le politiche macroprudenziali: una discussione dei principali temi.* Occasional Papers, Banca d'Italia, n.271.

Angelini, P., Neri, S., & Panetta, F. (2014). The interaction between capital requirements and monetary policy. *Journal of Money, Credit and Banking, 46*(6), 1073–1112.

Angelini, P., Nicoletti-Altimari, S., & Visco, I. (2012). Macroprudential, microprudential and monetary policies: Conflicts, complementarities and trade-offs. In A. Dombret & O. Lucius (Eds.), *Stability of the financial system—Illusion or feasible concept.* Cheltenham: Edward Elgar.

Balgova, M., Nies, M., & Plekhanov, A. (2016, October). *The economic impact of reducing nonperforming loans.* Working Paper No. 193, European Bank for Reconstruction and Development.

Beck, T. (2015). *Bank capital—Panacea for a crisis-free banking system?* European Economy, Banks, Regulation and the real Sector, No. 1.

Bernanke, B., & Blinder, A. S. (1988). Credit, money an aggregated demand. *The American Economic Review, 78*(2), 435–439.

Bernanke, B., Gertler, M., & Gilchrist, S. (1999). The financial accelerator in a quantitative business cycle framework. In J. Taylor & M. Woodford (Eds.), *Handbook of macroeconomics.* Amsterdam: Elsevier.

BIS—Bank of International Settlements. (2009). *Assessment of the macroeconomic impact of higher loss absorbency for global systemically important banks.* Report by the Macroeconomic Assessment Group jointly established by the Financial Stability Board and the Basel Committee on Banking Supervision.

Boeckx, J., de Sola Perea, M., & Peersman, G. (2016, October). *The transmission mechanism of credit support policies in the Euro Area.* Working Paper Research No. 302.

Borio, C., & Drehmann, M. (2009, March 29–46). Assessing the risk of banking crises—Revisited. *BIS Quarterly Review.*

Borio, C., & Zhu, H. (2012). Capital regulation, risk-taking and monetary policy: A missing link in the transmission mechanism? *Journal of Financial Stability, 8*(4), 236–251.

Bridges, J., Gregory, D., Nielsen, M., Pezzini, S., Radia, A., & Spaltro, M. (2014, January). *The impact of capital requirements on bank lending.* WP no. 486. Bank of England.

Brunnermeier, M. K., & Schnabel, I. (2014). *Bubbles and central banks: Historical perspectives.* New York: Mimeo.

Caballero, R. J., Hoshi, T., & Kashyap, A. K. (2008). Zombie lending and depressed restructuring in Japan. *American Economic Review, 98*(5), 1943–1977.

Calomiris, C. (2013). Reforming banks without destroying their productivity and value. *Journal of Applied Corporate Finance, 25,* 14–19.

Capgemini. (2014). *Impact of regulation on bank lending.*

Carosio, G. (2010). *Financial stability and macroprudential supervision: Challenges for central banks.* Paper presented at the 38th OENB Economics Conference.

Cecchetti, S., & Kohler, M. (2012). *When capital adequacy and interest rate policy are substitutes (and when they are not).* BIS Working Paper No. 379.

Ciccarelli, M., Maddaloni, A., & Peydró, J.-L. (2013). Heterogeneous transmission mechanism: Monetary policy and financial fragility in the Eurozone. *Economic Policy, 28*(75), 459–512.

Clerc, L. (2015). *Higher capital requirements for GSIBs: Systemic risk vs. lending to the real economy*. European Economy. Banks, Regulation and the Real Sector, No. 1.

Cohen, B. H., & Scatigna, M. (2014). *Banks and capital requirements: Channels of adjustment*. BIS Monetary and Economic Department. Working Papers No. 443.

Colombini, F., & Calabrò, A. (2011). *Crisi finanziarie, Banche e Stati*. Torino: Utet.

Constâncio, V. (2017, May). Macroprudential policy in a changing financial system, speech delivered at the second ECB Macroprudential Policy and Research Conference, Frankfurt am Main.

Crockett, A. D. (2000, September). *Marrying the micro- and macroprudential dimensions of financial stability*. Remarks before the Eleventh International Conference of Banking Supervisors, Basel.

Cucinelli, D. (2015). The impact of non-performing loans on bank lending behaviour: Evidence from the Italian banking sector. *Eurasian Journal of Business and Economics, 8*, 59–71.

de Larosière, J. (2009). Report by the High level group on financial supervision in the EU, Bruxelles.

Den Haan, W. J., Sumner, S. W., & Yamashiro, G. M. (2007). Bank loan portfolios and the monetary transmission mechanism. *Journal of Monetary Economics, 54*(3), 904–924.

Diamond, D., & Rajan, R. (2009). *The credit crisis: Conjectures about causes and remedies*. NBER Working Paper, No. 14379.

Ediz, T., Michael, I., & Perraudin, W. (1998, October). The impact of capital requirements on UK bank behaviour. *FRBNY Economic Policy Review*.

ESRB. (2014). *Handbook on operationalizing macro-prudential policies in the banking sector*.

ESRB. (2015). *Report on a review of macro-prudential policy in the EU one year after the introduction of the CRD/CRR*.

ECB—European Central Bank. (2011). *Monetary policy of the ECB*.

ECB—European Central Bank. (2013, January). The euro area Bank Lending Survey.

ECB—European Central Bank. (2014, March). *Forward-looking reaction to bank regulation*. Working Paper series n. 1645.

ECB—European Central Bank (2016, November). Survey on the access to finance of enterprises in the euro area—April to September 2016.

ECB—European Central Bank. (2017a, January). *The euro area Bank Lending Survey*.

ECB—European Central Bank. (2017b, May). *Financial stability review*.

Fell, J., Grodzicki, M., Martin, R., & O'Brien, E. (2016, November). Addressing market failures in the resolution of nonperforming loans in the euro area. *Financial Stability Review*, BCE.

Francis, W., & Osborne, M. (2009). *Bank regulation, capital and credit supply: Measuring the impact of prudential standards.* FSA Occasional Paper Series, 36.

Hanson, S. G., Kashyap, A. K., & Stein, J. C. (2011). A Macroprudential Approach to Financial Regulation. *Journal of Economic Perspectives, 25*(1), 3–28.

IIF—Institute of International Finance. (2011, September). The cumulative impact on the global economy of changes in the financial regulatory framework, Washington, DC.

IMF—International Monetary Found. (2016, October). Global financial stability report.

Jiménez, G., Ongena, S., Peydró, J.-L., & Saurina, J. (2014). Hazardous times for monetary policy: What do twenty-three million bank loans say about the effects of monetary policy on credit risk-taking? *Econometrica, 82*(2), 463–505.

Kannan, P., Rabanal, P., & Scott, A. (2011). Recurring patterns in the run-up to house price busts. *Applied Economics Letters, 18*(2), 107–113.

Kwan, S., & Eisenbeis, R. (1995). An analysis of inefficiencies in banking. *Journal of Banking and Finance, 19*, 733–734.

Lim, C., Columba, F., Costa, A., Kongsamut, P., Otani, A., Saiyid, M., et al. (2011). *Macroprudential policy: What instruments and how to use them? Lessons from country experiences.* IMF Working Paper, 11, 238.

MAG—Macroeconomic Assessment Group. (2010). *Assessing the macroeconomic impact of the transition to stronger capital and liquidity requirements.* BIS, Final Report.

Maddaloni, A., & Peydró, J.-L. (2011). Bank risk-taking, securitisation, supervision and low interest rates: Evidence from the Euro-area and the U.S. lending standards. *The Review of Financial Studies, 24*(6), 2121–2165.

Mishkin, F. (1995). Symposium on the monetary transmission mechanism. *The Journal of Economic Perspective, 9*, 3–10.

Myers, S. C. (1977). Determinants of corporate borrowing. *Journal of Financial Economics, 5*(2), 147–175.

Panetta, F. (2014, June). *On the special role of macroprudential policy in the euro area.* Remarks given at De Nederlandsche Bank, Amsterdam.

Panetta, F., Angelini, P., Albertazzi, U., Columba, F., Cornacchia, W., & Di Cesare, A. (2009). *Financial sector pro-cyclicality—Lessons from the crisis, Banca d'Italia.* Occasional papers, No. 44.

Peek, J., & Rosengren, E. (2000). Collateral damage: Effects of the Japanese bank crisis on real activity in the United States. *American Economic Review, 90*, 30–45.

Rabin, A. A., & Jeager, L. B. (1997). The monetary transmission mechanism. *The Eastern Economic Journal, 23*(3), 293–299.

Reinhart, C. M., & Rogoff, K. S. (2008). Is the 2007 US sub-prime financial crisis so different? An international historical comparison. *American Economic Review, 98*(2), 339–344.

Rochet J. C. (2015). *The bank capital controversy, European economy.* Banks, Regulation and the Real sector, No. 1.

Roger, S., & Vitek, F. (2012, February). *The global macroeconomic costs of raising bank capital adequacy requirements.* IMF Working Paper 12(44).

Taylor, A. M. (2015). *Credit, financial stability, and the macroeconomy.* NBER Working Paper, 21039.

White, W. R. (2009). *Should monetary policy "lean or clean?", Federal Reserve Bank of Dallas, globalization and monetary policy institute.* Working Paper No. 34.

Yellen, J. L. (2011). Macroprudential supervision and monetary policy in the post-crisis world. *Business Economics, 46*(1), 3–12.

CHAPTER 9

Capital Raising in European Banks

Antonella Cappiello and Paola Ferretti

9.1 Introduction

The continuing tension in the European financial markets is accompanied by the requests by the competent authorities to strengthen the capital base of the European banks. Several initiatives have been carried out to this end during the recent years. This chapter aims at describing the various steps of the recapitalisation process of the European banking system. Additionally, the chapter gives an overview of recapitalisation operations for a sample of European banks during the period 2012–2016. The analysis is designed to assess whether the capital increase genuinely contributed to the soundness of banks or whether a more balanced solution would be to focus jointly on different drivers to achieve this goal, *in primis* the improvement of the risk management and efficiency.

9.2 EBA Recommendations

Taking into account the continuing tension in the European financial markets, as well as the resulting measures to restore confidence in the EU banking sector, on 26 October 2011, members of the European Council came to an agreement on the necessity to strengthen the capital base of the banks.

A. Cappiello (✉) • P. Ferretti
Department of Economics and Management, University of Pisa, Pisa, Italy

F. Colombini (ed.), *Raising Capital or Improving Risk Management and Efficiency?*, https://doi.org/10.1007/978-3-319-71749-4_9

In implementing the agreement, on 8 December 2011, EBA issued a Recommendation referring to 71 major European banks. In particular, the national supervisory authorities were required to ask intermediaries, where necessary, to create an exceptional and temporary capital buffer (set by Core Tier 1/RWAs), to be brought to 9% by the end of June 2012, after having taken into account capital requirements deriving from the assessment of sovereign exposures, reflecting market prices as of 30 September 2011.

The request to set up a capital buffer had two objectives: (1) to reduce the risk perceived by investors on the soundness of the banks (counterparty risk), heightened by the acute tensions of sovereign debt, and to restore market confidence in the banking sector, and (2) to create an additional capital buffer to allow banks to cope with possible shocks while still financing the real economy.

The exceptional and temporary nature of the buffer was due to the fact that it was only to be maintained until the 2011 Recommendation had been revoked or amended. This happened on 22 July 2013, when the EBA published a new Recommendation, which exceeded and abolished the previous one, requiring the competent authorities to assess the banks' recapitalisation plans for the transition towards the full implementation and application of CRDIV-CRR/2013, taking into account the gradual implementation of new requirements while considering the impact of stressful situations on the feasibility of the plans.

Although the market conditions had improved since the EBA issued the first Recommendation, the preservation of a transitional level of capital became necessary and was justified by the increasing volatility of the financial market. Therefore, credit institutions were then required to preserve their capital levels and thus maintain a nominal amount of the Core Tier 1 ratio, denominated in the reference currency (e.g. the euro) corresponding to the amount of capital needed to meet the requirements of the 2011 Recommendation, accounting for the 9% of the RWAs.

Following a decision by the Board of Supervisors on 15 December 2014, the EBA Recommendation of July 2013 was abrogated, because since 2011 many EU banks have significantly strengthened their capital position and have already shown that they were able to meet the fully loaded minimum capital requirements set by CRDIV-CRR/2013, including the capital conservation buffer.

In regard to the first EBA Recommendation, it is important to emphasise, first, that the underlying exercise was not a stress test and therefore did not attempt to quantify potential losses in an adverse scenario caused by exposures to sovereign issuers of public debt securities. Conversely, it originated from the assessment of such exposures at market prices (mark-to-market), in order to understand the differences between the amounts entered in the financial statements to be covered by the creation of temporary capital reserves.

To meet the capital objective, banks had to first use private resources, which could have potentially come from retained earnings, reduced bonus payments, new issuance of common equity, contingent capital and liability management measures.

There were 71 banks that participated in the exercise (large European banks). Of these, only 37 showed a shortfall of €115 bln, of which three (Dexia, France/Belgium; Volksbank, Austria; and WestLB, Germany) had undergone a deep restructuring, six Greek banks were subject to a specific national Programme, and one (Bankia, Spain) started restructuring. In the end, 27 remained, with a total shortfall of €76 bln.

The shortfall was to be covered by the end of June 2012, through the issuance of higher-quality capital elements and by a series of limited actions meant to reduce the RWAs without affecting the lending flows to the real economy. Therefore, the banks implemented the necessary measures to comply with the Recommendation by submitting their capital plans to the national supervisory authorities in coordination with EBA by 20 January 2012.

On 3 October 2012, EBA published a report that presented the final results based on the data provided by banks, on the basis of financial statements up to 30 June. The vast majority of participating banks showed a Core Tier 1 ratio of more than 9%, including the 27 banks which had presented a capital deficit, due to a complete recapitalisation they carried out, for an amount of €115.7 bln (EBA, 2012).

Overall, taking into account the capital strengthening of the 34 sample banks that did not show an initial shortfall, and of the capital injection already implemented into the Greek and Spanish banks involved in the exercise, capital increases of more than €200 bln from December 2012 to June 2012 were recorded. Compliance with the Recommendation was mainly obtained through direct capital measures (retained earnings, new capital issuances, and liability management measures) and, to a lesser extent, through actions that influence RWAs. Particularly, the 27 banks addressed their recapitalisation of €115.7 bln for €83.2 bln through direct capital measures equal to 72% of the amount of the recapitalisation, and

€32.5 bln through measures that affected RWAs, by reducing them, which represented the remaining 28% of the recapitalisation amount. This led to a surplus of €39.9 bln on the initial deficit, and therefore, the capital measures used by the banks were more than sufficient to cover the initial deficit and reach the 9% objective of the Core Tier 1 ratio. Compared to September 2011, the 27 banks increased their core capital by 12.6%.

With reference to the other 34 banks that participated in the capital exercise but did not show any initial shortfall, the Core Tier 1 positions up to 30 June 2012 increased by €47 bln, which were divided as follows: €37 bln through measures of direct capital and €10 bln through impacts on RWAs.

Another aspect that deserves to be analysed is related to the changes in the capital positions of the banks participating in the capital exercise at the end of June. The final report demonstrated that the average Core Tier 1 ratio, after accounting for the buffer against sovereign exposures of the 61 banks, increased to 10.7% with the following breakdown: the 27 banks with an initial deficit reported an average Core Tier 1 ratio of 9.7%; the other 34 banks reported an average Core Tier 1 ratio of 11.5%.

Although the external environment continued to be very complex, recapitalisation helped to strengthen the capital base of the banking system as a whole and put the banks in a stronger position to continue lending to the real economy. The EBA Recommendation, as part of a comprehensive set of policy measures, proved therefore to be a necessary step towards restoring confidence in the EU banking system.

However, the exercise carried out by EBA presented some weak points, as well as aspects that can be criticised, particularly in regard to methodology and equal treatment of banks operating in different countries.

As far as methodological issues are concerned, the first critical point is that the exercise was based on a capital ratio consisting of variables (both numerator and denominator) calculated on a non-homogeneous basis in different European countries. In particular, the RWAs calculation was based on internal risk assessment models defined by individual banks and subject to validation procedures that may vary greatly between European countries.

A second methodological aspect concerns the application of mark-to-market to the entire portfolio of government securities (including those held until maturity, thus making the approach too stringent) and to the government security exposure of all eurozone countries and not only to the exposures of those countries really exposed to the sovereign debt crisis.

This circumstance was, in fact, beneficial for the German and French banks whose capital gains on the relevant exposures towards the government securities of their respective countries generated significant savings in terms of capital absorption.

With regard to the second type of issues (the equal treatment of banks operating in different countries), one element concerns the diversity of the business profile of the institutes involved in the EBA exercise. In fact, the regulation on capital requirements subjected the credit risk to a much more severe and rigorous treatment than the market risk. In calculating the capital ratios, this could penalise banks that concentrate more on the traditional banking business of lending to households and enterprises, such as Italian banks, compared to those orientated more in trading and investment banking.

Finally, a general aspect that gave rise to doubts and concerns among banks involved the setting of a particularly high threshold of a 9% Core Tier 1 ratio (higher than the 7% foreseen by Basel III). Even though we assume there was homogeneity among countries in the Core Tier 1 ratio calculation methodology, a 9% threshold was very high, as it required banks to make considerable efforts in order to obtain new resources in a context of strong market turmoil and uncertainty in the regulatory framework.

Additionally, a major increase in the Core Tier 1 ratio during a recession phase could have had profound pro-cyclical effects, as it would have forced banks, which could not gather new resources, to reduce their credit supply, accelerating the cycle trend; it would have been an opposite approach to that of the countercyclical buffer of Basel III.

9.3 Comprehensive Assessment: Rationales and Features

The economic slowdown and tensions in the international financial markets have had significant impacts on banks and consequently on the process of lending to the real economy. To restrict the scope of the negative phenomena, the supervisory authorities in Europe have adopted specific measures to enhance banks' soundness, especially through significant capital increases.

From the beginning of the financial crisis to the end of 2013, the raising of capital from the banks of the euro area amounted to about EUR

225 billion, to which 275 billion euro should be added in terms of state aid, for a total amount of more than 5% of the GDP of the area. Nevertheless, certain elements of weakness persisted, worsened by concerns about the overall riskiness of banks. In this context, the ECB has planned a comprehensive assessment regarding the robustness of the balance sheets and the risk profile of the European banking sector in view of the beginning, at the end of 2014, of the Single Supervisory Mechanism. In view of the European Banking Union and, in particular, in order to evaluate the adequacy of capital levels of the European banks, the ECB has carried out, in the period from November 2013 to October 2014, a comprehensive check-up on the balance sheets of banks. This assessment has involved 130 banks (with 120 significant ones) of 18 member states, representing approximately the 85% of the total assets of the euro area.

Among the objectives of the comprehensive assessment, we may note the quality improvement of the information available on the situation of banks (transparency), the identification of possible corrective actions to deal with capital shortfalls (correction), and the assurance of solidity and reliability of banks (strengthening of confidence).

The comprehensive assessment, innovative in scope and complexity, was conducted with a single methodology defined by the ECB at the European level with the aim of ensuring the level playing field. With a view to a unified banking system at the regulatory level, it is in fact essential to ensure banks the same treatment in order not to create distortions.

The comprehensive assessment has been structured in three main and complementary steps: (1) supervisory risk assessment, (2) asset quality review (AQR), and (3) stress test.

To determine the quantitative outcome of the exercise, a reference parameter was used for the Common Equity Tier 1 ratio, providing for the AQR and the baseline scenario of the stress test a minimum threshold of 8%, higher than the minimum requirement provided by Basel III (4.5%, as it is increased by 2.5% on the grounds of capital conservation buffer) and a further 1% to take account of the systemic relevance of significant banks. For the adverse stress test scenario, the threshold has been instead lowered to 5.5%.

In case banks had not reached the minimum requirements, they were asked to take corrective measures to be implemented in six months as regards the shortfalls related to the AQR or in the baseline scenario, and nine months in the case of shortfalls of the adverse scenario.

The capital shortfall should be filled with capital injections, and in the case of their inadequacy or delayed availability, it is possible to resort to public intervention. Other corrective measures planned were based on the reconfiguration of funding and the disposal of non-core assets.

For the AQR, a risk-based approach was adopted in order to focus on the individual balance sheet items considered too risky or not very transparent.

The AQR was articulated in three phases:

1. Selection of portfolios, that is, the identification of groups of loans or securities uniform per type of counterparty and risk degree.
2. Execution, which involved a series of accounting control activities, including the validation of data integrity, the sampling of exposures, the on-site document revision, the evaluation of the guarantees, and the recalculation of the provisions.
3. Data collection, which has aimed to ensure the consistency of the results so that they were comparable.

Regarding the stress test, as a tool used by the supervisory authorities to assess the resilience of the intermediaries upon the occurrence of particular scenarios (even extreme and hardly probable, though plausible), the ECB has decided to carry out this test to assess how the European banking system would respond to particular stress situations and subsequently propose appropriate corrective actions to return the sector to a situation of equilibrium.

In the context of comprehensive assessment, the stress test has intended to provide a perspective view of the solvency capacity of the banks on the basis of two assumptions, baseline and adverse scenario, using and also integrating the information of the AQR.

In the stress test, the reference parameter was also the CET1 ratio, which, as it has already been said, in the baseline scenario was to remain above the threshold of 8%, whereas in the adverse scenario this threshold was reduced to 5.5%.

The stress scenarios have considered the evolution of a series of key variables, including economic growth, inflation, and long-term interest rates, and the evolution of the prices of real and financial assets. The assumptions concerning these variables have represented, then, the external framework of reference for the banks. The robustness of the bank balance sheets was also assessed with reference to a vast collection of losses arising from the investment risks (e.g. credit, sovereign, market) and refinancing.

The projections of the banks were subjected to requirements defined in a centralised manner, in order to ensure prudence and high-quality results. For example, it has been assumed that the total value of exposures, the maturity, and the combination of products remained unchanged in the horizon of the stress test (static balance sheet assumption). The values considered, therefore, were those entered in the balance sheet at 31 December 2013, without taking account of any measures to strengthen capital undertaken by banks during 2014. Any shortfall of a bank arising out of the exercise was therefore identified in the maximum value that emerged from the AQR, baseline or adverse stress test, and not from the actual capital needs of the bank. The static balance sheet assumption, on the other hand, has increased the severity of the financial year because it is assumed that the banks could not undertake actions of risk mitigation such as the recomposition of the balance sheet towards less risky activities that absorb less capital.

As it has already been mentioned, the stress tests were integrated with the results arising from the AQR; the main integrations have focused on the amount of the initial stock of performing and non-performing exposures, risk parameters, and capital available to the bank in order to cope with the additional losses expected in the stress time horizon. This had particular importance in case the review of the asset quality had highlighted the need for additional provisions, because they would have required to slash the starting value of the assets used in the stress test and would have increased the estimates of loss along the time horizon of the exercise (2014–2016).

Finally, as it was for the AQR, the robustness of the results of the stress test was assessed by means of a rigorous process of quality assurance. This was meant to verify both the correct application of the methodology and the degree of consistency between the results presented by the banks and the shocks assumed.

9.3.1 The Main Results of the Comprehensive Assessment

As already noted, the comprehensive assessment was completed on 26 October 2014, in conjunction with the full assumption of supervisory powers by the ECB, which took place on 4 November. The following are the main results (ECB, 2014).

As regards the AQR, it coincided with a detailed analysis of over 800 specific portfolios, corresponding to 57% of the RWAs of banks. This has led, among other things, to examine over 119,000 borrowers, to verify the assessment of approximately 170,000 guarantees, to develop 765 models to "refute" internal estimates of provisions and the reassessment of over 5,000 among the most complex exposures at fair value.

As a result of the AQR, the adjustments made to the accounting values of the assets of the banks participating on 31 December 2013 amounted to 47.5 billion euros. Furthermore, the outstanding amounts of the NPLs for participating banks have increased by 135.9 billion euros, because the definition of NPLs, traced back on a harmonised and comparable framework, also included the assessment of forbearance.

In addition to generating adjustments of the accounting values, the results of the AQR have also been used for the projection of the capital adequacy of banks in stress test scenarios (join up). According to the projections of the adverse scenario, the capital of banks fell by about 215.5 billion euros (22% of capital held), divided into 33.8 billion due to the AQR and 181.7 billion due to the stress test. A further decrease (equal to 47.2 billion) was due to the increase of the RWAs. Taking this into account, the overall reduction of capital was 262.7 billion euros in the adverse scenario.

In percentage terms, the reduction of capital stood at 2.5%, divided into 0.4% due to the AQR and 2.1% due to the stress test, whereas the impact of the rise of the RWAs stood at 0.8%, due almost entirely to the stress test. Consequently, the average Common Equity Tier 1 ratio fell from 11.8% at the end of 2013 to 8.4% at the end of 2016.

Another aspect to consider concerns the comparison of solvency ratio projections of the various banks with the threshold defined by the exercise (CET1 at 8%). Twenty-five banks out of 130 (Table 9.1) showed an overall capital shortfall of 24.62 billion euros.

9.4 The Stress Test of 2016

The stress test carried out by the EBA in 2016 was aimed primarily at identifying the vulnerability of the European banks and indicating sustainable solutions, providing support to the supervisory assessments with regard to bank capitalisation plans in the medium term. Unlike preceding stress test (2011 and 2014), the stress test of 2016 is not of a pass/fail type, in that it does not establish a minimum threshold of capital to be respected through the activation of capital strengthening measures. The

Table 9.1 Banks and shortfalls

	Banks	*CET1 ratio adverse scenario*	*Capital shortfall (bln €)*	*Capital raised (bln €)*	*Capital shortfall post capital raised (bln €)*
1	Monte dei Paschi di Siena (IT)	−0.1%	4.25	2.14	2.11
2	Eurobank (GR)	−6.4%	4.63	2.86	1.76
3	Banco Comercial Portugues (PT)	3.0%	1.14	−0.01	1.15
4	National Bank of Greece (GR)	−0.4%	3.43	2.50	0.93
5	Oesterreichischer Volksbanken-Verbund (AT)	2.1%	0.86	0.00	0.86
6	Permanent tsb (IE)	1.0%	0.85	0.00	0.85
7	Banca Carige (IT)	−2.4%	1.83	1.02	0.81
8	Dexia (BE)	5.0%	0.34	0.00	0.34
9	Banca Popolare di Vicenza (IT)	3.2%	0.68	0.46	0.22
10	Hellenic Bank (GR)	−0.5%	0.28	0.10	0.18
11	Banca Popolare di Milano (IT)	4.0%	0.68	0.52	0.17
12	Nova Ljubljanska Banka (SI)	5.0%	0.03	0.00	0.03
13	Nova Kreditna Banka Maribor (SI)	4.4%	0.03	0.00	0.03
14	Cooperative Central Bank (CY)	−8.0%	1.17	1.50	0.0
15	Bank of Cyprus (CY)	1.5%	0.92	1.00	0.0
16	Veneto Banca (IT)	2.7%	0.71	0.74	0.0
17	Banco Popolare (IT)	4.7%	0.69	1.76	0.0
18	Piraeus Bank (GR)	4.4%	0.66	1.00	0.0
19	Credito Valtellinese (IT)	3.5%	0.38	0.42	0.0
20	Banca Popolare di Sondrio (IT)	4.2%	0.32	0.34	0.0
21	Münchener Hypothekenbank (DE)	2.9%	0.23	0.41	0.0
22	AXA Bank Europe (BE)	3.4%	0.20	0.20	0.0
23	Caisse de Refinancement de l'Habitat (FR)	5.5%	0.13	0.25	0.0
24	Banca Popolare dell'Emilia Romagna	5.2%	0.13	0.76	0.0
25	Liberbank	5.6%	0.03	0.64	0.0
	Totals	2.1%	24.62	18.59	9.47

Source: ECB (2014)

results have shown only one element for the quantification of the capital of Pillar 2 as a result of the Supervisory Review and Evaluation Process (SREP) in which the supervisory authority examines the individual risk profiles and the levels of capitalisation of banks.

Similarly to the exercises conducted in the past, the EBA has maintained the static balance sheet principle. Therefore it did not take into account any capitalisation measure adopted after 31 December 2015.

The stress test is based on a common methodology and scenarios and was accompanied by harmonised models that captured the starting data and the results of the stress tests in order to allow a rigorous assessment and a comparison between the participating banks. There were 51 banks, representing approximately 70% of the total assets of the euro area, thus located: 37 in the euro area and 14 in Denmark, Hungary, Norway, Poland, Sweden, and the United Kingdom.

The news of the 2016 stress test also focused on the types of risk considered. In addition to market and credit risk and the cost of funding, it considered (1) the contract risk, that is, the risk that fraudulent behaviour may determine penalties or costs for the bank; (2) the currency risk, which refers to the impact of currency oscillations on the quality of credit in foreign currency; and (3) the interest rate risk, which assesses the influence of zero or negative interest rates on the profitability of the bank (ESRB, 2016).

The approach followed was a bottom-up type, in which the banks are required to project the impact of well-defined scenarios, subject however to strict constraints as well as a thorough examination by the competent authorities.

The simulation was carried out based on the data of the balance sheet at the end of 2015, and the common macroeconomic scenarios were applied in a three-year time period from the end of 2016 to the end of 2018. For the assumptions of the baseline scenario (formulated by the European Commission) and for the adverse scenario (defined by the European Systemic Risk Board—ESRB), refer to Table 9.2.

As a result of the substantial efforts made since 2011 to strengthen the capital base of the EU banking system, the starting point for the 2016 stress test was an average ratio of the CET1 of 13.2% at the end of 2015 (12.6% fully loaded), which represents a capital situation that is much more robust as regards the previous stress tests. From December 2013 to December 2015, in fact, the CET1 capital on a transitional basis increased by approximately 180 billion euros for the banks analysed and over 260 billion euros compared to December 2010.

Table 9.2 Macroeconomic scenarios (percentage values)

	Baseline scenario			*Deviation*			*Adverse scenario*		
	2016	*2017*	*2018*	*2016*	*2017*	*2018*	*2016*	*2017*	*2018*
Real GDP growth rate									
European Union	2.0	2.1	1.7	−3.2	−3.3	−1.0	−1.2	−1.3	0.7
Euro area	1.8	1.9	1.7	−2.8	−3.2	−1.1	−1.0	−1.3	0.6
Inflation rate									
European Union	1.1	1.6	2.0	−2.0	−1.9	−2.1	−0.9	−0.2	−0.2
Euro area	1.0	1.6	1.9	−1.9	−1.7	−1.9	−0.9	−0.1	−0.1
Unemployment rate									
European Union	9.2	8.9	8.9	0.7	1.9	2.8	9.9	10.8	11.6
Euro area	10.6	10.3	10.1	0.4	1.4	2.3	11.0	11.7	12.4

Source: own processing on the European Systemic Risk Board data (ESRB, 2016)

The impact of the adverse scenario has brought the CET1 ratio of banks from 13.2% to 9.4% at the end of 2018. This decrease was determined mainly by a capital reduction of 269 billion euros, even if on the other hand the RWAs grew by 10% with an impact on the CET1 ratio of 120 percentage points. Since a part of the decline has been led by the transitional provisions of the requirements of the CRDIV/CRR during the projection period, the impact on the fully implemented baseline was less: the fully loaded CET1 ratio in fact decreased from 12.6% in 2015 to 9.2% in 2018.

The main driver of the impact of the adverse scenario is given by the losses on loans equal to −349 billion euros, with a negative impact of 370 baseline points on the CET1 ratio. The other losses are attributable to operational risk, with a negative impact of 110 baseline points (equal to −105 billion euros), mainly driven by conduct risk (−80 baseline points, −71 billion euros) and market risk in all portfolios, including counterparty risk (−98 billion euros, equal to −100 baseline points). Positive or negative effects on capital decrease are also derived from a combination of other factors such as net interest income, fees and commissions, and administrative costs.

In the adverse scenario, therefore, the capital fell by an average of 3.8 percentage points, in a greater variation than that of 2.6 percentage points in the 2014 stress test. The difference is in part attributable to the more rigorous methodology adopted and the greater severity of the adverse scenario, this time also projected on a horizon of three years and the static balance sheet assumption. Thanks to a higher level of capital and other improvements made from 2014, the final ratio of CET1 in the adverse scenario has nevertheless reached on average 9.2%, exceeding the 8.5% of 2014. With one exception (Monte dei Paschi di Siena), all banks have shown CET1 levels well above the reference parameter of 5.5% used in 2014 for the adverse scenario assumption, to attest to the solidity of overall capitalisation levels of the banks examined.

9.5 Some Evidence from a Sample of European Banks

After having outlined the various steps of the bank recapitalisation process required by the European authorities, it is helpful to analyse a sample of banks in order to investigate the sequence of actions undertaken to reinforce the bank's capital base.

We therefore examined a sample period extending from 2012 to 2016, investigating the first five banks found to be the best (DNB Bank, NV BNG, Svenska Handelsbanken, Swedbank, NRW.Bank) in the framework of the 2016 EBA stress test and the five worst banks (MPS, Banco Popular, UniCredit, Allied Irish Bank, Deutsche Bank).

In the following tables, we report for each bank the capital composition for each year considered. For this purpose, the data presented refer to the Common Equity Tier 1, to the Additional Tier 1, to Tier 1, to Tier 2, and to the Total Capital, as well as to the risk-weighted assets for determination of the respective ratios (Tables from 9.3 to 9.12).

Table 9.3 MPS: own funds (thousands) and ratios

	2012	*2013*	*2014*	*2015*	*2016*
Common Equity Tier 1 (CET1)			6,607,509	8,503,145	5,353,399
Additional Tier 1(AT1)			0	598,309	0
Tier 1	8,917,368	8,973,104	6,607,509	9,101,454	5,353,399
Tier 2	4,164,247	3,865,560	3,292,608	2,196,269	1,463,924
Total Capital	12,799,835	12,838,664	9,900,117	11,297,723	6,817,323
RWAs	92,828,000	84,499,150	76,220,330	70,828,477	65,521,653
CET1 capital ratio	0.00%	0.00%	8.67%	12.01%	8.17%
Tier 1 capital ratio	9.61%	10.62%	8.67%	12.85%	8.17%
Total capital ratio	13.79%	15.19%	12.99%	15.95%	10.40%

Source: own processing (Annual Reports)

Table 9.4 Banco Popular: own funds (thousands) and ratios

	2012	*2013*	*2014*	*2015*	*2016*
Common Equity Tier 1 (CET1)			9,217,569	9,974,748	7,808,140
Additional Tier 1(AT1)			0	0	0
Tier 1	9,099,553	9,658,894	9,217,569	9,974,748	7,808,140
Tier 2	688,562	219,965	365,303	546,124	655,167
Total Capital	9,788,115	9,878,859	9,582,872	10,520,872	8,463,307
RWAs	88,756,823	80,607,207	80,112,663	76,087,403	64,372,232
CET1 capital ratio	0.00%	0.00%	11.51%	13.11%	12.13%
Tier 1 capital ratio	10.25%	11.98%	11.51%	13.11%	12.13%
Total capital ratio	11.03%	12.26%	11.96%	13.83%	13.15%

Source: own processing (Annual Reports)

Table 9.5 UniCredit: own funds (thousands) and ratios

	2012	*2013*	*2014*	*2015*	*2016*
Common Equity Tier 1 (CET1)			41,997,688	41,375,158	31,537,202
Additional Tier 1(AT1)			3,501,611	3,544,906	3,467,648
Tier 1	48,868,274	42,737,233	45,499,299	44,920,064	35,004,850
Tier 2	14,342,603	14,913,926	9,357,508	106,586,616	10,144,917
Total Capital	62,018,395	57,651,159	54,856,807	55,578,680	45,149,767
RWAs	427,126,757	423,738,575	409,222,601	390,598,859	387,135,931
CET1 capital ratio	0.00%	0.00%	10.26%	10.59%	8.15%
Tier 1 capital ratio	11.44%	10.09%	11.12%	11.50%	9.04%
Total capital ratio	14.52%	13.61%	13.41%	14.23%	11.66%

Source: own processing (Annual Reports)

Table 9.6 Allied Irish Bank: own funds (thousands) and ratios

	2012	*2013*	*2014*	*2015*	*2016*
Common Equity Tier 1 (CET1)			9,717	9,285	10,307
Additional Tier 1(AT1)			–	494	485
Tier 1	10,755	8926	9717	9779	10,792
Tier 2	1910	1410	1008	1269	980
Total Capital	12,591	10,336	10,725	11,048	11,772
RWAs	71,417	62,395	59,114	58,549	54,235
CET1 capital ratio	0.00%	0.00%	16.44%	15.86%	19.00%
Tier 1 capital ratio	15.06%	14.31%	16.44%	16.70%	19.90%
Total capital ratio	17.63%	16.57%	18.14%	18.87%	21.71%

Source: own processing (Annual Reports)

Table 9.7 Deutsche Bank: own funds (thousands) and ratios

	2012	*2013*	*2014*	*2015*	*2016*
Common Equity Tier 1 (CET1)	37,957	38,534	60,103	52,429	47,782
Additional Tier 1(AT1)	12,526	12,182	3794	5793	7703
Tier 1	50,483	50,717	63,898	58,222	55,486
Tier 2	6532	4747	4395	6299	6672
Total Capital	57,015	55,464	68,293	64,522	62,158
RWAs	333,605	300,369	396,648	397,382	356,235
CET1 capital ratio	11.38%	12.83%	15.15%	13.19%	13.41%
Tier 1 capital ratio	15.13%	16.88%	16.11%	14.65%	15.58%
Total capital ratio	17.09%	18.47%	17.22%	16.24%	17.45%

Source: own processing (Annual Reports)

Table 9.8 DNB Bank: own funds (thousands) and ratios

	2012	*2013*	*2014*	*2015*	*2016*
Common Equity Tier 1 (CET1)	103,047	114,770	129,915	150,889	163,388
Additional Tier 1(AT1)	3162	3515	4028	10,267	17,471
Tier 1	106,209	118,285	133,944	161,156	180,860
Tier 2	15,740	21,165	24,115	27,887	26,851
Total Capital	121,949	139,450	158,058	189,043	207,711
RWAs	984,137	1,004,716	1,038,396	1,056,731	1,040,888
CET1 capital ratio	10.47%	11.42%	12.51%	14.28%	15.70%
Tier 1 capital ratio	10.79%	11.77%	12.90%	15.25%	17.38%
Total capital ratio	12.39%	13.88%	15.22%	17.89%	19.96%

Source: own processing (Annual Reports)

Table 9.9 NV BNG: own funds (thousands) and ratios

	2012	*2013*	*2014*	*2015*	*2016*
Common Equity Tier 1 (CET1)			2770	2988	3200
Additional Tier 1(AT1)			–	424	733
Tier 1	2576	2806	2770	3412	3933
Tier 2	–	4	–	–	–
Total Capital	2576	2810	2770	3412	3933
RWAs	11,729	11,530	11,681	12,797	12,328
CET1 capital ratio	0.00%	0.00%	23.71%	23.35%	25.96%
Tier 1 capital ratio	21.96%	24.34%	23.71%	26.66%	31.90%
Total capital ratio	21.96%	24.37%	23.71%	26.66%	31.90%

Source: own processing (Annual Reports)

Table 9.10 Svenska Handelsbanken: own funds (thousands) and ratios

	2012	*2013*	*2014*	*2015*	*2016*
Common Equity Tier 1 (CET1)	89,535	98,084	100,535	115,240	
Additional Tier 1(AT1)	10,602	8,043	11,933	12,768	
Tier 1	102,333	100,137	106,127	112,468	128,008
Tier 2	5487	269	16,731	16,021	16,225
Total Capital	101,879	100,406	122,858	128,489	144,233
RWAs	1,006,219	1,016,192	480,388	473,132	458,787
CET1 capital ratio	0.00%	8.81%	20.42%	21.25%	25.12%
Tier 1 capital ratio	10.17%	9.85%	22.09%	23.77%	27.90%
Total capital ratio	10.12%	9.88%	25.57%	27.16%	31.44%

Source: own processing (Annual Reports)

Table 9.11 Swedbank: own funds (thousands) and ratios

	2012	*2013*	*2014*	*2015*	*2016*
Common Equity Tier 1 (CET1)	80,697	84,606	87,916	93,926	98,679
Additional Tier 1(AT1)	6270	4009	4998	10,624	14,281
Tier 1	86,967	88,615	92,914	104,550	112,960
Tier 2	7082	2157	12,674	13,269	12,229
Total Capital	91,155	90,772	105,588	117,819	125,189
RWAs	464,339	451,931	414,214	389,098	394,135
CET1 capital ratio	17.38%	18.72%	21.22%	24.14%	25.04%
Tier 1 capital ratio	18.73%	19.61%	22.43%	26.87%	28.66%
Total capital ratio	19.63%	20.09%	25.49%	30.28%	31.76%

Source: own processing (Annual Reports)

Table 9.12 NRW.Bank: own funds (thousands) and ratios

	2012	*2013*	*2014*	*2015*	*2016*
Common Equity Tier 1 (CET1)			18,254	18,384	18,393
Additional Tier 1(AT1)					
Tier 1	16,655	17,091			
Tier 2	1833	2033			
Total Capital	18,488	19,124	19,991	20,063	20,023
RWAs	41,710	38,825	45,528	43,171	44,044
CET1 capital ratio	0.00%	0.00%		42.58%	41.76%
Tier 1 capital ratio	39.93%	44.02%	0.00%	0.00%	0.00%
Total capital ratio	44.33%	49.26%	43.91%	46.47%	45.46%

Source: own processing (Annual Reports)

Focusing on the period 2014–2016 and on the main capital ratio, the CET1 ratio, it is clear that among the five best banks, NRW.Bank showed extremely high levels of capitalisation as compared to the other four, which were, additionally, characterised by a fairly low degree of variability. On the other hand, MPS was among the five worst banks, with a CET1 which, in 2016, showed a markedly decreased CET1 as compared to 2015 (Fig. 9.1).

The critical condition of some positions is further confirmed by the analysis conducted with regard to the values of the CET1 ratio considered in the adverse scenario of the 2016 stress test (Fig. 9.2).

The general result of the analysis we carried out shows the greater weakness of the Italian banking system as compared to the great European countries. In particular, MPS, at the end of the simulation period, was the only bank with a negative CET1 (−2.23%) among those examined. The overall situation of the bank is adversely affected by the high level of NPLs, which exposes MPS to a potentially strong risk in the event of an economic crisis, such as that simulated by the stress test. This means that in

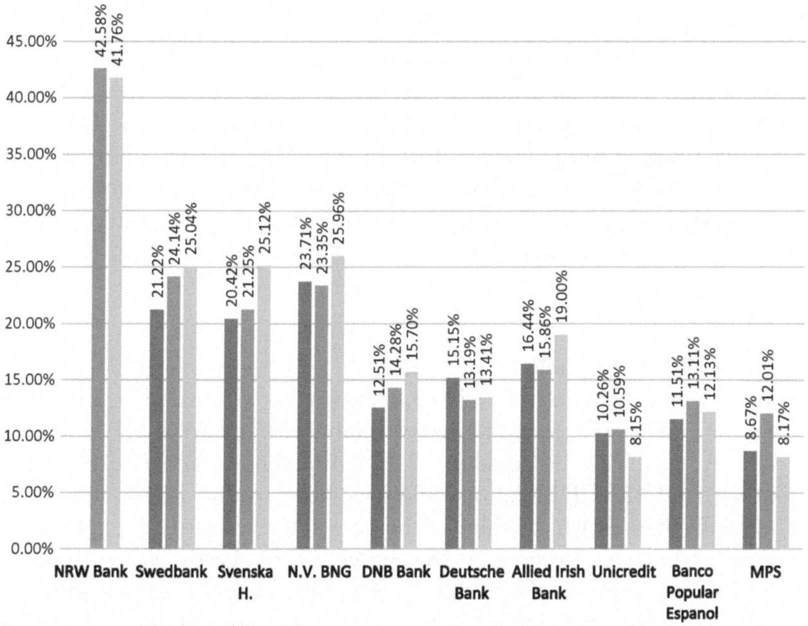

Source: own processing (Annual Reports)

Fig. 9.1 CET1 ratio 2014–2016

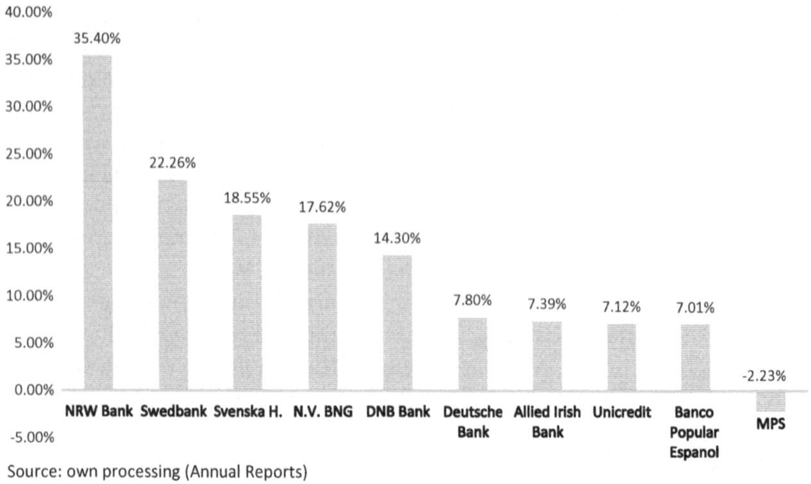

Fig. 9.2 CET1 ratio (2018 adverse scenario)

such a case the bank would be insolvent and would therefore have to be saved or forced into bankruptcy.

Discussion has long revolved around the issue of how to achieve a definitive solution of the bank's situation. The MPS management and the Italian government have proposed a variety of solutions (for a more extensive overview of the MPS question, see Box 9.1), focusing attention on recapitalisation operations.

Box 9.1 MPS recapitalisation

The adverse scenario of the 2016 stress test, as we have seen, shows for the end of 2018 a significant worsening with regard to MPS capital, with a CET1 ratio equal to −2.23%. In the basic scenario, on the other hand, the CET1 ratio would have been around 12.2%, fundamentally in line with the value of the ratio at the reference date of the time period considered (31 December 2015). Partly also on the basis of these results, the ECB has asked MPS to adopt suitable measures to solve the bank's problems and, in particular, that of the quality of credit.

The plan set up by the bank to address this issue ("Project Charles") has not been completed because it has not been possible to raise funds in the market in order to complete the recapitalisation.

On 23 December 2016, the Italian Government adopted the Law Decree n. 237/2016 containing measures involving state aid for the liquidity and capital of banks. This measure was designed to avoid the eventuality that the hypothetical difficulties of a bank (such as those emerging from a stress test) could translate into genuine difficulties, with consequences for the bank itself and for the overall stability of the financial system.

On the same date, MPS requested special liquidity support measures (i.e. state guarantees for new issues of debt); on 30 December the bank forwarded to the Ministry of the Economy and Finance, and also to the ECB and the Bank of Italy, a request for the granting of precautionary recapitalisation.

It should be noted that as early as 2015, the Single Supervision Mechanism (SSM) had asked MPS to present a plan for capital enhancement, which at the time was designed to fulfil the task of remedying the capital shortfall that had been highlighted by the comprehensive assessment. The SSM had also asked MPS to undertake the necessary actions in order to solve the problem of the quality of credit and to engage in the definitive clean-up and revival of the group. These actions were to include operations of aggregation, but this proposal was not performed due to the difficulty of finding a partner. In June 2015 the bank, upon the authorisation of SSM, proceeded to carry out a capital increase of three million euros, of which 1.1 million was appropriated for repayment of state aid received in 2013 and the remainder to cover the shortfall.

Precautionary recapitalisation, as laid down by the BRRD Directive, is a measure that can be adopted in order to avoid or to remedy a severe disorder in the economy of a Member State and to preserve financial stability. This state support has the nature of a one-off, precautionary and temporary measure: it can be granted only on condition that the bank is solvent and that the state intervention is approved by the European Commission on the basis of the rules on state aid.

The Communication of the EU Commission on state aid to the banking sector ("Banking Communication"), issued in 2013, allows state support only after the capital instruments have been converted into shares, among which subordinate bonds are included (burden-sharing principle).

The amount of precautionary capital that a bank may request from the State is the amount that is necessary to cover the capital requirement deriving from the adverse scenario of a stress test.

On 23 December 2016, in the light of the results of the stress tests that were made known by the EBA in the previous July, the ECB quantified for MPS a regulatory capital requirement of 8.8 billion, with reference to the adverse scenario. The amount was determined as follows: 6.3 billion in order to realign the CET1 ratio with the 8% threshold (from the −2.23% indicated by the results of the stress test in the adverse scenario) and 2.5 billion to reach the 11.5% threshold of the total capital ratio.

9.6 Conclusions

Our analysis shows an intense process of recapitalisation of the European banks, also according to the initiatives adopted by the supervisory authorities. Nevertheless, significant weaknesses still exist as in the cases of the worst banks of our sample. This could mean that although recapitalisation is of crucial importance, it cannot, alone, restore a situation of equilibrium. To this end, what is required is that the capital increase must be accompanied by more extensive measures, such as interventions concerning the business model, governance, and, mainly, the improvement in risk management and efficiency. Achieving better risk management and higher efficiency will create structural premises to reinforce the individual bank capacity for profit generation in the medium and long term.

Acknowledgments This chapter is the result of the joint effort of the two authors, who equally contributed to the work.

References

EBA. (2012, October). *Final report on the implementation of capital plans following the EBA's 2011 Recommendation on the creation of temporary capital buffers to restore market confidence.*

ECB. (2014, October). *Aggregate report on comprehensive assessment*, Frankfurt.

ESRB—European Systemic Risk Board Data. (2016, January). *Adverse macro-financial scenario for the EBA 2016 EU-wide bank stress testing exercise.*

CHAPTER 10

Banking Regulation and Supervision in the USA

Paola Ferretti

10.1 Introduction

Regulation and supervision in the USA, similarly to other contexts, constitute two distinct yet complementary activities, without a strict legal separation.

Regulation defines the framework of rules within which financial intermediaries can carry out their business. Once the rules have been defined, supervision guarantees that they will be respected: the supervision provides the necessary assurance that financial institutions will operate in a safe and sound manner by monitoring, inspecting, and examining them.

Overall, financial regulation aims to protect borrowers and investors who are participating in financial markets and to mitigate financial instability. US banking regulation is traditionally focused on prudence.

This chapter aims to outline the distinctive elements of banking regulation and supervision in the USA, highlighting the structure of the Federal Reserve System, its main areas of intervention, and the tools utilised to achieve the above-stated objectives.

P. Ferretti (✉)
Department of Economics and Management, University of Pisa, Pisa, Italy

F. Colombini (ed.), *Raising Capital or Improving Risk Management and Efficiency?*, https://doi.org/10.1007/978-3-319-71749-4_10

10.2 The Federal Reserve System, Regulation, and Supervision

The Federal Reserve System supervises and regulates a wide range of financial institutions and activities. The Federal Reserve works in conjunction with other federal and state authorities (e.g. the Office of the Comptroller of the Currency, the Federal Deposit Insurance Corporation, the Office of Thrift Supervision, and the banking departments of various states) to ensure that financial institutions safely manage their operations and provide fair and equitable services to consumers.

Particularly, the Federal Reserve is responsible for supervising and regulating certain segments of the US financial sector to ensure safe and sound business practices and compliance with existing laws and regulations (Bernanke, 2006; Economic and Monetary Affairs, 2015). The Federal Reserve performs different tasks designed to promote effective operation of the economy. Specifically, it carries out monetary policy, promotes stability of the financial system, and seeks to minimise systemic risks. Additionally, it ensures the safety and soundness of intermediaries and monitors their impact on the financial system as a whole; it also fosters payment and settlement system safety and efficiency and supports consumer protection and community development.

The Federal Reserve System was set up in 1913; as the central bank of the USA, it has three key components: the Federal Reserve Board, the 12 regional Federal Reserve Banks, and the Federal Open Market Committee.

The Federal Reserve Board is an agency of the federal government. It reports to Congress, which oversees both the Federal Reserve System as a whole and also its components. The Board provides general guidance for the system, by guiding all aspects of the Federal Reserve System and all its activities; furthermore, it oversees the 12 Reserve Banks, sharing with them the responsibility for supervising and regulating certain financial institutions and activities.

As operating arms of the Federal Reserve System, the 12 Reserve Banks are private institutions, non-profit organisations, owned privately by their member bank intermediaries; they independently appoint boards composed of bankers and local business leaders. Each Reserve Bank operates within its own geographic area (district) of the USA and gathers information about the businesses and the needs of local communities in its region; these data are then factored into monetary policy decisions and other decisions made by the Reserve Board. Among the specific responsibilities of the Reserve Banks, the following (among others) must be mentioned: supervision of the state member banks (state-chartered banks that are members of the Federal Reserve System), as well as of bank and thrift holding companies and non-bank financial intermediaries regarded as systemically important; lending to depository intermediaries in order to guarantee adequate levels of liquidity in the financial market; provision of financial services; examination of financial institutions in order to guarantee compliance with federal consumer protection and lending regulations as well as promoting local community development.

Lastly, the Federal Open Market Committee consists of seven members of the Reserve Board and five Reserve Bank Presidents. The Chair of the Board is the Chair of the Federal Open Market Committee. Among other tasks, the Committee opens market operations that set US monetary policy to promote maximum employment, stable prices, and moderate long-term interest rates in the US economy.

Hence, the overall purpose of the Federal Reserve is to regulate and supervise financial institutions. This objective is achieved by setting up micro-prudential regulation and supervision applied to banks, holding companies and their affiliates, and also to other intermediaries, including non-bank financial companies designated to be subjected to prudential standards. Furthermore, the Federal Reserve engages in macro-prudential regulation and supervision aimed to promote the stability of the financial system as a whole. The micro-prudential and macro-prudential approaches should be considered from a complementary perspective, in the sense that in an overall perspective, the financial system has greater stability if its components are sound. It is nevertheless possible to identify several specific features. On one side, the micro-prudential approach aims to ensure the safety and soundness of each individual intermediary through in-depth examination and inspection of the structure, operation, and compliance of the institution supervised. On the other side, the macro-prudential approach focuses on the soundness and resilience of the financial system and therefore seeks to assess how the actions of a given institution can have an impact on other institutions and on the overall economic and financial system of the USA. As is known, the macro-prudential approach became extremely important on a global scale in the wake of the 2007–2009 financial crisis, which made it clear that the financial regulatory agencies—including, therefore, the Federal Reserve—must also take into account risks that can arise on the systemic level, as well as those pertaining to individual intermediaries (Masera, 2010). A too-narrow focus on the soundness of individual financial institutions makes it harder to detect and mitigate potential threats to financial stability that cut across many firms and markets (Board of Governors of the Federal Reserve System, 2016).

However, the traditional approach the Federal Reserve adhered to is that of micro-prudential supervision, which can be achieved by evaluation of the risk management system of a given intermediary, and also of its financial conditions and its compliance with laws and regulations. The purpose of these assessments is to allow an overall assessment of the stability of the single intermediary and its overall risk exposure, the adequacy of its corporate governance, and the quality of its board of directors and management; furthermore, such checks may allow identification of the operative areas where corrective action is required, thus making it possible for appropriate action to be undertaken.

The Federal Reserve follows a risk-based approach to consolidated supervision, aiming to identify the greatest risks and the emerging risks that could endanger the supervised institution. Additionally, the Federal Reserve's approach seeks to assess the intermediary's capacity to identify, measure, monitor, and control such risks (Flannery, 1998). For the largest institutions, whose size and operational complexity have considerably increased over the years, the risk-based approach is carried out mainly through a continuous process of on-site supervision rather than point-in-time examinations.

In order to reinforce supervision of the largest and most complex financial institutions, in 2010 the Federal Reserve set up the Large Institution Supervision Coordinating Committee (LISCC), entrusted with the task of coordinating supervisory activities and assessing the conditions of these operators (Yellen, 2015). Thus every year, LISCC carries out the Comprehensive Capital Analysis and Review of the largest banks. In the light of the financial crisis, it was decided that these assessments should be carried out in order to ensure that every large institution maintains a rigorous, forward-looking capital planning approach which will genuinely consider all the risks undertaken and also to make sure each institution has sufficient capital to allow continuation of its functions throughout times of economic and financial distress. Additionally, LISCC performs the Comprehensive Liquidity Annual Review which is designed to evaluate the liquidity position and liquidity risk position; finally, LISCC is also entrusted with performing the Supervisory Assessment of Recovery and Resolution Preparedness.

The results of the process of examination or inspection are the object of a specific report drawn up by the Federal Reserve. The report includes, among other things, ratings (such as CAMELS, see Sect. 10.4) on an intermediary's overall health conditions. If the intermediary is found to have problems with regard to stability or compliance, the Federal Reserve is authorised to impose ad hoc corrective measures.

10.3 Regulation and Supervision in the Light of the Financial Crisis

In the light of the 2007–2009 financial crisis (Colombini, 2012a, 2012b), as already mentioned, the Federal Reserve has defined frameworks and supervision programmes for the largest and most complex institutions. Specifically, the Federal Reserve carries out an annual assessment on whether the large financial firms (e.g. those with $50 billion or more in consolidated total assets) are sufficiently capitalised to cope with losses occurring during periods of stress and whether they can, at the same time, meet their commitments towards their creditors as well as continue to be active in financing the economy.

The annual assessment described here consists of two programmes: the above-mentioned Comprehensive Capital Analysis and Review and the Dodd-Frank Act supervisory stress testing. The latter constitutes a quantitative evaluation of the impact of stressful economic and financial market conditions on financial institutions. It is performed in the framework of the Dodd-Frank Wall Street Reform and Consumer protection Act (Dodd-Frank Act passed in 2010 and subsequently modified and integrated) as well as in harmony with the rules issued by the Reserve Board. The aim of the programme is to ascertain whether the capital ratios of the intermediaries are likely to undergo significant variations when they are subjected to stress. The results of this supervisory stress testing not only have the effect of prompting action in the form of capital planning for individual intermediaries, but they also integrate the quantitative assessment that forms part of the Comprehensive Capital Analysis and Review (Board of Governors of the Federal Reserve System, 2017).

The Dodd-Frank Act, as a fundamental element of the post-crisis reform process (Colombini, 2010), has—among other things—confirmed the importance of the macro-prudential approach to supervision and regulation as a means of reinforcing the financial system and reducing the probability of future crises and has endowed the Federal Reserve with greater responsibilities (Murphy, 2013). These include the task, as mentioned above, of carrying out an annual supervisory stress test. On the basis of the Dodd-Frank Act, the institutions subjected to the supervisory stress test are also required to undergo their own stress tests and to transmit the results to the Federal Reserve. The supervisory stress tests and the company-run stress tests, taken together, aim to provide the various stakeholders of the institution (management, public, supervisors, etc.) with the information they need in order to be able to understand the possible effect that stress conditions may have on the institution's capacity to cope with losses without, at the same time, interrupting its support for the economy.

During the supervisory stress test, the Federal Reserve focuses on balance sheets, risk-weighted assets (RWAs), net income, and the resulting post-stress capital levels and regulatory capital ratios. In performing the test, a set of capital action assumptions prescribed in the Dodd-Frank Act stress test rules are generally utilised. The projections are based on three macroeconomic scenarios (baseline, adverse, and severely adverse); the use of common capital action assumptions and scenarios enhances the comparability of the supervisory and company-run results (Board of Governors of the Federal Reserve System, 2017).

Finally, it should be noted that in order to underline the relevance of capital adequacy (further emphasised on the international level by the various Basel agreements, against which there are some coordination problems; see Acharya, 2011; Calandra Buonaura, 2013), the Dodd-Frank Act establishes a minimum leverage and risk-based requirements on a consolidated basis (Murphy, 2013) for certain institutions (e.g. bank holding companies, savings and loan holding companies, non-bank financial companies supervised by the Federal Reserve). Certain requirements are also laid down with regard to liquidity.

As a result of some differences between Basel III and the rules laid down in the Dodd-Frank Act, concerns may arise insofar as the full effectiveness of the capital requirements (and liquidity standards; Barth, Prabha, & Wihlborg, 2015) is concerned. Simply stated, it is a question of solving certain conflicts, such as that pertaining to the rating agencies, whose role has been confirmed by Basel III but not by the Dodd-Frank Act. Failure to solve such conflicts would make it difficult to achieve a fair level playing field on the international level. Attention should also be paid to the need to understand potential differences in the conceivable gap in the timescale and manner of transposition of Basel III to the USA and other countries (Masera, 2013). The drawback could result in the possibility of regulatory arbitrage and, in the last resort, of the development of a shadow banking system. Shadow banking, as is well known, represented an important source of unregulated risk during the 2007–2009 financial crisis.

10.4 The CAMELS Rating: Features and Goals

As noted above, the Federal Reserve examines the safety and soundness of financial stability in institutions by means of on-site bank examination in complement with off-site monitoring (Bernanke, 2007; Cole & Gunther, 1998). The latter aims to monitor the financial conditions and performance of institutions in order to identify those that may need closer scrutiny. The analysis can be based on judgemental assessment on periodic financial and other data relating to institutions' activities (supervisory screens) or statistical tests pertaining to financial ratios (econometric models). The aim is to identify weak institutions with poor or deteriorating financial profiles and thus to recognise as soon as possible any adverse trends developing in the banking system. Moreover, as the backbone of the supervisory process (Pettway & Sinkey, 1980), the on-site examination includes regular visits, interviews with management for assessment of the accuracy of the financial statements, accounting records, internal controls, and compliance with laws and regulations. At the end of these examinations, the Federal Reserve assigns a composite rating on the basis of the findings collected through on-site inspections; this rating is basically determined in line with the CAMELS rating system.

First defined in the 1970s, the CAMELS rating system is an indispensable tool for examiners and regulators, because it allows assessment of an institution's health conditions by examining various different aspects of its activities (Barr, Killgo, Siems, & Zimmel, 2002). The assessment is based on numerous information sources, such as financial statement, funding sources, macroeconomic data, budget, and cash flows. In other words, an institution's financial performance is evaluated from a number of different perspectives. Thus CAMELS is a highly accurate tool for use as a performance evaluator for banks and is capable of predicting failures (Barker & Holdsworth, 1993; Salhuteru & Wattimena, 2015).

CAMELS is a rating that is not disclosed to the public, in order to avoid—in the case of adverse judgements—negative repercussions that would damage the reputation of an individual bank, hampering attempts by the latter to operate and compete on the market.

CAMELS is the acronym for the following components: C = capital adequacy; A = asset quality; M = management quality; E = earning ability; L = liquidity; S = sensitivity to market risk. It is important to note that the last among these areas of investigation (sensitivity to market risk) was introduced at a later date (in 1996), to take into account the interest rate risk and, in particular, to achieve a rating that would succeed in pinpointing the potential effects that variations in the interest rate can have on capital (Baral, 2005; Dincer, Gencer, Orhan, & Sahinbas, 2011; Doumpos & Zopounidis, 2009; Swindle, 1995).

The CAMELS rating includes a score for each of its six components and an overall numeric composite or synthetic rating. This latter, assigned as an abridgement of the component ratings, is considered as the prime indicator of an institution's financial conditions, though it involves a certain degree of subjectivity. It is not the arithmetic mean of the six components, but it is an estimate which allows each component to be weighted to a variable extent, as a function of the specific situation of the institution considered. In other words, it reflects the interrelationship and divergent impact of its components.

In both cases (rating of the individual components and synthetic rating), the scale of judgements ranges from 1 (best rating with the lowest risk and the lowest concern of the supervisors) to 5 (worst rating with the highest risk and the highest concern). The meanings of these gradations are as follows:

- Rating 1: Sound in every aspect; strong performance. Any weaknesses are minor and can be managed in an ordinary manner by the management. No supervisory response is required.
- Rating 2: Fundamentally sound; satisfactory performance. Only moderate weaknesses are present. Supervisory response is limited.
- Rating 3: Some degree of supervisory concern; fair performance. Weaknesses may range from moderate to severe. This is to be considered as a watch category, requiring more than normal supervision.
- Rating 4: Unsafe and unsound practices or conditions; marginal performance, significantly below average. Presence of serious financial or managerial deficiencies, which could impair future viability of the institution. In this case, close supervision is required.
- Rating 5: Extremely unsafe and unsound practices or conditions; unsatisfactory performance which is critically deficient. The risk of failure in the short term is high. Constant supervision is called for.

With regard to the individual components that are taken into consideration for purposes of the CAMELS rating, the following observations should be noted.

C—Capital Adequacy

The centrality of capital adequacy is by now a well-known and consolidated concept. Its evaluation can be based on a number of factors, analysing such aspects as capital level, quality, and composition of capital; comparison with international (Basel agreements) and local supervisory requirements; the ability of management to address emerging needs for additional capital; growth trends and forecasts; level and trend of risk-weighted assets; quality, type, liquidity, and diversification of assets; loan concentrations; economic environment; and so on.

A—Asset Quality

This component reflects the exposure—both current and potential—to risk associated with the assets of a given institution. It thus provides insight into the management's ability to measure, monitor, and control the credit risk of the portfolio as a whole. The assessment of this area of analysis is based on examination of factors such as the distribution, severity, and trend of non-performing loans, loan concentration, adequacy of allowance for loan losses policies, and credit administration.

M—Management Quality

This indicator expresses the ability of the board of directors and management to identify, measure, monitor, and control the risks of the institution that is being analysed. Sound management is one of the most important factors behind financial institutions' performance. Therefore, the management component is generally regarded as the most important element for the purpose of determining composite rating. For instance, it is fundamental to assess how well management fulfils its roles and addresses its responsibilities. Other factors taken into consideration include the following: the management's capacity to plan and respond appropriately to changes in the business conditions and/or the launch of new products and entry into new markets; compliance with laws and regulations; the adequacy of audits and internal controls designed, among other aims, to promote effective operations and reliable financial and regulatory reporting; appropriateness of compensation policies.

E—Earning Ability

This rating evaluates the quality and quantity of both current and future earnings, in relation to the ability to provide retained earnings to capital.

As an example, earnings may be affected by inadequately managed risks; their quality may be diminished by undue reliance on extraordinary or non-recurring gains. Finally, future earnings may be adversely affected by an inappropriate prediction of operating expenses or by a weak risk management. The factors considered therefore bear a relation to the stability of earnings, and also to the quality and source of earnings, the level of expenses, and the adequacy of future earnings under a variety of economic conditions.

L—Liquidity

In order to assess this component, it is crucial to examine the current and future sources of liquidity compared to funding needs. For this purpose, the elements taken into consideration include the trend and stability of deposits, reliance on volatile sources of funds, convertibility of assets into cash without loss, access to securitisation and to money markets, and the establishment of contingency funding plans.

S—Sensitivity to Market Risk

This module refers to the hypothesis that variations in market conditions could adversely impact on earnings and/or economic capital. Market risk refers, in particular, to risk exposure associated with changes in interest rates, foreign exchange rates, commodity prices, equity prices, and so on. This component is analysed in terms of the management's ability to identify, measure, monitor, and control market risk.

The possibility of using a framework that is capable of evaluating the overall performance of the financial institutions is very important, especially in the current operative context, which has already for quite some time been characterised by a worldwide integration. As we have seen, by virtue of the CAMELS model, it becomes possible to express the financial performance of the intermediaries by investigating various different profiles of the activity carried out (capital, asset quality, management, earnings, liquidity, and market risk). These are factors that allow qualitative and quantitative analysis to be performed and which make it possible to express the overall strength of the institution. Furthermore, CAMELS generates information in terms of compliance and of the degree of supervisory concern and type of supervisory response that must be generated in order to minimise the adverse effects on banks. During the years of the financial crisis, this model was applied in the USA in order to assess which institutions needed special help in order to avert a negative impact on the entire financial system (systemic risk).

The relevance of the CAMELS model should also be considered with reference to the European context. Specifically, in recent years, the European banking supervisors (Colombini, 2015) have extended the analysis of financial situations to include a broader perspective than mere risk analysis (PWC, 2015). By making a comprehensive assessment, the aim is to include additional aspects, such as business and organisation. Thus it would appear that the new philosophy of the European supervisors is moving towards a model similar to CAMELS. Although there exists no declaration by the Single Supervisory Mechanism authorities that explicitly states such an assertion, the most recent decisions do seem to reflect the contents of the CAMELS model. This can be seen, for instance, in the case of capital adequacy, examined from a variety of perspectives, which among other issues also include stress testing. The centrality of capital adequacy is further emphasised by the decisions of the ECB in matters concerning SREP (Supervisory Review and Evaluation Process), as well as the ICAAP (Internal Capital Adequacy Assessment Process), and the restrictions on the dividend policy. Moreover, the European authorities' focus on asset quality is confirmed by the asset quality review, carried out for the first time by the ECB in 2014 as a preliminary step prior to introduction of the single supervisory system. Actions designed on the one hand to improve banking governance (Colombini, 2014) and, on the other, to reinforce earnings bear a relation to the M (management quality) and E (earning ability) of the CAMELS model, as well as to the actions performed with regard to liquidity (e.g. ILAAP—Internal Liquidity Adequacy Assessment Process).

Basically, then, the review system set up by the ECB to determine the SREP rating seems to be influenced by the line of reasoning underlying the CAMELS (ECB, 2013). In this context it should be borne in mind that SREP investigates the risk profiles of each bank from various different angles: the business model, governance and risk management, the capital position, and liquidity position (Reply, 2017). For each profile the banks receive a risk level score (from 1, the lowest level of risk, to 4, the highest risk); in addition banks receive a global score as average of the scores of the four components. The global score is used as a basis for determination (if necessary) of further capital requirements in addition to the Basel requirements (ECB, 2017).

Despite the above-mentioned strengths, together with the by now well-established popularity over the world (Rostami, 2015), there are some criticisms about CAMELS model. Among others, the critical aspects were pointed out by Hirtle & Lopez (1999), who noted that CAMELS is highly confidential and only exposed to institutions' management, for the purpose of protecting the business strategies. According to others (e.g. Gaytán & Johnson, 2002), the model is only parallel with the performance of the bank at the time of the examination, while variables in banks are highly volatile to market forces. In effect, tools like CAMELS are very useful if the analyses on the institutions are performed at frequent intervals and the financial conditions are stable. If this is not the case, the limit of such models could reside precisely in the fact of not succeeding in expressing the longer period conditions of the institutions. Consequently, the results would be of little avail as early indicators of future problems (Sahajwala & Van den Bergh, 2000).

10.5 Conclusions

Banking regulation and supervision in the USA are characterised by a certain complexity as well as well-developed tools for the assessment of the banks, like the CAMELS rating. This is a model created by the federal regulators to assess the overall performance of banks by analysing different perspectives (capital, asset, management, earnings, and sensitivity to market risk).

Recently the relevance of an overall assessment of the banks pushed the European supervisors towards an extension of the analysis of bank situations, in order to include not only the capital adequacy but also additional aspects, such as the business model, governance and risk management, risks to capital and to liquidity, and funding. It would appear, in other words, that the new rational of the European supervision is moving towards a model similar to CAMELS.

References

Acharya, V. V. (2011, August). *The Dodd-Frank Act and Basel III. Intentions, unintended consequences, transition risks, and lessons for India*. Working Paper IGC, International Growth Centre.

Baral, K. J. (2005). Health check-up of commercial banks in the framework of CAMEL: A case study of joint venture banks in Nepal. *Journal of Nepalese Business Studies, 2*(1), 41–55.

Barker, D., & Holdsworth, D. (1993). *The causes of bank failures in the 1980s.* Research Paper N. 9325, Federal Reserve Bank of New York.

Barr, R. S., Killgo, K. A., Siems, T. F., & Zimmel, S. (2002). Evaluating the productive efficiency and performance of U.S. commercial banks. *Managerial Finance, 28*(8), 3–25.

Barth, J. R., Prabha, A. P., & Wihlborg, C. (2015). *The Dodd-Frank act: Key features, implementation progress, and financial system impact.* Santa Monica: Milken Institute.

Bernanke, B. S. (2006, October 16). *Bank regulation and supervision—Balancing benefits and costs.*

Bernanke, B. S. (2007, October 11). *Central banking and bank supervision in the United States.*

Board of Governors of the Federal Reserve System. (2016). The federal reserve system. *Purposes & Functions.* https://doi.org/10.17016/0199-9729.10

Board of Governors of the Federal Reserve System. (2017, June). Dodd-frank act stress test 2017: Supervisory stress test. *Methodology and Results.*

Calandra Buonaura, V. (2013, Novembre 30). *L'attività degli intermediari finanziari nella regolamentazione sovranazionale.* Orizzonti del diritto commerciale.

Cole, R. A., & Gunther, J. W. (1998). Predicting bank failures: A comparison of on-and off-site monitoring systems. The value of a government monitor for U.S. banking firms. *Journal of Financial Services Research, 13*(2), 103–117.

Colombini, F. (2010). La crisi finanziaria e la riforma Obama. *Rivista Trimestrale di Diritto dell'Economia, 3*, 201–225.

Colombini, F. (2012a). Financial crises. Where do we stand? *Law and Economics Yearly Review, 1*(2), 234–262.

Colombini, F. (2012b). Banche, stati e banche centrali nelle crisi finanziarie. *Rivista Trimestrale di Diritto dell'Economia, 3*, 160–185.

Colombini, F. (2014). Bank governance. Lessons from the financial crises. *Law and Economics Yearly Review, 3*(2), 273–295.

Colombini, F. (2015). Risk, regulation, supervision and crises in the European Banking Union. *Law and Economics Yearly Review, 4*(2), 236–273.

Dincer, H., Gencer, G., Orhan, N., & Sahinbas, K. (2011). A performance evaluation of the Turkish banking sector after the global crisis via CAMELS ratios. *Procedia—Social and Behavioral Sciences, 24*, 1530–1545.

Doumpos, M., & Zopounidis, C. (2009). *A multicriteria bank rating system.* European Working Group "Multiple Criteria Decision Aiding, Spring, Series 3, 19, pp. 17–19.

ECB. (2013, November). *Structural characteristics of the euro area and US banking sectors: Key distinguishing features.*

ECB. (2017, March). *Annual report on supervisory activities.*

Economic and Monetary Affairs. (2015). *Overview and structure of financial supervision and regulation in the US.*
Flannery, M. J. (1998). Using market information in prudential bank supervision: A review of the U.S. empirical evidence. *Journal of Money, Credit and Banking, 30*(3), 273–305.
Gaytán, A., & Johnson, C. A. (2002). *A review of the literature on early warning systems for banking crises.* Central Bank of Chile, Working Paper n. 183.
Hirtle, B. J., & Lopez, J. A. (1999). Supervisory information and the frequency of bank examinations. *Federal Reserve Bank of New York Economic Policy Review, 5,* 1–20.
Masera, R. (2010). Reforming financial systems after the crisis: A comparison of EU and USA, PSL. *Quarterly Review, 63*(255), 299–362.
Masera, R. (2013). US Basel III Final Rule on banks' capital requirements: A different-size-fits-all approach, PSL. *Quarterly Review, 66*(267), 387–402.
Murphy, E. V. (2013, January 30). *Who regulates whom and how? An overview of U.S. financial regulatory policy for banking and securities markets.*
Pettway, R. H., & Sinkey, J. F. (1980). Establishing on-site bank examination priorities: An early-warning system using accounting and market information. *The Journal of Finance, 35*(1), 137–150.
PWC—PricewaterhouseCoopers. (2015, December). *The Banking Union, moving forward.*
Reply. (2017, February). *SSM SREP.* Where are we after the first two exercises?
Rostami, M. (2015). Determination of Camels model on bank's performance. *International Journal of Multidisciplinary Research and Development, 2*(10), 652–664.
Sahajwala, R., & Van den Bergh, P. (2000). *Supervisory risk assessment and early warning systems, Basel committee on banking supervision.* Working Paper, N. 4.
Salhuteru, F., & Wattimena, F. (2015). Performance with CAMELS ratios towards earnings management practices in state banks and private banks. *Advances in Social Sciences Research Journal, 2*(3), 301–314.
Swindle, C. S. (1995). Using CAMEL ratings to evaluate regulator effectiveness at commercial banks. *Journal of Financial Services research, 9*(2), 123–141.
Yellen, I. (2015, March 3). *Improving the oversight of large financial institutions.* Speech at the Citizens Budget Commission, New York, Board of Governors of the Federal Reserve System.

CHAPTER 11

Raising Capital or Improving Risk Management and Efficiency

Fabiano Colombini

11.1 Introduction

Solvency concerns the bank's ability to honour its debts at any cost. This, in turn, presupposes the availability of monetary resources during crisis periods. Solvency is measured by the ratio between capital and total deposits or total assets, or better, of assets exposed to risk. The latter concept basically reproposes that of capital adequacy.

The solvency risk concerns the different ability of banks to settle their debts at any cost. Solvency is achieved by means of systematically higher asset values as compared to liabilities, thereby indicating positive levels of the bank's capital. This highlights the problem of growth of profit and of a bank's recourse to market instruments in order to develop its capital and its monetary resources and production volumes. The expansion path starts from the raising of capital and positive performance, which in turn increases sound business and generation of profit.

Capital raising creates premises for solvency, stability, business evolution and business growth in individual banks in Europe and worldwide. Capital raising is inspired by regulation and, at the same time, by supervision.

F. Colombini (✉)
Department of Economics and Management, University of Pisa, Pisa, Italy

F. Colombini (ed.), *Raising Capital or Improving Risk Management and Efficiency?*, https://doi.org/10.1007/978-3-319-71749-4_11

Bank management is conducted through choices concerning the actual current situation and the future situation. Capital represents a key variable in business, but the improvement of risk management and efficiency constitutes the best reply as a means of reinforcing structural conditions for survival. This chapter aims to investigate these elements in order to express critical issues and critical points for the evolution of individual banks and their business.

11.2 Raising Capital: A Measure for Solvency

On closer inspection, insolvency arises from an excessive risk level, which brings about reductions in value of financial asset portfolios (Johnson, 1993; Kohn, 2004; Saunders & Cornett, 2008). This testifies to a problem of appropriate choices for risk identification, measurement and control, as well as the need to minimise the impact on a bank's capital and to ensure its survival on the market.

Maintenance of solvency presupposes management choices based on appropriate principles of rigour and, above all, on accuracy in credit risk assessment. It is also necessary to ensure the creation of a loan portfolio which, over time, will prove capable of restoring and renewing cash flow, together with the ordinary cash flow arising from interest collection.

Solvency has close links to liquidity because the sources of liquidity arise from assets, liabilities and off-balance sheet items (OBSIs) and from the costs and revenue trend, because the sources of solvency are directly affected by asset and liability values and by achievement of profit.

Solvency is also linked to management of the other risks, as their impact influences the economic outcome and leads to fluctuations in the value of assets and liabilities. Raising capital will be able to offset the solvency at a given time and not in the medium and long term. Therefore regulatory and supervisory authorities require capital to protect the bank from insolvency, which is measured at a given time period. Evolution of competition, inputs, output, costs and revenue allows banks to create conditions in which the level of capital may not be inadequate for the evolution of economy.

Increasing capital constraints by regulation and supervision stresses the use of capital in order to solve bank problems: is this a rational approach or should it be investigated more deeply? Capital constraints should be able to mitigate the insolvency risk, but this is only a quantitative solution in order to absorb losses which have been generated by bank management.

Raising capital usually implies a deterioration in asset values and costs and revenue, attributable to poor quality in corporate governance as well as in risk management and efficiency.

It is important to stress that improvement in risk management and efficiency represents the structural conditions that are necessary to recreate the premises for a shift towards positive trends in costs and revenue and, at the same time, in the evolution of assets, liabilities and capital. This is the key point to pursue in the evolution of management conditions through European banks.

Raising capital is the most widespread regulatory and supervisory measure concerning banking intermediaries in the evolution of banking systems in Europe. In what direction will banks evolve after the raising of capital? The future of a well-capitalised and well-managed bank will be less unstable and less unpredictable than that of a poorly capitalised and badly managed bank. Competition can create growth problems for production volumes, reducing the basis for the bank's profit. Raising capital will change the dividend distribution and, at the same time, the distinction between the payout ratio and the retention ratio: profit will thus be split into the part for distribution and the part for retention.

In this context, supervisory authorities should create an organisation unit for monitoring the level and evolution of capital absorbed by individual banks in Europe and the number of capital procedures to reinforce the bank capital. The greater the number of procedures for raising capital and the more frequent the recapitalisation, the more serious the problems of individual banks are likely to be. This is a sign of intrinsic weakness of the individual bank, and the raising of capital imposed by regulation and by supervision in different time periods can be considered the clear signal. The problem, however, is the wasting of capital which can be measured only in the case of problems, crises or failures incurred with bank exits from the market.

11.3 Raising Capital: Nature and Stability

Raising the level of capital and improving risk management and efficiency allow individual banks to achieve structural and solid reinforcement over time: the bank will be more solid and thus better able to offset adverse events and stay on the market. This is a purely statistical observation, which is important but at the same time is not sufficient to grant insight into the genuine current status and future evolution, as capital plays a crucial role for banking business strategies.

Turnover of loans can be high or slow: in the former of these two cases it has a good impact on liquidity, in the latter case it has a bad impact on liquidity, underlying the relative strategies to set up. It is important to pursue an adequate level of turnover in order to obtain a genuine impact on liquidity and management of the individual bank.

In this framework, capital management is designed to encourage the growth of available resources, reinforce the bank's business wealth and ensure respect for adequacy criteria. Its development and management constitute a premise for solvency and profitability.

Bank financial structure rests to a large extent on indebtedness, rather than capital. The following types of indebtedness can be distinguished: short-term, medium-term or long-term maturities, fixed or indexed interest rate and the consequent financial charges that reduce the level of profits; the bank's capital, on the other hand, is characterised by indeterminate maturity, an oscillating rate of return and dividends that affect the distribution of profits.

The peculiarity of bank financial structure is associated with the trust and reputation acquired on the market. The acquisition of trust and reputation facilitates the issue and placement of a bank's liabilities: accordingly, indebtedness may rise considerably to high levels. Changes in the financial structure and, therefore, the utilisation of instruments involving debt and capital respond to different needs on the part of the public: essentially, these divergent needs involve insufficient—or, alternatively, a vast quantity—of information concerning business areas.

The strategic role of capital arises from the protection awarded to depositors and purchasers of liabilities in the hypothesis of failed repayment of credits, which would reduce the value of a bank's assets and could lead to its insolvency and bankruptcy, since there exist well-known problems of adverse selection and moral hazard that can generate negative outcomes and ensuing chain reactions.

Capital is regarded as the bulwark of the stability and solidity of commercial banks for three fundamental reasons: absorption of fluctuations in value of the assets, stabilisation in the sources of financing and absence of contractually established remuneration constraints (Berger, Herring, & Szegö, 1995; Pecchioli, 1987; Pringle, 1974; Taggart & Greenbaum, 1978).

Differences among risks, when the latter are related to different business areas, lead to unequal requirements as regards capital and processes aimed at increasing capital within banks (Lindquist, 2004). Information asymmetries, the extent of available instruments, the danger of massive and rapid requests to convert deposits into money must be taken into account when a bank seeks to identify the suitable level of capital.

A capital increase creates the premises for development of intermediated and productive volumes, providing positive influence on the formative process of the profit and loss account. Furthermore, the increased incidence of capital versus liabilities reinforces the degree of solidity of the bank's financial situation and, therefore, the solvency of individual banks.

The increase in capital and available resources is reflected in the effects on investments, regarding especially investment in new technologies.

With regard to commercial banks, for a medium and long time period horizon there exists a direct relation, as can easily be noted, between the expansion of capital and that of loans. This progressively enhances available resources and also ensures protection of buyers of liabilities (Gunther & Moore, 1993; Moore, 1992).

The increase in capital is linked to the following aspects: retention of profits for reserve formation, placement of shares on the market and creation of subordinate liabilities.

In screening and monitoring concerning the range of loans, the bank aims to encourage the size development of companies and, at the same time, to create the premises for economic growth. By granting loans to reliable clients, the bank pursues its own interests but also pursues the general interest consisting in the reinforcement of enterprises which, more than others, contribute to economic growth while maintaining solid bases for the future.

In European banks, capital is a tool used very frequently by regulatory and supervisory authorities essentially with the aim of creating a protection against bad events and negative impacts on the economic account. Raising capital is useful but at the same time creates remuneration problems and investment problems.

Therefore the "walls" against bad events should be able to provide safety and soundness for just a period of time. Changing production and distribution processes, rationalising costs and revenue and profits leading to best practices of risk management and efficiency constitute the true and real tools to activate for restoring and improving the internal conditions of individual banks and, as a consequence, of the banking system.

Banks in Europe have a loan portfolio distinguished by good loans and bad loans. The good loans create turnover and, at the same time, return rates; in contrast, bad loans create problems for repayment in capital and interest. Increasing deterioration worsens the economic conditions and liquidity conditions of the bank.

11.4 Raising Capital: Bank Business Evolution

Banks pursue the objective of expansion of on and off-balance sheet items and volumes over time in order to create the premises for profits and positive performance. Banking balance sheets have grown rapidly in a low interest rate environment and in the presence of a surge in innovative instruments (Acharya, Cooley, Richardson, & Walter, 2010; Wang, 2017).

Banks take deposits and make loans to individuals and firms (commercial banking). Some banks engage in underwriting, dealing, market making of securities and derivatives, management of personal and real estate property, consultancy, mergers and acquisitions, financial planning, custody and administration of securities, intermediation and selling of securities, derivatives, investment trusts and real estate investment trusts, pension funds and insurance policies (investment banking).

The evolution of the banking business has underlined the shift from commercial banking to investment banking and therefore an increase in the range of risks and in total risk. The process of identification, measurement and management of risks is of crucial importance in creating and maintaining conditions for profits and solvency. This shift is evident when looking at the assets side, the liabilities side and income sources as the share of net interest income falls and non-interest income rises.

The universal model in the banking sector combines commercial banking with investment banking and can be regarded as a critical issue for managing risks at a sustainable level for the individual institution and for the whole financial system.

Large banks tend to apply the universal banking model in the European Union (EU) for production diversification and also for risk diversification, adopting jointly the instruments of commercial banking and investment banking. Moreover, the expansion of business areas leads to a corresponding increase in the range of risks, with the result that risk management assumes a progressively more significant role. As a consequence of the links among different business areas, a bank may encounter difficulty in estimating its total risk exposure; accordingly, many banks engage in risk transfer as a practice for management of asset classes at higher credit risk.

The systematic use of this practice has negative repercussions on the two classical banking activities: screening and monitoring. Screening and monitoring reduce or, in a very optimistic assumption, completely eliminate the problems, respectively, of information asymmetry *ex ante* and, therefore, of adverse selection and the problem of information asymmetry *ex post* and, therefore, of moral hazard.

A considerable number of banks have undertaken the development of business areas which are parallel to the classical areas of raising and lending funds. Many of these developments frequently involve high leverage areas, as in the case of derivatives (Colombini, 1999, 2004; Colombini & Calabrò, 2010). Restoring rational choices in the context of commercial banks constitutes a requirement for medium and long period of financial stability, awarding less importance to growth of their capital.

Dealing and market making of securities, derivatives and proprietary trading have become increasingly important over time. There has also been a remarkable growth in derivatives, especially in the over-the-counter (OTC) market. Since the beginning of the third millennium, securitisation markets have grown rapidly and created the shadow banking system, built up essentially by special purpose vehicles (SPVs) and structured investment vehicles (SIVs).

Extensive recourse to leverage and, at the same time, the development of the phenomenon of the shadow banking system (Claessens, Ratnovski, & Singh, 2012; Gorton & Metrick, 2010; Lemma, 2016; Stein, 2010) imply avoidance of capital requirements, in a bank context, through the constitution of off-balance sheet vehicles. The latter, in particular, run up debts on the market of commercial papers such as short-term securities and use the achieved resources to purchase long-term securities, such as asset-backed securities (ABS). The difference between the return on purchased securities and the cost of financing through commercial papers creates grounds for the attainment of profits by means of special purpose vehicles.

The shadow banking system represents one of the main ways in which vast quantity of risk generated and transferred is rendered opaque by banks (Pozsar, Adrian, Ashcraft, & Boesky, 2012). It is important to introduce greater transparency into financial intermediaries' balance sheets, above all as regards OBSIs, which, in the light of financial crises on a global scale, highlight irrationalities in the banks' management.

An adequate level of capital is necessary according to the regulations (Basel I, II, III and the forthcoming IV) and to the supervisory framework:

the former represents the prudential line while the latter (i.e. the supervisory framework) is in the discretional line. Prudence versus discretion: two different and opposite views create capital constraints and therefore contribute to the level of bank's capital.

Regulation imposes capital constraints by establishing capital coefficients for their achievement and respect through time periods (prudential view). Supervision intervenes generally when critical adjustments are necessary (discretional view). Whereas regulation is operational, reflecting changes through time, supervision is operational from time to time, checking the asset and liability values and costs and revenue trend of the given bank and, if necessary, making the decision to intervene. There is a remarkable point that should be emphasised: the time lag between the origin of the critical situations and the supervisory decision to impose the raising of capital is usually too long for several reasons, and this interval of time leads to deterioration in bank values.

Therefore, the level of bank capital is the final result of free choices, regulatory constraints and supervisory constraints. The free component involves a very restricted area as an individual decision: is this bureaucratic procedure underlining a rational approach? This is not clear and it appears to be based on a plurality of bodies and on a plurality of calculations with reference to the composition of the risk-weighted assets (RWAs) and the off-balance sheet items (OBSIs).

Available details seem to testify to the complexity and bureaucratic approach to distinguishing between banks with low or adequate level of capital. Credit risk and solvency risk are important in order to estimate capital needs for the present and future time. Therefore, the level of capital is a crucial variable for the business areas, as well as for the lending and investment process and development of the bank in question. Strategic and operational choices contribute to achieving good or bad results according to the professional skills and capacity of the management and the reactions of competition and markets.

In this framework, the performance considers the results achieved in different business areas. It examines the construction and analysis of a series of financial, capital and economic indicators, and in particular, the focus on profits.

The contraction in net interest income drives bank intermediaries to reinforce their non-interest income through a larger range of products. This causes an extension in instruments and business areas and the consequent increase in risk range and mutual interrelations.

Responsibility for bad or good results is attributed to administrators of the bank. Therefore, in a crisis or bank-failure event, the responsibility falls primarily on the administrators, especially at the high bank levels, who are responsible for decision-making and choices regarding instruments, bank business, bank areas and risk management. Thus a sort of automatism should be introduced in the application of financial penalties on the administrators by the supervisory authorities, especially at the top level of the bank in question, who should be instructed to "fix" the damage on the basis of new and more severe rules in the event of crisis or bank failure. They should be very clearly aware of the warning signs and of initiatives to prevent or offset the worsening of bank situation.

Due to the fact that recent financial crises have dramatically focused attention on the adverse impact of bank crises on banking, and on the economy, a tool against any morally hazardous behaviour is required. In this context, the new proposal concerns the creation of various precautionary funds fed through a percentage of administrators' high salaries, to be used in the event of crisis or bank failure, and to be returned in the event of no crisis or bank failure. Administrators, especially at the top level, are always held responsible for crisis or failure, and therefore the bail-in should have a more serious and more incisive effect on the category in question.

Also necessary is a complete revision of corporate governance bank models, as well as a turnover of top management, raising the level of professional competence and capacities with the introduction of operators capable of accurately evaluating the risk-return relation in the medium and long term.

11.5 Regulation: Critical Issues

The application of Basel III and the forthcoming Basel IV are inspired, as in the past, by prudential logic stressing progressive corrections and inadequacies in regulatory measures in the EU. Basel III has introduced higher and better levels of capital, in the framework of risk-weighted assets, and, at the same time, the liquidity risk and the leverage to be implemented progressively over time. It can thus be regarded as based on a prudential approach.

It does not exclude additional capital corrections for the banks which are subject to AQR, stress tests, on-site inspections and the SREP evaluation carried out by the supervisory unit at the ECB. Accordingly, this can be regarded as adopting a discretionary approach which highlights overlapping and excessive regulations and uncertainties for banks in the EU.

The transition to Basel III and recent additional steps show that the previous Basel I and Basel II regulations proved to be inadequate and unable of preventing the birth and the effects of subprime mortgage financial crisis and sovereign debt crisis in Europe, which produced serious repercussions on financial stability and economic growth.

The application of Basel III implies compliance with capital requirements indicated as equal for all banks and checked and reformulated in several cases by the supervisory authorities through additional corrections, thus increasing the impact on capital.

Balance sheet assets and off-balance sheet items, even when classified, are considered for subsequent evaluation and inclusion in the denominator for the capital requirement calculation.

Ratings are used to assess the creditworthiness of borrowers who approach a bank and become customers. The application of ratings leads to the creation of different classes and different weighting coefficients, ranging from low values for not particularly risky loans to increasingly high values for risky loans, raising capital requirement differences.

The risk-based approach postulates the subdivision of the loan portfolio into different classes. For each class or class set, rating intervals are identified, which imply the application of increasingly high weighting coefficients upon the worsening of the associated rating interval.

Thus the loan portfolio is split into different classes and class sets for the internal application of percentage weighting coefficients on the basis of rating assignments.

The bank's choices should be set according to rigorous principles, selecting the best customers for their positive effects on the credit risk, the lightest impacts on capital absorption and, therefore, the best stimulations for intermediated and production volumes.

Therefore, with equal rating interval, the uniform coefficient approach does not take into account this non-homogeneity in loan diversification which is often important for the resulting credit loss effects and the consequent impact on the economic account and on capital.

The types of capital ratios, and adherence thereto, sometimes necessitate a forcing in management choices. Their imposition has spread in various countries, mainly aiming at stability through internal reinforcement in crisis situations.

Taking a closer look, capital ratios neither eliminate nor lower corporate risks, which may even suffer increases; they merely create the premises for the reduction or elimination of losses occurring in negative events. This is a crucial point: regulatory and supervisory capital requirements do not contribute to shifts or reductions in the level and range of bank risks but create the resources for more greater absorption of losses in negative events. Therefore, bank survival relies on the financial operators' skills and professional capacity for rationality and sound risk management over time.

Capital ratios meet the need for prediction and allocation of an adequate level of capital, essentially with regard to negative impacts and losses caused by credit, market and operational risks. Capital is considered the main aid to commercial banking stability and solidity for three reasons: absorption of asset value fluctuation, stabilisation of financing sources and absence of contractual remuneration constraints (Berger, Herring, & Szegö, 1995; Pecchioli, 1987; Pringle, 1974; Taggart & Greenbaum, 1978).

The main target for supervisory authorities, distinguishing between the significant banks, as examined by the supervisory unit at the ECB, and the less significant banks, as examined by the national competent authorities, is the setting of higher capital levels in relation to higher risk levels of financial instrument types, thus reducing the incentive for moral hazard. However, the effects of capital ratios on moral hazard are not entirely uniform, diverging according to the theoretical model followed.

Real guarantees, personal guarantees, credit derivatives and balance sheet compensations stress credit risk mitigation and, thus, benefits for the estimation of capital requirements.

Capital coefficients imply the calculation of ratios between the regulatory capital and balance sheet asset and off-balance sheet item types, appropriately risk-weighted. The total capital used is greater than the strict capital account, including not only the real capital but also any subordinated debts, as the latter are bound to periodical remuneration, and subject to repayment obligation.

The standardised model on credit risk postulates the partition of balance sheet assets and off-balance sheet instruments into classes for the application of the weights established by the regulatory authorities, in the same way for all banks.

The reactions and behaviour of individual banks differ widely. These distinctions are weakly justified by the uniform and generalised capital ratio application due to the lack of assessment for each instrument on the portfolio risk, and also to the identical weight assigned to different loans within the same class.

It also follows that the results achieved are the outcome of initial starting situations which postulate different levels of capital and different levels of composition of business areas and related instruments.

Each class incorporates diversity in its instruments and in the composition of customers, but this also gives rise to risk differences. In addition, the degree of correlation between different asset instruments is not taken into account, ignoring the postulates of diversification (Grenadier & Hall, 1996; Santomero, 1991; Shaefer, 1987).

The different capacity of individual banks to create a diversified lending portfolio is not taken into account (Colombini, 2008). An ideal system should consider the increase in risk to the portfolio arising from the introduction of assets instead of limiting itself to a mere capital addition. Thus the risk associated with different financial instruments should be correctly appreciated.

Even individual banks' capacity to select and monitor loans to customers is neglected, despite the existence of differences in methods and choices which influence the concrete risk of each individual loan and of the portfolio as a whole. A uniform coefficient application does not take into account these differences in risk screening and risk monitoring, which often prove to be fundamental in the subsequent credit loss and consequent impact on the economic account.

In the framework of the theory of information asymmetries, the position of individual bank intermediaries for news and data collection and the production of information is necessarily very different. Accordingly, higher or lower costs will be involved. The creation and archiving of data on customer relations, as well as bank capacity to produce information and the related costs, reflect the strengths and weaknesses in comparison and competition with other similar intermediaries.

Therefore classes are rather broad; they do not take into account the existence of diversification, nor the benefits of methods of screening and monitoring; furthermore, they present substantial static elements and are essentially set up for the creation of conditions of control performed by supervisory authorities.

At the base of the internal models, there is the value at risk (VaR), which constitutes the maximum potential loss affecting a portfolio of financial instruments in a precise time interval, calculated assuming a determined probability. VaR considers the impact of the variations in market factors on the value of each single financial instrument, such as interest rates and exchange rates.

The internal model on credit risk introduces internal ratings for the appreciation of balance sheet assets and off-balance sheet items. This model reflects evaluations and calculations from individual banks and makes it necessary to obtain the approval of supervisory authorities.

The internal model presupposes individual banks' best capacity for risk appreciation and management, in comparison with the standardised model, drawn up and imposed by the supervisory authorities. The problem lies in the trade-off evaluation, between setting and realisation expenses, together with consequent capital constraints on one side and benefits inherent in the best risk management on the other.

This model allows VaR calculation, identifying individual banks' credit risk exposure and, therefore, the amount of capital, following the indications provided by the supervisory authorities for construction and operation.

Therefore, the identification of individual banks' best position in credit risk measurement and control does not imply a restriction in the role of supervisory authorities, which remain constantly committed to an *ex ante* and *ex post* verification of the characteristics and results of banks' internal models.

The internal model of market risks, in turn, postulates the best capacity of individual banks' risk appreciation in comparison with the standardised model drawn up by the supervisory authorities. The issue lies in the joint appreciation of setting and realisation expenses and the consequent capital constraint on one side and benefits inherent in best management of risk on the other.

This model permits VaR calculation which identifies the market risk exposure for individual banks, and, therefore, the capital amount, thus complying with the indications provided by supervisory authorities for construction and operation. A central issue lies in the imposed requirements check which proves to be very complex, feeding outflanking possibilities and lack of capital growth. Such a circumstance raises the issue of introducing capital ratios for uniform application and, at the same time, of a simple check by supervisory authorities (Bliss, 1995).

The process of financial innovation must also be taken into account, and, in particular, financial instruments for credit and market risk coverage such as swaps, options and futures must be adequately included in the set of rules.

More generally, the different levels of trust and benefit of risk management raise different strategic answers, inherent in the changed balance sheet assets and off-balance sheet items for the reduction of potential loss and/or for the growth of capital which is suitable for their coverage.

The performance considers the results achieved in various different business areas. The aim is to construct and analyse a series of financial, capital and economic indicators and, in particular, the focus on profit.

In this framework, the pre-commitment approach means a solution to the capital requirement issue, left unresolved by the models based purely on VaR application. This would allow preventive definition of the capital necessary to cover negative impacts caused by market risks, calculating exactly the potential loss (Considine, 1998; Kupiec & O'Brien, 1995).

This model postulates the identification of the time period and the level of potential loss and implies the application of bank penalties if errors are encountered, essentially reflecting canons and internal needs. The introduction of penalties and time intervals for the check should create the necessary incentives for a correct and rational setting. The pre-commitment approach is distinct from previous approaches and allows full freedom in individual banks' choice of parameters.

Moreover, the application of the pre-commitment approach presupposes the solution of certain aspects such as penalty modalities, check frequency and consequent penalties introduced by supervisory authorities, isolated or joint use of other models, possible link between potential loss predetermination and capital growth (Bliss, 1995).

11.6 Supervision: Critical Issues

The various Basel I, Basel II and Basel III and the forthcoming Basel IV rules progressively tend to an increase in the compliance costs of individual banks while disregarding the fact that banks differ greatly between small and medium banks in comparison with the largest banking institutions. The issue for banks is the use of rational and rigorous methods for the management of business areas and related risks, from the viewpoint of producing profits in the short, medium and long term. The establishment of more and more rules introduces greater complexity in bank regulation and, at the same time, increases compliance costs. Therefore a comparison of costs and benefits arising from the introduction of regulation should be performed.

The habitual focus on increasing capital is not the correct approach, because it makes use of a unitary attitude, that is, the "one size fits all" approach (Bliss, 1995), to banks which are profoundly different in their business areas and risk range. Rules essentially consider a loss coverage issue through an adequate capital level, and this is a very different matter from the actual ability to manage the entire risk range.

Increasing the number and complexity of rules tends to introduce further complications in the task of supervision, but the main aim of supervision is still that of checking and ensuring control over the application of the rules in European banks. A banking crisis requires supervision initiatives which usually involve the raising of capital as a standard approach to build up a "wall" against the worsening or failure of the situation of a bank.

Therefore supervisory capital constraints, together with regulatory capital constraints, imply a reduction of the capacity to lend to the economy and do not introduce improvements in risk management.

Quantitative data should be gathered and updated over time on banks that are experiencing a period of difficulties or which are undergoing supervisory imposition of capital. Records should also be kept with regard to the time periods involved, in order to trace recurrent events and, potentially, to predict which banks are likely need new capital again in the future and which banks will improve and achieve stability. The repetition of supervisory capital raising from time to time for the same banks is an adverse phenomenon, as it points to survival by capital raising and unstable internal conditions. Such a situation is a signal of poor quality management. Therefore, the supervisory measures are unsatisfactory and do not represent definitive solutions for banks in trouble; furthermore, in no way the issue of the lack of internal capacity for adding new resources to improve the quality of management is taken into consideration.

In a medium and long time perspective, a correspondence between capital erosion and bad management will become evident. Thus macro supervision will highlight the problem of "wasting capital" and the absence of ultimate solutions. Moreover, building up and checking quantitative data at the central level of the ECB for significant banks and the national level of NCAs for less significant banks will provide insight into the evolution of the European banking system.

Supervision is characterised by gathering and analysing information, checking bank evolution, drawing up an assessment on the bank. The result can be expressed in the overall SREP which reflects the supervisors' overall assessment on the bank's viability. The SREP is built up on quantitative and non-quantitative requirements: the principle applied is that an increase in risk should be matched by the raising of capital in banks involved.

In the USA, supervisors use CAMELS, which is a highly accurate tool for use as a performance evaluator for banks and is capable of predicting failures (Barker & Holdsworth, 1993; Salhuteru & Wattimena, 2015). CAMELS is a rating that is not disclosed to the public, in order to avoid—in the case of adverse judgements—negative repercussions that would damage the reputation of an individual bank, hampering attempts by the latter to operate and compete on the market.

In this framework it is important to stress the elements composing CAMELS for performance evaluation. In the perspective of reviewing the European supervision procedure, CAMELS is distinguished by the characteristic of considering a number of large and useful indicators for assessing an individual bank's viability.

The most important issue for a bank is the accurate and rational ability to identify, measure and manage the entire risk range, in a manner closely related to the bank's business areas. Attention should focus on instruments for a positive impact on profit production and on simple and risk-adjusted performance indicators.

It is in the coordination of ideas and actions on a European level that it becomes possible to improve the potential of financial and economic systems, reducing the global imbalance between creditor and debtor countries which can exacerbate geopolitical tensions.

The creation of the banking union and the experimental ECB asset quality review concerning significant banks lay the foundations for uniform analysis and modes of risk assessment ways for banks in Europe.

The single supervision rule postulates control over bank capital ratios on the basis of Basel III and the forthcoming Basel IV application and control over economic, financial and capital trends. Problematic situations are monitored as soon as difficulties become evident, from their initial phase onwards; the development of an asset quality review also plays an important role, together with stress tests and the SREP as an overall indicator for identifying weaknesses, poor initiatives and bad practices.

However, the ECB alone cannot create strong premises for economic development in Europe. Political choices are necessary in order to move towards structural economic reforms in the short term, to be followed by much more solid integration, removing all sources of uncertainty affecting finance and economics (Andenas & Supino, 2015; Capriglione & Sacco Ginevri, 2015; McCormick, 2015).

11.7 Improving Risk Management and Efficiency

Capital raising for satisfying regulatory and supervisory capital requirements contributes to increasing the capital level and therefore the absorption capacity in the event of unexpected losses. A higher level of capital will be able to handle negative economic results and bank survival: solvency can be measured at given times.

Improving risk management and efficiency allows banks to achieve structural conditions to recreate positive premises towards positive trends in costs and revenue and, at the same time, in the evolution of assets, liabilities and capital. This is the key point to pursue in the evolution of management conditions within European banks and within world banks.

There is a relationship between risk management and efficiency: improving risk management allows creation of the best conditions that will lead to bank efficiency, as it implies costs' reductions and, in good experiences, revenue increases and, consequently, a more effective reshaping of costs and revenue in the composition of the profit and loss account. This means that improved risk management can be considered as a good premise for improving both bank efficiency and the bank soundness and survival capacity. Additionally, an increase in bank resilience will enable a bank to reinforce its efficiency and economic account, moving from one position to another along a path of modernisation of business models with upgraded production and distribution conditions. These improvements constitute indicators of better survival capacity.

In this framework, the financial crises that arose in 2007 in the USA and extended throughout the world resulted in a marked number of bank failures in the USA and the world. This is a feature that led to reductions in bank industries, but, at the same time, it reinforced bank resilience, as much as poor quality banks were unable to continue their business in many parts of the world.

Financial crises and bank failures thus highlight the inefficiency of many banks. There is a need for the overall banking system to evolve towards greater efficiency in production, distribution and shaping of average curves and marginal curves, not only in the context of Italian but also in European and worldwide banks.

This is a crucial point that must be addressed in order to create the best evolution of production lines, distribution, shape of average curves and marginal curves of all banks. Emphasis should also be placed on the crucial point of improving risk management and efficiency in the evolution of regulation and supervision, within both European and world banks. Thus incentives should be created to improve risk management, especially credit risk, with greater awareness of the crucial role of better efficiency.

Building up new regulatory rules and new supervisory procedures based purely on capital raising will not be sufficient to create good conditions for the sound evolution of banks in Europe and worldwide. Capital raising can be useful to satisfy the need for solvency risk measurement at a given time; on the other hand, when moving through time periods the situation can change within a short or medium length of time, recreating adverse economic results. In particular, the capital problem may reappear, creating a vicious circle in which both capital need and capital "wasting" will be intensified.

In short, reinforcing capital at the actual time for a negative event incurred is in many cases not sufficient to create a good solution for the individual bank from a micro supervisory and a macro supervisory perspective: it merely increases bank problems with the same banks from time to time.

This is a clear-cut indication of a larger problem which calls for an internal solution by reviewing and changing: governance, business models, production, distribution, costs, revenue and management. It thus requires close and complimentary interaction between the bank and its quality management. As should be clear from the foregoing discussion, the solution will not lie in simple capital raising, thereby merely satisfying the new regulations and supervision requirements. The real solution depends on a genuine capacity for internal structural changes, moving towards increasingly sound risk management procedures and better procedures for all types of efficiency (see Chap. 4).

Along this route, regulators and supervisors should be urged to promote the adoption of modern risk management models and modern efficiency models in order to reshape the structural conditions of bank management. The aim should be to ensure competent and effective management not only throughout good periods but also during economic downturns.

Incentives for structural changes as mentioned above should be included in new regulatory and supervisory lines, promoting structural changes towards better risk management and better efficiency models. As an example, regulatory authorities could allow the efficient banks, especially on the plane of X-efficiency with high quality management, to benefit from greater flexibility on capital leverage. As another example, regulatory authorities could allow efficient banks with high quality loan screening and monitoring procedures to benefit from more flexible capital requirements. Uniformity in capital ratios will not, in itself, create conditions for excellent screening and monitoring methods, and the application of the "one size fits all" is not adequate for modern times. Therefore changes, incentives and competition constitute lines for reshaping regulation in Europe. They are inspired by the two fundamental lines of change, namely, risk management and efficiency.

11.8 Conclusions

The crucial importance of capital, risk management and efficiency in European banks is confirmed by the investigation which has been carried out.

Capital adequacy is to be taken into consideration for the composition of assets, liabilities and off-balance sheet items and for absorption of unexpected losses produced only in the event of irrational choices and, in particular, in the event of risk management presenting weaknesses and irrationalities.

Skills and tools are very important in risk management, as they can exercise a positive impact on the pursuit of profit or a negative impact in the event of a loss.

The credit risk in a banking context must be well managed and maintained at low levels, and its negative impact should not exceed that of other risk-related choices tending towards an increase in risk exposure.

Joint development of commercial banking and investment banking provides opportunities for profit; such a development is risky only in the event of irrational risk management.

The extent and duration of economic crises are closely related to the rise and effects of financial crises and thus to the requirement of adequate short-term initiatives to counteract recessive economic pushes. European banks have undergone a prolonged period of financial and economic crisis, which has led to substantial changes in the evolution of the banking business, composition of assets and liabilities and off-balance sheet items and in the profit and loss account.

The extensive presence of NPLs in banking due to financial crises and related economic recessions has generated the credit crunch towards enterprises, especially those of small and medium size. Accordingly, the possibility of progressive reduction of NPLs, at economic conditions, is being explored, essentially by means of loan sales and bad bank creation.

This would make it possible to move towards more favourable conditions for loan granting and economic development.

Quality criteria for risk analysis and evaluation, and, especially, for credit risk assessment through asset quality review, stress tests, on-site inspections and SREP assessment carried out by the ECB Banking Supervision over European banks, are of notable importance. The SREP assessment considers and evaluates the following aspects: the business model, governance, risk management, risks to capital, risks to liquidity. The overall SREP score reflects the supervisor's assessment of the bank's viability.

It is particularly important to make progress in supervisory cooperation between the ECB and the NCAs for improvement of performance in supervision of large banks, but even more so with regard to the supervision of small- and medium-sized banks, as these constitute the backbone of the banking system in terms of the number involved across Europe. The information is gathered and implemented at different national levels, and ensuring uniform criteria will not be easy, especially since different methodologies and different practices were used in the past as compared to the present-day set-up. The building of a ground of uniform principles requires hard work to be done in conjunction with supervisory authorities at a central level and at a national level. Without appropriate coordination, medium and small banks in different countries will be supervised and treated in different ways by NCAs whose operators differ in skills and competences.

The importance of public debt levels for individual states has given rise to the demands for privatisations and sale of public assets in order to reduce the public debt. This would allow the recreation of margins to support the economy as a result of the decrease in interest expenditure. This expenditure is already being reduced in many countries due to the contraction of return and interest rates as a consequence of conventional and unconventional measures adopted in Europe—especially the quantitative easing of the ECB.

The plainest example is given by economic recessions which have gripped the majority of the economies of various members of the EU for an overall period of eight years, including the subprime mortgage financial crisis and the sovereign debt crisis. These difficulties, which were most acute between 2007 and 2014 but also beyond, were examined in a political framework; answers were put forward in an economic and financial framework, but the outcome was not particularly effective in the course of time and not very different from the German model of austerity, with obvious results in a European context.

The following issues, outlined in brief here below, represent important issues that need to be taken into consideration in order to complete the broad picture of capital raising:

- importance of public debt reductions in European countries;
- capital level requirement to offset the solvency risk at a given time in banks;
- improving risk management and efficiency as the key issue in order to create structural premises for a bank positive evolution in the future time;
- toxic assets in European large banks from the subprime mortgage financial crisis still constitute a weak factor in order to achieve profit;
- supervisory expectations on NPLs in bank balance sheet stated by the Banking Supervision becoming *de facto* new discretional rules;
- importance of analysis and comprehension of the negative aspects of the bail-in and therefore profound and radical changes of the rules applied through the bail-in within the EU;
- more freedom and discretion in the choices of European banks, with the introduction of a widespread pre-commitment approach in risk management.

In this context, political choices in the financial and economic field considering the importance of the timing of their adoption and consequent impact are less effective in the presence of indecisions and uncertainties.

The analysis provided in this book examined capital raising as the main tool in the context of prudential rules in regulation and discretional rules in supervision. This is a crucial point which calls for a profound change in line with improvement of risk management and efficiency in the banking industries. It is a crucial point in order to create better internal conditions and premises for reinforcing the banks' resilience.

Bank capital is composed of three elements: capital constraints by regulation, capital constraints by supervision and free capital by bank choices. Bank discretional margins are very restricted and the influence of public authorities is substantial: it exerts an adverse effect on the quality banks that are capable of rational screening and monitoring and, at the same time, of sound risk management and efficiency, thereby achieving a good performance. Changes, incentives and recreating structural conditions postulate new and innovative measures built up by regulatory and also supervisory authorities.

The raising of capital is the main tool used by regulation on a prudential application and by supervision on a discretional application in order to maintain the viability of the banking system. Capital requirements are calculated through Basel III and the forthcoming Basel IV and are also imposed as an additional tool through discretional decisions by supervisory authorities. This is a sort of "recurrent stressing" for implementation by banks in order to pursue the stability objective. It is important to point out that raising of capital is useful only to hedge the solvency risk at the specific date involved and only if the solvency risk is correctly estimated.

Looking at only the capital level is misleading as it is unable to create the premises for a sound and stable bank at a future time. Improving risk management through the identification, measurement and management of all risks linked with bank instruments and bank business areas is the best strategy to achieve structural reinforcement and, therefore, to ensure the soundness of individual banks and the banking system in the medium and long term.

This strategy can be completed by an improvement of efficiency in the various forms of cost, revenue and profit, as this would be in line with the structural premises for sound and viable conditions leading to better frameworks for the economic account from one period of time to another.

References

Acharya, V. V., Cooley, T. F., Richardson, M. P., & Walter, I. (2010). *Regulating wall street: The Dodd Franck Act and the new architecture of global finance*. New York: Wiley.

Andenas, M., & Supino, I. (2015). Politics and finance with reference to the European institutional frame. *Law and Economics Yearly Review, 1*, 144–160.

Barker, D., & Holdsworth, D. (1993). *The causes of bank failures in the 1980s* (No. 9325). Federal Reserve Bank of New York.

Berger, A. N., Herring, R. J., & Szegö, G. P. (1995). The role of capital in financial institutions. *Journal of Banking & Finance, 19*(3), 393–430.

Bliss, R. R. (1995). Risk-based bank capital: Issues and solutions. *Economic Review-Federal Reserve Bank of Atlanta, 80*(5), 32.

Capriglione, F., & Sacco Ginevri, A. (2015). Politics and finance in the European Union. *Law and Economics Yearly Review, 1*, 4–109.

Claessens, S., Ratnovski, L., & Singh, M. M. (2012). *Shadow banking: Economics and policy* (12). International Monetary Fund.
Colombini F. (1999). Strumenti derivati e intermediari finanziari. *Rivista Bancaria,* 1.
Colombini, F. (2004). Strumenti fuori bilancio negli intermediari bancari. La recente esperienza italiana. Rivista Bancaria, 4.
Colombini, F. (2008). *Intermediari, mercati e strumenti finanziari. Economia e integrazione*. Torino: Utet.
Colombini, F., & Calabrò, A. (2010). Risk management e derivatives. Strategie bancarie. *Banche e Banchieri,* 4.
Considine, J. (1998). Pilot exercise-pre-commitment: Approach to market risk. *Economic Policy Review,* No 3.
Grenadier, S. R., & Hall, B. J. (1996). Risk-based capital standards and the riskiness of bank portfolios: Credit and factor risks. *Regional Science and Urban Economics, 26*(3), 433–464.
Gorton, G., & Metrick, A. (2010). Regulating the shadow banking system. *Brookings Papers on Economic Activity, 2010*(2), 261–297.
Gunther, J. W., & Moore, R. M. (1993). The long-run relationship between bank capital and lending. *In Financial Industry Studies.* Federal Reserve Bank of Dallas, 3.
Johnson, H. J. (1993). *Financial institutions and markets. A global perspective.* New York: McGraw-Hill.
Kohn, M. (2004). *Financial institutions and markets.* Oxford: Oxford University Press.
Kupiec, P. H., & O'Brien, J. M. (1995, July). *A pre-commitment approach to capital requirements for market risk.* Finance and Economics Discussion Series, 36. Washington, DC: Board of Governors of the Federal Reserve System.
Lemma, V. (2016). *The Shadow Banking System: Creating Transparency in the Financial Markets.* London: Palgrave Macmillan.
Lindquist, K. G. (2004). Banks' buffer capital: How important is risk. *Journal of International Money and Finance, 23*(3), 493–513.
McCormick, R. (2015). The influence of politics on regulatory and cultural change in the financial sector after the financial crisis: A UK perspective. *Law and Economics Yearly Review, 4*(1), 110–123.
Moore, R. R. (1992). *The role of bank capital in bank loan growth: Market and accounting measures* (No. 92-3). Federal Reserve Bank of Dallas.
Pecchioli, R. M. (1987). *Prudential supervision in banking.* Paris: OECD.
Pozsar, Z., Adrian, T., Ashcraft, A., Boesky, H. (2012). *Shadow banking.* FRBNY Staff Reports, 458, 2012.
Pringle, J. J. (1974). The capital decision in commercial banks. *The Journal of Finance, 29*(3), 779–795.

Salhuteru, F., & Wattimena, F. (2015). Bank performance with CAMELS ratios towards earnings management practices in state banks and private banks. *Advances in Social Sciences Research Journal, 2*(3), 301–314.

Santomero, A. M. (1991). The bank capital issue. In Wihlborg, C., Fratianni, M., Willett T. D. (Eds.), *Financial regulation and monetary arrangements after 1992*. Amsterdam: North-Holland.

Saunders, A., & Cornett, M. M. (2008). *Financial institutions management. A risk management approach*. Boston: McGraw-Hill/Irwin.

Shaefer, S. M. (1987). The design of bank regulation and supervision: Some lessons from the theory of finance. In R. Portes & A. K. Swoboda (Eds.), *Threats to international financial stability*. Cambridge: Cambridge University Press.

Stein, J. C. (2010). Securitization, shadow banking & financial fragility. *Daedalus, 139*(4), 41–51.

Taggart, R. A., & Greenbaum, S. I. (1978). Bank capital and public regulation. *Journal of Money, Credit and Banking, 10*(2), 158–169.

Wang, J. C. (2017). Bank's search for yield in the low interest rate environment: A tale of regulatory adaptation, Federal Reserve Bank of Boston.

Index

F. Colombini (ed.), *Raising Capital or Improving Risk Management and Efficiency?*, https://doi.org/10.1007/978-3-319-71749-4

The manufacturer's authorised representative in the EU is Springer Nature Customer Service Centre GmbH, Europaplatz 3, 69115 Heidelberg, Germany. If you have any concerns regarding our products, please contact ProductSafety@springernature.com

Printed and bound by CPI Group (UK) Ltd, Croydon, CR0 4YY
05/10/2026
02228140-0002